GRADE 5

An inspirational real-world program for gifted learners

By Melanie L. Bondy

Edited by Shanda Blue Easterday MFA, PhD

Printed by: Data Reproductions Corporation
Auburn Hills, Michigan

DEDICATION

To my dad, George Betka, who taught me how to make life a song, be "the captain"
and stick to the job while enjoying the vacations.

ACKNOWLEDGMENTS

For their support and encouragement: Scott and Brendan Bondy, Richard and Marilyn Bondy and Alvina Betka.

For being wonderful educational role models: Dr. Alan Quick, Joseph Jeanette, Wayne Wrona and Dr. Ronald O'Hara.

For being the most dedicated hard-working teachers I have ever had the pleasure of working with:
Kristen Rabideau and Heidi Felstead.

To the principals who believed in me: Sara O'Hara, Laura Holbert and Kurt Swearingen.

To the L'Anse Creuse Public Schools superintendent, Dr. DiAnne Pellerin, who recognized the benefits of this program and
encouraged me to present it outside of my school and district.

To the students who gave me the honor of being able to share their projects with others: Elizabeth Boschma,
Kristen Boschma, Adrianna Katsimpalis, Ariel Katsimpalis, Marissa Krause, Lauren Marino, Kelsey Nucci,
Nicole Paul, Sarah Trerice and Brooke Will.

To the educational editors who gave their valuable time to review the Envision program: Kristen Rabideau,
Denise Pechman, Suzanne Hellner and Dr. Alan Quick, and to Marjorie D. Podzielinski for her valuable input.

To Joyce Kindermann and John Kozak, for talking business with me when I first began this journey.

To my graphic artists, Frank Ciolino and Michael Bartello, for their exceptional talent, ideas and dedication.

To my editor, Shanda Blue Easterday, for her perseverance, hard work and belief in the Envision program.

Bondy, Melanie L.

Envision, Grade 5: Melanie L. Bondy: edited by Stephen Welch and Shanda Blue Easterday.

Cover and book design by Frank Ciolino, and Michael Bartello: seesponge.com.

Spanish translation and editing by Laura McCarthy, Thelma Ortiz and Bella Lile.

Printed in the United States of America, Data Reproductions Corporation.

Referenced with permission: *Taxonomy of Educational Objectives: Book 1: Cognitive Domain*, Benjamin S. Bloom, Ed.
Copyright © 1956, 1984. Pearson Allyn and Bacon, Boston, MA.

Mind Vine Press, LLC
70727 Copper Boulevard, Lawton, MI 49065

mindvinepress.com

ISBN 978-0-9786715-9-4

TABLE OF CONTENTS

AUTHOR LETTER:
A SOLUTION TO TEACHING
GIFTED STUDENTS

A SOLUTION TO TEACHING GIFTED STUDENTS

Teaching has always meant more than presenting lessons, assigning homework and grading papers. Today, educators are asked to micromanage a host of objectives and topics that stretch far beyond the standard core curriculum. While tackling these new responsibilities, teachers must still contend with the challenge of educating an often under-served population of students: the gifted, whose needs are substantially different from those of most of their classmates.

As a teacher, I struggled to provide the best education I could for all my students. In my first class, of thirty-five students, I had five students who were in a cluster group for the gifted. I worked long hours to find and create innovative lessons for the thirty non-gifted students, and then endeavored to adapt each lesson to accommodate my five cluster students.

I was fortunate, in that first year of teaching, to take part in a one-year training program for teaching the gifted, and I learned of the available strategies for teaching gifted students. I looked forward to these strategies helping my gifted students excel in school, and I became motivated and energized to utilize them right away.

As I began implementing the techniques I had learned, which included supplying research projects, explorations, logic exercises and high-level thinking games, I believed these new exercises were sufficiently challenging my gifted students. After only about a week with each new activity, however, I noticed that they were becoming repetitive and mundane. The logic problems offered different scenarios, but all employed the same type of thinking. Once the students understood the first few problems, solving the rest became mechanical. In addition, the problems had little or no relationship to the students' personal lives.

The research projects and explorations I had so hopefully adopted proved, in a classroom setting, to be haphazardly grouped, difficult to manage, extremely broad and unclear in their requirements and too subject-specific to allow for much curriculum flexibility. They were also not in-depth enough to engage the students for more than a few weeks.

Of additional significance, I found that I had no valuable way of assessing—and therefore promoting—student advancement. The logic exercises, for example, included answer keys, but the keys offered no means to evaluate the levels of thinking associated with solving the problems. Answers were simply right or wrong. Similarly, the thinking games, explorations and research projects all defied useful assessment, leaving me to guess at where my students were and where they were poised to go. A colorful portfolio showcasing the end products of various broad activities and repetitive projects is a poor substitute for a thorough, convincing record of demonstrable advancement in high-level thinking.

Although the gifted students were enjoying their new extra activities, they were, in fact, being little more than entertained. At this point, though frustrated from researching and prepping materials that had proved to be of such limited value, I was unwilling to accept that "the best available" was the best I could offer my gifted students. I grew more determined than ever to find a solution to this nagging problem.

To solve the problem, I developed Envision, a gifted program that is exciting and challenging, that leads students through the highest levels of thinking and that appeals to diverse interests by having deep roots in the real world. Because Envision draws on all subject areas, students can work on their projects at any time of the day, during any class period, and still be connected to the general work of the class. Envision includes a climactic succession of related projects with concrete objectives.

Of special importance to me is that each student's progress is subject to clear, consistent, unambiguous assessment at predetermined stages from start to finish. Also, the program is ambitious enough in its depth and scope to engage, challenge and reward gifted students all year long. Finally, Envision is a program that gifted students work on with minimal oversight, which encourages independent learning and, as a practical concern, allows more time for the teacher to address other classroom needs.

PROGRAM INTRODUCTION:
THE ENVISION EXPERIENCE

THE ENVISION EXPERIENCE

What is Envision?

Envision is a real-world independent study program for gifted and talented students who are not sufficiently challenged by the standard curriculum. It includes a series of four multidisciplinary projects, one for each quarter, and is designed to span the entire school year.

What type of class can use Envision?

Intended to complement or replace the standard curriculum, the projects integrate advanced academic study with real-world experience and problem solving. Because the projects are not subject-specific, drawing as they do from all disciplines, they can be integrated easily into any type of classroom curriculum. The Envision program is also flexible enough to be used in a regular education classroom that has gifted and talented students or in a classroom of only gifted students.

Which students can participate in Envision?

Students who participate in the program are those who are identified, based on school or district criteria, as being gifted, talented or advanced learners.

IMPORTANT!

Almost positively, especially after seeing the first projects completed, your non-gifted students will want to participate in the Envision program. Allowing these students to participate in Envision will not only excite and motivate them even more about school, but will also make you feel good knowing that you are providing the best opportunities for all of your students. Even non-gifted students can take on the Envision challenges and will probably surprise you with their level of enthusiasm and learning.

Allowing non-gifted students to participate may require some extra work on your part. For instance, you may choose to modify the Student Instruction Guides, you may have more photocopying to do and you may need to hold a larger Project Expo. However, expanding participation to more students will greatly reward both you and them.

Can the projects be implemented in any order?

While any one project can be taught independently from the other three, the program is most effective when all four are undertaken in chronological order and as a series. The order in which the projects are implemented is determined after considering the levels of Benjamin S. Bloom's Taxonomy of Educational Objectives (Bloom, 1956, 1984) contained in each project, the complexity of each project's topic and the amount of work required for each project.

The first project in the series is designed to familiarize students with a new style of learning, and, for that reason, has a lighter topic. The second and third projects' topics are more complex in their subject matter, which adds an extra dimension of challenge for experienced Envision learners. The fourth and final project is designed with the end of the school year in mind. Its topic is lighter, yet the objectives continue to challenge students in new, creative ways. There are detailed descriptions of the projects in the last section of this introduction.

THE ENVISION EXPERIENCE

How are the student materials organized?

At the beginning of the quarter, Envision students receive a Student Instruction Guide containing all the instruction needed for the upcoming project. The instruction guide allows students to work on their projects independently, guiding them step-by-step through the project.

If students need additional guidance along the way, a set of important Student Resource Cards is included and offers a wide range of supplemental instruction. The resource cards offer definitions, helpful tips and visual examples for certain tasks listed on the Student Instruction Guide.

Though the teacher introduces the program and is available for periodic guidance, encouragement and assessment, the Student Instruction Guide and the resource cards enable students to work largely on their own and at their own pace. This structure encourages independent learning on the part of the Envision student, while allowing the teacher ample time to attend to his or her regular responsibilities.

At the completion of each project, students receive a Student Self-Assessment, which gives them the opportunity to reflect on and assess their own work.

How are the teacher materials organized?

Following this introduction, you will find a Teacher Instruction Guide. The Teacher Instruction Guide is also presented in a step-by-step format and explains project implementation from start to finish. It includes detailed instructions, examples and references to all the forms and materials you will use along the way.

In addition to the Teacher Instruction Guide are four Project Appendices. The appendices contain all the letters, charts, invitations, signs, certificates and assessments needed to complete the Envision program. These reproducible forms are grouped by project and are provided in order of use.

What additional materials does the program include?

The entire Envision program package is thorough and complete. In addition to this manual, the package contains all additional supplemental materials needed to integrate Envision smoothly into any classroom. The materials include Project Expo Posters, a Bulletin Board Banner, the Student Resource Cards previously discussed and a specially designed CD. The CD contains all the PDF files of forms, in color and with typeable fields. There is also useful information for both teachers and students at mindvinepress.com.

What is Bloom's Taxonomy of Educational Objectives?

Benjamin S. Bloom's Taxonomy of Educational Objectives is a model that presents thinking as occurring at six levels, and ranks those levels from the least complex, or the lowest level, to the most abstract, or the highest level. The type of cognition that occurs at any given level distinguishes that level from the others. At the lower end, in Bloom's original 1956 Taxonomy, are Knowledge, Comprehension and Application, in rising order. At the higher end are Analysis, Synthesis and, ultimately, Evaluation.

Over the decades, however, educators who have worked with Bloom's Taxonomy have made a significant change to the hierarchy of cognitive activities. In most educational circles, Synthesis now ranks above Evaluation as the highest level, making Evaluation the second highest.

THE ENVISION EXPERIENCE

What distinguishes each of the Bloom's levels?

A practical way to understand these six levels of thinking and how they relate to one another is to know the cognitive activity that occurs at each level, and the skills associated with each cognitive activity.

Knowledge, at the lowest cognitive level, involves recalling something previously encountered, but does not involve understanding or applying that knowledge. Related skills include memorizing, listing, defining, quoting, naming, simple labeling, locating, and knowing who, when, where, what and how many.

Comprehension requires that a student understand knowledge, such as the nature of an important event, for example, rather than merely when and where the event occurred. Comprehension does not, however, require the student to apply that knowledge to other knowledge, such as a similar event. Related skills include summarizing, describing, estimating, interpreting, outlining, collecting, demonstrating and understanding how as opposed to simply how many.

Application happens when a student uses learned knowledge to solve new problems in new situations. Related skills include calculating, solving, experimenting, resolving and answering.

Analysis, the first of the three highest-level activities, occurs when a student dissects a concept or object into its component parts and examines those parts separately and in relation to one another or to the whole. Related skills include separating, ordering, diagramming, classifying, dividing, comparing, contrasting and finding patterns.

Evaluation means offering an opinion on the value of information, events, or concepts based on specific criteria. Related skills include assessing, ranking, persuading, judging, supporting and refuting.

Synthesis, widely considered the most abstract kind of thinking, occurs when a student can restructure the parts of a whole into something new. The ability to create something new from what has been learned requires a thorough understanding of the subject matter, an understanding of its applications and its parts, and an evaluative opinion regarding each part's importance and relevance to the whole. Related skills include integrating, revising, rearranging, substituting, designing, composing, building, organizing, interviewing, hypothesizing and inventing.

IMPORTANT!

The levels described above are cumulative. For example, the highest level of thinking, Synthesis, incorporates all other levels of thinking: Knowledge, Comprehension, Application, Analysis and Evaluation. Please to keep this in mind when reviewing each Envision project's connection to Bloom's Taxonomy discussed below.

What is Envision's connection to Bloom's Taxonomy?

As mentioned above, each project teaches a specific, varied set of advanced objectives that have been carefully selected and organized according to Benjamin S. Bloom's widely accepted and updated Taxonomy of Educational Objectives. Although the projects incorporate all levels of thinking, the bulk of the objectives for each project focuses on exercising the three highest levels.

If you would like to see each project's connection to the Bloom's Taxonomy levels, go to the beginning of each project appendix:

- Appendix 1: "Travel Passport and Bloom's Taxonomy"
- Appendix 2: "Career Aspiration and Bloom's Taxonomy"
- Appendix 3: "Financial Adventure and Bloom's Taxonomy"
- Appendix 4: "Knowledge Quest and Bloom's Taxonomy"

THE ENVISION EXPERIENCE

What are the other available Envision programs and projects?

In addition to Envision Singles, Mind Vine Press offers grade-level sets of Envision programs. Each Envision Complete Grade Level Program comes with the Envision teacher guide and four complete projects that include pre-cut Student Resource Cards, teacher forms and customizable CD. The Complete Grade Level Programs also come with five color posters and a bulletin board banner.

Complete Envision Programs Available

Envision: Grade 3 Complete Program

 Pet Parade: Choose and research a pet to adopt or purchase in the future.

 Giving Journey: Choose a gift for someone and create a plan to work for it.

 Discovery Science: Design and conduct a scientific experiment.

 Curiosity Expedition: Research an exciting topic of your choice.

Envision: Grade 4 Complete Program

 Design a complete, personalized dream backyard using one acre of land.

 Acquire an awareness of an environmental issue and have a voice in the matter.

 Interact and learn within the community while planning and performing a service.

 Develop a detailed plan of healthy habits by which to live.

THE ENVISION EXPERIENCE

Envision: Grade 5 Complete Program

 Plan every aspect of a trip from start to finish within a specified budget.

 Research a career and all of the education required to accomplish this major life goal.

 Plan personal finances and purchases based on the starting salary of a chosen career.

 Thoroughly investigate and report on a meaningful and relevant topic of choice.

Envision Singles Available

Envision Single: Career Aspiration, Appropriate for Grades 5-8

 Research a career and all of the education required to accomplish this major life goal.

Envision Single: Backyard Getaway, Appropriate for Grades 4-7

 Design a complete, personalized dream backyard using one acre of land.

Envision Single: Pet Parade, Appropriate for Grades 3-6

 Choose and research a pet to adopt or purchase in the future.

Envision Single: Party Plan, Appropriate for Grades 2-3

 Plan a themed party to celebrate a special event.

For detailed descriptions and ordering information, please visit mindvinepress.com.

THE ENVISION EXPERIENCE

What are the four Envision projects?

For each Envision project, students are guided to create a comprehensive portfolio, a formal classroom presentation and an exhibit presented at an Envision project expo.

Travel Passport (Project 1): As the first project in the series, Travel Passport immediately engages students in the Envision program by being as much fun as it is educational. Students have the challenge of planning every aspect of an imaginary trip, to a destination of their choice, while managing a travel budget.

Students will research and make decisions about such matters as where and when to travel, modes of transportation, types of accommodations and which sites to visit. Students will create a daily travel itinerary, a travel expense chart and a computer-generated graph showing statistical information related to their destination. After carefully planning their trip, students will imagine they have returned and then write a creative memoir in which they reflect on their journey. All of this written material will be collected in a portfolio.

Each student will then design and create an exhibit that captures and conveys the highlights of his or her trip. The exhibit will include maps, brochures, photos, a self-created postcard and a three-dimensional visual that represents a particularly memorable aspect of the student's fictitious experience. As part of an in-class presentation and the concluding project expo, each student will dress in clothes that relate to his or her destination.

Career Aspiration (Project 2): The second Envision project is designed to enlighten students about where education can lead them in life. Students have the opportunity to take a career interest inventory, chose a potential career, research it and not only select, but investigate the education or training needed to reach this major life goal.

In the project portfolio, students create computer-generated charts, graphs and a brochure detailing information related to their education or training. The students then research and identify a number of career-related matters, such as salary, on-the-job duties and contributions to society. In order to enhance the reality of the project, students interview someone in their chosen career field. The portfolio is finalized when students have sought an actual job posting and completed a resume, cover letter and employment application.

The project exhibit will showcase their portfolios and be a visually appealing advertisement for their careers and educations. Students are encouraged to include brochures, photos, on-the-job tools and any other visuals they gathered over the course of the project. As part of an in-class presentation and the concluding project expo, each student will dress in clothes that relate to his or her career.

THE ENVISION EXPERIENCE

Financial Adventure (Project 3): The third Envision project educates students on the importance and fundamentals of personal finance. Students have the rewarding experience of formally accepting a job offer from their chosen career field from Project 2, Career Aspiration, and acquiring the tools necessary to build a financial plan for their future.

Armed with their starting salary and a specified spending amount, students will delve into decision-making skills such as buying vs. renting a home, the use of cash vs. credit, budgeting income vs. outgoing expenses, allotting for savings and investments and making imaginary purchases for necessities and discretionary items. The rationale for each of these decisions will be supported by computer-generated charts, graphs and written explanations.

At their project exhibit, students will share their portfolio, a floor plan or three-dimensional model of their future home and a display board that depicts their budgeted expenses and purchased items.

Knowledge Quest (Project 4): The final project of the year energizes students with the opportunity to select and thoroughly analyze any topic of interest that they have the desire to learn about.

Students will create a semantic map to guide their research and note taking. They will also record a hot list of useful websites, write a bibliography, compose and conduct a survey and classify their survey results by designing a double bar graph. All of their findings will be reported in a newspaper format that requires a combination of various informational text structures, standard newspaper elements and computerized text features.

For the project exhibit, each student will design a game, create an illustration that predicts the future of his or her topic and arrange a display board related to the topic of study. Students will also prepare demonstrations that teach something about their fields of study. As part of an in-class presentation and the concluding project expo, each student will dress in clothes that relate to his or her topic.

With the Envision program, you will be confident that your gifted students are continually being fully challenged at high levels while being enriched with the freedoms of choice and creative expression. Envision will inspire their educational experiences on a daily basis. Your gifted students will look forward to each new Envision learning endeavor and, most importantly, to their own futures.

TEACHER INSTRUCTION GUIDE FOR PROJECT IMPLEMENTATION

TEACHER INSTRUCTION GUIDE

You are now ready to begin implementing the Envision program in your classroom. This Teacher Instruction Guide serves as a comprehensive checklist for every step necessary to achieve success. The instruction guide is based on a school year comprised of four ten-week quarters, but can be modified to suit your needs.

IMPORTANT!

Because the project format for each ten-week term is the same, you will use this instruction guide for implementing each of the four Envision projects.

 Every step in the Teacher Instruction Guide includes detailed instructions and visual examples. Because you will start with the Travel Passport Project, the examples included in this guide are based on Travel Passport.

STEP 1
Planning and Preparing for the Quarter

The first form, the Teacher Planning Guide, allows you to plan every stage of each project from start to finish. Setting dates and times for project events well in advance will guarantee the best possible outcome.

Students should be given an entire quarter or about ten weeks to work on and complete each project. This ten-week period can be slightly flexible, give or take a week, as needed.

Note: The Teacher Instruction Guide walks you through the entire project implementation process. Forms you will use are included with each step in the order they are needed. It is best to do the photocopying as you proceed with each step, rather than copying everything up front, since many forms will need to be filled in prior to photocopying. Located in each project Appendix is a Teacher Copy Chart that lists each form you will need, when you will need it, and how many copies you will need.

TEACHER INSTRUCTION GUIDE

1.1 Copy one Teacher Planning Guide.

1.2 Use the guidelines below, along with the chart that follows, to guide you in filling out your personal Teacher Planning Guide. It may be helpful to start with Week 10 and work in reverse.

Week 1 Preparation, Introduction, Implementation:
- 30 minutes outside of class for initial planning and preparing (Steps 1.1-1.2).
- 15 minutes outside of class to prepare for Project Introduction (2.1-2.3).
- 20 minutes of class time for Project Introduction (2.4-2.7). The Project Introduction should be at least one day prior to Project Implementation (below).
- 20 minutes outside of class to prepare for Project Implementation (3.1-3.6).
- 30 minutes of class time for Project Implementation (3.7-3.17).

Weeks 2, 4 and 6: No teacher preparation or scheduled events. Students continue to work on their projects during these weeks.

Weeks 3, 5, 7 Checkpoint Meetings:
- 10 minutes outside of class to prepare for the Checkpoint Meetings (4.1-4.2).
- 10 minutes of class time to distribute Checkpoint Organizers (4.3-4.6). Distribute the Checkpoint Organizers two to three days prior to the Checkpoint Meetings (below).
- 10 minutes of class time, per every five to six Envision students, to conduct Checkpoint Meetings (4.7-4.12).

Week 8 Preparation, Invitations:
- 10 minutes outside of class to prepare for the Project Expo (5.1-5.2).
- 10 minutes of class time to Invite Families to the Project Expo (5.3-5.4).
- 60 minutes outside of class to continue preparation for the Project Expo (5.5-5.11).

Week 9 Preparation, Classroom Presentations, Classroom Expo, Student Self-Assessment:
- 30 minutes outside of class, plus an optional store trip, to prepare for the Classroom Presentations and Project Expo (5.12-5.15). Prepare two to three days prior to Classroom Presentations (below).
- 5 minutes of class time, per Envision student, to conduct the Classroom Presentations (6A.1-6A.13 or 6B.1-6B.12). The Classroom Presentations should be on the same day and during the same time block as the Classroom Expo and Student Self-Assessment (below).
- 5 minutes of class time, per each Envision student, plus an additional 10 minutes for the Classroom Expo and Student Self-Assessment (7A.1-7A.9 or 7B.1-7B.10).

Week 10 Final Preparation, Project Expo, Teacher Assessment:
- 45 minutes outside of class to complete Final Preparation for the Project Expo (8.1-8.10). This preparation will need to be done on the day of the Project Expo.
- 60 minutes of class time to conduct the Project Expo (9.1-9.4). Scheduling the expo in the evening ensures better attendance by parents.
- 2 store trips plus 10 minutes outside of class per each Envision student, for the Conclusion and Teacher Assessment (10.1-10.8).
- 15 minutes of class time for Student Review (10.9-10.10).

Decide on a Travel Passport travel budget for your students. The recommended maximum amount is $3000 per student. This amount allows for planned travel either within the United States or abroad. The recommended minimum amount is $2800 per student. Setting a minimum-spending amount ensures that students will not simply choose a local attraction, bank the remainder of the money and finish the project too quickly. Record your budget amounts at the bottom of the Teacher Planning Guide for future reference.

TEACHER PLANNING GUIDE

Events scheduled with the class are in black.

Week	Event (Step Numbers)	Time Required
1	Planning and Preparing for the Quarter (1.1-1.2)	30 min.
	Prepare for Project Introduction (2.1-2.3)	15 min.
	Project Introduction (2.4-2.7)	20 min.
	Preparation for Project Implementation (3.1-3.6)	20 min.
	Project Implementation (3.7-3.17)	30 min.
2	No teacher preparation during this week. Students continue to work on their projects.	
3	Preparation for the Checkpoint Meetings (4.1-4.2)	10 min.
	Distribute Checkpoint Organizers (4.3-4.6)	10 min.
	Checkpoint Meetings (4.7-4.12)	10 min.
4	No teacher preparation during this week. Students continue to work on their projects.	
5	Preparation for the Checkpoint Meetings (4.1-4.2)	10 min.
	Distribute Checkpoint Organizers (4.3-4.6)	10 min.
	Checkpoint Meetings (4.7-4.12)	10 min.
6	No teacher preparation during this week. Students continue to work on their projects.	
7	Preparation for the Checkpoint Meetings (4.1-4.2)	10 min.
	Distribute Checkpoint Organizers (4.3-4.6)	10 min.
	Checkpoint Meetings (4.7-4.12)	10 min.
8	Preparation for the Project Expo (5.1-5.2)	10 min.
	Invite Families to the Project Expo (5.3-5.4)	10 min.
	Preparation for the Project Expo Ctd. (5.5-5.11)	60 min.
9	Preparation for Classroom Presentations and the Project Expo (5.12-5.15)	30 min. (+ store: optional)
	Classroom Presentations (6A.1-6A.13 or 6B.1-6B.12)	5 min. per Envision student
	Classroom Expo and Student Self-Assessment (7A.1-7A.9 or 7B.1-7B.10)	5 min. per Envision student + 10 min.
10	Final Preparation for the Project Expo (8.1-8.10)	45 min.
	Project Expo (9.1-9.4)	60 min.
	Conclusion and Teacher Assessment (10.1-10.8)	2 trips to store +10 min./student
	Student Review (10.9-10.10)	15 min.

Maximum Travel Passport budget amount: $3,000 • Minimum Travel Passport budget amount: $2,800

STEP 2
Student Introduction

IMPORTANT!

If you would like to see each project's specific connections to the Bloom's Taxonomy levels, you will find a document at the beginning of each Project Appendix.

AND

If you would like to utilize the Spanish translations, you will find the documents at the end of each Project Appendix. For each project, the parent letter/s, Student Commitment Contract, Student Instruction Guide, and Expo invitation have been translated.

Prepare for Project Introduction:

2.1 Make a copy of one Parent Envision Introduction Letter (Travel Passport Introduction only), one Parent Project Introduction Letter, one Student Project Introduction Letter and one Student Instruction Guide.

2.2 Using the information from your Teacher Planning Guide, complete the Parent Envision Introduction Letter (Travel Passport only), Parent Project Introduction Letter and Student Project Introduction Letter.

IMPORTANT!

When completing the information on the forms, remember that there are two options:

1. You may choose to photocopy the form from the corresponding appendix and fill in the blanks by hand.

OR

2. You may use the CD to type in the blanks, then print the form in color or black and white.

2.3 Copy a completed Parent Envision Introduction Letter (Travel Passport only), and a Parent Project Introduction Letter for each student. Do not make multiple copies of the Student Introduction Letter or Student Instruction Guide at this time. You will need only one of each of these right now.

Project Introduction:

2.4 Bring your gifted students together and, referring to the Parent Envision Introduction Letter, give them an overview of the Envision Program.

2.5 Read aloud the Student Introduction Letter to give students an overview of the project. Refer to the Student Instruction Guide to highlight some of the project tasks.

2.6 Travel Passport Only: To each student, hand out one Parent Envision Introduction Letter to take home. Explain that the bottom portion of it contains an Envision Permission Form that the parent should sign, detach and return to you as soon as possible.

2.7 To each student, hand out one Parent Project Introduction Letter to take home.

introduction letter

Dear Parent(s),

I am happy to inform you that your child has been invited to participate in an advanced academic program called Envision. I am sending you this letter to explain the program and ask for your permission to include your child in this special opportunity.

Envision is an exciting, yearlong program designed for students who are not sufficiently challenged by the standard grade-level curriculum. The focus of the program is on developing high-level critical thinking and creativity, and encourages students to *envision* how they might achieve their goals for the future. Envision guides students through four real-world-based projects, one for each quarter of the school year.

In chronological order, the four projects are: Travel Passport, Career Aspiration, Financial Adventure and Knowledge Quest. Travel Passport allows students to choose a destination and fully plan and coordinate an imaginary trip. Career Aspiration engages students in thinking concretely about possible academic and career choices they will face later in life. The third project, Financial Adventure, helps students discover the realities of personal finance, from housing expenses and paying bills, to making purchases and saving and investing for the future. Finally, Knowledge Quest allows students to research, in depth, any topic they are interested in and want to know more about. Each project introduces new ideas, new vocabulary, new technology and new challenges.

Students will work on Envision during class time, free time and at home.

To give permission for your child to participate in Envision, simply sign the Envision Permission Form at the bottom of this letter, detach it and return the form to me. If you want your child to participate in Envision, please read the attached Parent Travel Passport Introduction Letter. The letter introduces you to the first project, informs you of important dates and requests permission for your child's continued participation. You will receive a Parent Project Introduction Letter at the beginning of each quarter with the start of each new project.

Envision promises to be a wonderful learning opportunity for your child. I look forward to hearing from you. Please feel free to contact me if you have any questions.

Sincerely,

Mrs. Bondy

269-978-7227 · bondyme@school.org

- -

permission form

Please fill out this section, detach and return as soon as possible.   Date: <u>September 6, 2XXX</u>

❏ I have read the Parent Envision Introduction Letter and give my child permission to participate in the Envision program.

❏ I have read the Parent Envision Introduction Letter and do not give my child permission to participate in the Envision program.

Child's Name: <u>Alyssa Good</u>   Parent's Signature: <u>Joanne Good</u>

TRAVEL PASSPORT

parent travel passport introduction letter

Dear Parent(s),

Welcome to Travel Passport, an Envision project that will challenge and inspire your child. Travel Passport gives your child an imaginary allowance to "travel" anywhere in the world. The challenge is that your child will plan, budget and document every aspect of the trip.

For this project, your child will conduct research on his or her travel destination and then make numerous informed decisions regarding concerns such as where, when and how to travel; where to stay; what to visit; and how to prepare for his or her absence from home. Your child will then create a daily itinerary, a travel-expense chart, a computer-generated graph of travel-related facts or statistics and a fictional travel memoir regarding his or her travel "experiences." Lastly, your child will build an exhibit that presents key aspects of his or her travels, and will give a brief formal presentation to the class.

A Student Instruction Guide will be provided to guide your child, step by step, through this process. The Instruction Guide is a comprehensive list of project requirements and is designed to engage higher-level thinking. The guide also refers to helpful Resource Cards, that provide additional explanations, ideas, tips and directions. There will be a set of these cards to which your child can refer in our classroom.

Travel Passport is designed to be worked on independently during class time, free time and at home. By scheduling several Checkpoint Meeting dates throughout the quarter, I will be able to monitor each student's progress. On these dates, I will meet with each student to discuss accomplishments and plan goals for the next checkpoint. I will also address any difficulties students might be having.

Travel Passport will conclude with a Project Expo. The expo will be your child's opportunity to share his or her finished project with family, friends and other guests. You will receive a detailed invitation to the Project Expo later in the quarter.

Dates to Remember:

Checkpoint 1: *September 18, 2XXX*

Checkpoint 2: *October 2, 2XXX*

Checkpoint 3: *October 16, 2XXX*

Classroom Presentation: *November 1, 2XXX*

Travel Passport Expo: *November 7, 2XXX 6:30 - 7:30 pm*

Sincerely,

Mrs. Bondy

269-978-7227 · bondyme@school.org

TRAVEL PASSPORT

student travel passport introduction letter

Dear Student,

Welcome to Travel Passport! This is the first project you will embark on as part of the Envision Program experience. Travel Passport is about taking a journey – a journey of the imagination. It is also a very real journey of discovery, research and creativity.

The project begins with your receiving an imaginary travel budget of $3,000. You will be required to spend at least $2,800. Keeping these amounts in mind, you will choose a real travel destination, one that you can reach and enjoy within your budget. Your destination should be a place of special interest to you.

This project contains four components. The first will be to research and write about your destination and your trip. You will organize this information in a project portfolio. The second will be to create an exhibit of your trip as if you had already gone and come home. The third will be to share your completed portfolio and exhibit with your classmates. To do this, you will give a brief formal presentation. During your presentation, you will explain key aspects of your trip. Fourth is the Project Expo, an event that celebrates your hard work and achievements. This final component allows you the opportunity to invite family and friends to share in your success.

You will work on Travel Passport throughout the school day and, of course, during your free time and at home. Generally, you will be expected to work on your own. You will consult with me periodically at Checkpoint Meetings to discuss your progress and receive guidance. Between the checkpoints, feel free to discuss your project with other Envision students.

The attached Student Instruction Guide contains all the information you will need to complete the required Travel Passport Project successfully. The Instruction Guide will challenge you to be resourceful, organized and to think at a higher level.

Dates to Remember:

Checkpoint 1: *September 18, 2XXX*

Checkpoint 2: *October 2, 2XXX*

Checkpoint 3: *October 16, 2XXX*

Classroom Presentation: *November 1, 2XXX*

Travel Passport Expo: *November 7, 2XXX 6:30 - 7:30 pm*

After reading this introduction, you are now ready to begin thinking about your travel destination and planning your adventure. Good luck and have fun!

Sincerely,

Mrs. Bondy

269-978-7227 · bondyme@school.org

STUDENT INSTRUCTION GUIDE

Building Your Project Portfolio • Creating Your Exhibit
Presenting Your Project • Attending the Expo

CREATIVITY IS HIGHLY ENCOURAGED!

IMPORTANT!

Available resource cards are denoted by a numbered Travel Passport icon ![icon]. When you see one of these icons, you will know that there is a corresponding numbered resource card available that gives additional helpful information and depicts visual examples for your reference. Also, be sure to visit mindvinepress.com, trustworthy Internet sites, library reference materials and (if you like) a travel agent, for additional resources and examples.

COMPONENT 1

Building Your Project Portfolio Total Possible Portfolio Points: 66 out of 100 total possible for project

Get ready! It is now time to plan and make decisions about the trip of your dreams. This will be a wonderful experience and opportunity to engage your intellectual abilities as well as your imagination. Complete the numbered requirements below, in order, as they build upon one another and will guide you smoothly through the process. Bon voyage!

1. ✈ Questions (3 points each): Compose a paragraph or more for each bullet-pointed set of questions below. Write each paragraph on its own separate page. Title each page.

Note: You may write about yourself as if you were an adult, old enough to drive a car and rent a hotel room. You may "take along" a traveling companion, but the extra expenses must come out of your total travel budget.

• What is your specific travel destination
(city, state/province, country)? What is its absolute location in
latitude and longitude, and relative location in reference to surroundings, such as nearby
cities, geographical features or landmarks? Why is this destination of interest to you?

• When will you take your trip (time, day, month, year)? How long will you stay? How do costs, seasonal patterns and the destination itself affect or determine your choices about when to travel and how long to stay?

STEP 3
Project Implementation

Prepare for Project Implementation:

The Student Commitment Contract mentioned below ensures that students and their parents understand and are accountable for project work time and Checkpoint Meeting expectations. It creates a formal commitment to these expectations and an understanding that students could lose their Envision privileges if they do not follow them. It also reminds students and parents of important project dates.

3.1 Copy one Teacher Forms Checklist and one Student Commitment Contract.

3.2 Fill in the Envision student names on the Teacher Forms Checklist and set it aside for later use.

3.3 Using the event dates from your Teacher Planning Guide, complete the Student Commitment Contract.

3.4 Make a copy of the completed Student Commitment Contract for each Envision student.

3.5 Copy a completed Student Project Introduction Letter and Student Instruction Guide, both previously used in Step 2, for each of your gifted students. Staple the Student Project Introduction Letter and guide together as a packet, placing the introduction letter on top.

Note: You may also want to copy the smaller sized resource card pages in the corresponding Project Appendix to include with each student letter and guide. This is not necessary, since there is the classroom set of resource cards, but may be helpful to students when they work on Envision outside of the classroom.

FINANCIAL ADVENTURE ONLY:

Financial Adventure Only: Also copy and attach in this order and following the Student Instruction Guide: Financial Adventure Glossary, Roommate Questionnaire and Roommate Discussion Guide.

3.6 Decide on a specific location to keep the Project Resource Cards. Take out and set aside the set of cards for the project you are implementing.

TEACHER INSTRUCTION GUIDE

Project Implementation:

3.7 Use your Teacher Forms Checklist (Step 3.1) to record each signed Envision Permission Form (distributed in Step 2.6) that is returned to you.

3.8 Distribute a Student Commitment Contract (Step 3.4) to each of your Envision students.

3.9 Review the contract with your students and answer any questions they have.

3.10 Ask each student to sign the contract, thereby agreeing to its expectations.

3.11 Direct students to take their Student Commitment Contracts home to be signed by a parent and returned to you as soon as possible.

3.12 Distribute a student packet (Step 3.5) to each of your contracted Envision students.

3.13 Read the Student Introduction Letter and review the remainder of the student packet materials together.

3.14 Share two to three resource cards with the students and explain how they correspond to particular requirements on the Student Instruction Guide. Show students where the resource cards will be kept.

IMPORTANT!

Stress to students that the Student Instruction Guide gives only the essentials for the tasks, allowing for student creativity. However, the resource cards are available to lend additional support by supplying definitions, explanations, tips and visual examples.

3.15 Direct students to keep their materials in a safe, handy place. Let them know that they can now work on the project at school, during extra time and at home. Tell them it is their responsibility to bring their project materials back and forth each day.

3.16 Allow students to begin using available class time to work on Envision.

3.17 Record the receipt of the signed Student Commitment Contracts on the Teacher Forms Checklist as they are returned.

TEACHER FORMS CHECKLIST

use this checklist to record forms submitted by the students

student name	envision permission form	student commitment contract	student checkpoint organizer 1	student checkpoint organizer 2	student checkpoint organizer 3	expo invitation response number attending special equip. needed
1. Michael	✓					
2. Alysssa	✓					
3. Brian	✓					
4. Alex	✓					
5. Lauren	✓					
6. Brendan	✓					
7. Ella	✓					
8. Teagan	✓					
9. Earl	✓					
10.						
11.						
12.						
13.						
14.						
15.						
16.						
17.						
18.						
19.						
20.						
21.						
22.						
23.						
24.						
25.						

expectations

project work time

I agree to:

- be responsible for following my Student Instruction Guide to do my work.
- keep track of all my project materials.
- work hard on Envision without disturbing others.
- save my unanswered questions until my teacher is free to talk.

checkpoint meetings

I will come prepared with:

- my Student Instruction Guide.
- my completed Student Checkpoint Organizer.
- all of my project materials.

important dates and times

Checkpoint 1: _September 18, 2XXX_

Checkpoint 2: _October 2, 2XXX_

Checkpoint 3: _October 16, 2XXX_

Classroom Presentation: _November 1, 2XXX_

Travel Passport Expo: _November 7, 2XXX_
_6:30 - 7:30 pm_

signatures

I agree to:

- meet expectations on the dates listed above.
- complete each of the Travel Passport requirements to the best of my ability.
- bring my project work to school each day so that I can work on it during extra time.
- take my project work from school each night so that I can work on it at home.

I understand that the Envision Travel Passport Project is a special opportunity, and that if I do not meet the above expectations, I may be asked to return to normal classroom activities.

Student Signature: _Alyssa Good_   Date: _September 6, 2XXX_

Parent Signature: _Joanne Good_   Date: _September 6, 2XXX_

Please return this contract by: _September 7, 2XXX_

POSTCARD

DAILY ITINERARY

QUESTIONS

Each bulleted question for Component 1 should be answered on a separate sheet of paper. Each answer should be a paragraph or more in length. The question should be written clearly at the top of the page. Your answer should be well explained and include your thought process and reasoning. Once you have completed your answer, you may have extra white space on the page. Use this white space to demonstrate your creativity with art, borders or other finishing touches.

WHAT IS MY SPECIFIC TRAVEL DESTINATION?

I am going to Toronto! It is the capitol of the Canadian province of Ontario. Its relative location is 223.5 miles northeast of my home in Harrison Township, Michigan. It is on the north shore of Lake Ontario. Its absolute location is 43° 40′ North and 79° 22′ West.

I was debating whether to visit Toronto or the city of Calgary (located in the province of Alberta). I chose Toronto because it is much closer to my home, which makes the trip more affordable. It also has a tremendous variety of activities and is beautiful during the holiday season. Another great thing about Toronto is that things are close together and easy to get to. I won't waste a lot of time and money on day trips. Some interesting things I found out about Toronto while researching are…

STEP 4
Checkpoint Meetings

Although Envision is an independent study program, your interaction and guidance are crucial to each student's success. The checkpoint process assures students that they will have a scheduled time to receive your personal attention. It also allows them to share their accomplishments to date and ask any questions they may have. At each Checkpoint Meeting, you can assess progress and lend support and direction, encouraging the students to stay on track to meet upcoming deadlines. To help schedule and run your checkpoints smoothly, complete the following steps.

> **IMPORTANT!**
> You will revisit this section (Step 4) each time you plan to conduct a Checkpoint Meeting.

Preparation for Checkpoint Meetings:

4.1 Copy a Student Checkpoint Organizer for each of your Envision students.

4.2 Copy one Teacher Checkpoint Record and fill in your Envision student names.

Distribute Checkpoint Organizers:

4.3 Distribute the Student Checkpoint Organizers to your Envision students. Have each student fill in his or her name, the upcoming Checkpoint Date and the Travel Destination.

4.4 Explain to the students that in a few days you will be meeting with them to discuss their projects. Explain that they will each need to complete a Student Checkpoint Organizer and bring it on that day.

4.5 Read through the organizer with them and answer any questions.

4.6 Direct the students to complete their organizer over the next few days and bring it to the Checkpoint Meeting.

Checkpoint Meetings:

4.7 While your non-Envision students are working, ask a group of five to six Envision students to meet with you for a Checkpoint Meeting. Remind them to bring their completed Student Checkpoint Organizers, Student Instruction Guides and project materials.

4.8 Using the Student Checkpoint Organizers, allow each student to respond to each question. Ask students to expand on their answers when necessary. Offer assistance where needed.

4.9 Use your Teacher Checkpoint Record to record any notes you wish to make.

4.10 Conclude the meeting by collecting the Student Checkpoint Organizers to keep for your records.

4.11 Keep your Teacher Checkpoint Record for use at all Checkpoint Meetings and for your records.

4.12 Direct the first group of students to return to their seats and ask your next group of five to six Envision students to meet with you for a Checkpoint Meeting.

Repeat Steps 4.7 through 4.12 until each Envision student has met with you.

STUDENT CHECKPOINT ORGANIZER

Student Name: _Brendan_   Checkpoint Date: _September 18, 2XXX_

Travel Destination: _Paris, France_

directions

1. Using your Student Instruction Guide check off any requirements that you have completed up to this point.

2. Bring the following items to the Checkpoint Meeting:

• your Student Instruction Guide.

• your completed Student Checkpoint Organizer.

• all of your project materials.

questions

1. Which requirements have you completed up to this point?

All of my portfolio questions. They were fun!

2. Is there anything you need help with?

I'd like help deciding which 3-D visual to create: Eiffel Tower or Arc de Triomphe.

3. Is there anything else about your project that you would like to discuss?

Will you look over the rough draft of my travel memoir?

4. List at least three goals you expect to accomplish by the next checkpoint.

I plan to finish my itinerary, expense chart, graph and memoir by the next checkpoint.

TEACHER CHECKPOINT RECORD

student name	travel destination	checkpoint 1 notes	checkpoint 2 notes	checkpoint 3 notes
1. Michael	Monteverde, Costa Rica	Finished portfolio questions. Great start!		
2. Alysssa	Florence, Italy	Finished portfolio questions & itinerary!		
3. Brian	Orlando, Florida	Finished portfolio questions. Alex will assist Brian with computer graphs. Check back.		
4. Alex	Grand Canyon	Finished portfolio questions and memoir. Looks good!		
5. Lauren	Philadelphia, Pennsylvania	Finished portfolio questions 1-9. Working on question 10. Needs a binder.		
6. Brendan	Paris, France	Finished questions. Working on itinerary. Discussed 3-D visual: chose the tower.		
7. Ella	Washington, D.C.	Finished portfolio questions and itinerary. Excellent!		
8. Teagan	Frankfurt, Germany	Finished portfolio questions. Great start!		
9. Earl	Cairo, Egypt	Finished portfolio questions & memoir. Looks good!		
10.				

STEP 5
Preparing for the Project Expo and the Classroom Presentations

---

IMPORTANT!

The expo is an extremely important part of the Envision experience. While it requires a certain amount of work, it solidifies the entire experience for you, your students and your students' parents. It is very important that students have a special opportunity to shine and display all of the hard work they have done over the quarter. It is also extremely rewarding for you, who will not only be proud of the student accomplishments, but will also receive a lot of parent feedback at this time.

Preparation for the Project Expo:

5.1 Copy one Student Expo Invitation and use your Teacher Planning Guide to complete the expo information.

5.2 For each Envision student, copy a completed expo invitation and fold it accordingly.

Invite Families to the Project Expo:

5.3 Give a Student Expo Invitation to each Envision student. Point out to the students that there is an Expo Invitation Response included with the invitation for each family to sign, detach and return.

5.4 Send the Student Expo Invitations home with the students to their families.

Preparation for the Project Expo Continued:

5.5 As the expo responses are returned to you, record the information in the correct columns of the Teacher Forms Checklist.

5.6 Based on the Expo Invitation Responses, review whether any students will need special equipment, such as a computer or television. Reserve the equipment if necessary.

5.7 Based on the Expo Invitation Responses, find and reserve a large enough expo location (classroom, library, gymnasium or hallway) in which to host the expo. Be sure the location can accommodate any equipment required by the students.

5.8 Create a general plan for ordering, obtaining and serving refreshments (optional).

5.9 Copy a Student Certificate for each Envision student. Complete the certificates and set them aside for the Project Expo.

5.10 Copy a Student Name Sign for each Envision student. Complete each name sign and set it aside for the Project Expo.

5.11 Walk the route from the entrance of the Project Expo location building to the entrance of the Project Expo location itself. Count the number of Left and Right Arrow Signs you will need to post along the way. Make enough copies of each and set them aside for the Project Expo.

Preparation for Classroom Presentations and the Project Expo:

5.12 Copy a Teacher Assessment for each Envision student to use for Classroom Presentations.

5.13 Copy a Student Self-Assessment for each Envision student. Set them aside for Student Self-Assessment time.

IMPORTANT!

Be sure to keep the Student Self-Assessments separate from the Teacher Assessments. The main reason for this is so that students are assessing themselves without seeing the points you have already given. Students cannot complete their Self-Assessments prior to your Teacher Assessments because they need to wait until after they have given their Classroom Presentations.

5.14 Confirm your room and equipment reservations for the Project Expo.

5.15 Purchase any optional supplies or refreshments you will need for the Project Expo.

TRAVEL PASSPORT

YOU'RE INVITED!

EXPO INVITATION RESPONSE

Please fill out and return by: _Friday, Nov. 2_

Student Name: _____

Student Attending? ☐ Yes ☐ No

Number of Student Guests Attending: _____

Will your child need any special school equipment for

the expo (i.e.,computer or TV)? Please List: _____

_____

Thank you.

We look forward to seeing you at this special event!

PLEASE JOIN US FOR OUR ENVISION TRAVEL PASSPORT EXPO!

Why? _To view students' Envision accomplishments_

Who? _All are welcome - family and friends_

Where? _Mind Vine Elementary Gymnasium_

When? _Wednesday, Nov. 7, 2XXX · 6:30 pm - 7:30 pm_

Remember to bring your camera!

CERTIFICATE OF ACHIEVEMENT

Michael

AWARDED TO

November 7, 2XXX

DATE

Mrs. Bondy

SIGNATURE

envisi⊙n

TRAVEL PASSPORT PROJECT

Michael

STUDENT

envisi⊙n

travel passport expo

envision®

travel passport expo

envision®

31

TEACHER ASSESSMENT
TEACHER ASSESSMENT

TEACHER ASSESSMENT

Component 1: Building Your Project Portfolio
Total Possible Portfolio Points: 66 (out of 100 total possible for project)

Requirements	Possible Points	Teacher Points	Average Points
1. Questions			
What is your specific travel destination (city, state/province, country)? What is its absolute location (latitude and longitude) and relative location (refer to surroundings, such as nearby cities, geographical features or landmarks)? Why is this destination of interest to you?	3		
When will you take your trip (time, day, month, year)? How long will you stay? How do costs, seasonal patterns and the destination itself affect or determine your choices about when to travel and how long to stay?	3		
Will you travel alone or with a companion? What are the possible benefits and drawbacks of traveling alone, with a friend or with a family member? (Remember that your traveling companion's expenses will come out of your total travel budget.)	3		
What modes of transportation (car, plane, bicycle, train, boat) will you use for each stage of your trip? How do cost and timing affect or determine your choices of transportation?	3		
Where will you stay while traveling (hotel, resort, campground)? Will you stay in one place or move around? How do cost and location affect your choices of accommodations?	3		
What specific attractions or sites will you visit? What specific events or activities might you attend or partake in at each? How do cost, timing and location affect your choices?	3		
Where will you eat while on your trip (restaurants, fast food, vendors, at your place of accommodation)? How do cost, timing and location affect your dining choices?	3		
What clothes, special gear or special documents will you need for your trip? What arrangements need to be made to obtain these items?	3		
What souvenirs or keepsakes will you purchase while on your trip? How does your budget affect your choices?	3		
Will your trip cause you to miss any commitments at home? What responsibilities – such as chores or caring for a pet – do you have that will be taken care of by someone else while you are away? What arrangements have you made for these commitments and responsibilities while you are away? How does your budget affect your arrangements?	3		
2. Daily Itinerary: Organize a detailed daily itinerary for your trip beginning with the day you depart and concluding with the day of your return. Be sure to account for every part of each day.	5		
3. Expense Chart: Create an expense chart showing every good or service you have purchased or plan to purchase for or on your trip. Be sure to include taxes, tips and a total for each expense. Also, show your grand total for all your travel expenses. Be sure that you do not go over your budget. If you are under budget, explain what you will do with any leftover money.	8		

STUDENT SELF-ASSESSMENT
STUDENT SELF-ASSESSMENT

STUDENT SELF-ASSESSMENT

Component 1: Building Your Project Portfolio
Total Possible Portfolio Points: 66 (out of 100 total possible for project)

Requirements	Possible Points	Student Points
1. Questions		
What is your specific travel destination (city, state/province, country)? What is its absolute location (latitude and longitude) and relative location (refer to surroundings, such as nearby cities, geographical features or landmarks)? Why is this destination of interest to you?	3	
When will you take your trip (time, day, month, year)? How long will you stay? How do costs, seasonal patterns and the destination itself affect or determine your choices about when to travel and how long to stay?	3	
Will you travel alone or with a companion? What are the possible benefits and drawbacks of traveling alone, with a friend, or with a family member? (Remember that your traveling companion's expenses will come out of your total travel budget.	3	
What modes of transportation (car, plane, bicycle, train, boat) will you use for each stage of your trip? How do cost and timing affect or determine your choices of transportation?	3	
Where will you stay while traveling (hotel, resort, campground)? Will you stay in one place or move around? How do cost and location affect your choices of accommodations?	3	
What specific attractions or sites will you visit? What specific events or activities might you attend or partake in at each? How do cost, timing and location affect your choices?	3	
Where will you eat while on your trip (restaurants, fast food, vendors, at your place of accommodation)? How do cost, timing and location affect your dining choices?	3	
What clothes, special gear or special documents will you need for your trip? What arrangements need to be made to obtain these items?	3	
What souvenirs or keepsakes will you purchase while on your trip? How does your budget affect your choices?	3	
Will your trip cause you to miss any commitments at home? What responsibilities – such as chores or caring for a pet – do you have that will be taken care of by someone else while you are away? What arrangements have you made for these commitments and responsibilities while you are away? How does your budget affect your arrangements?	3	
2. Daily Itinerary: Organize a detailed daily itinerary for your trip beginning with the day you depart and concluding with the day of your return. Be sure to account for every part of each day.	5	
3. Expense Chart: Create an expense chart showing every good or service you have purchased or plan to purchase for or on your trip. Be sure to include taxes, tips and a total for each expense. Also, show your grand total for all your travel expenses. Be sure that you do not go over your budget. If you are under budget, explain what you will do with any leftover money.	8	

STEP 6
Conducting the Classroom Presentations

This is the first occasion for your Envision students to share their completed projects with an audience – in this case, you and the rest of the class. It is the only opportunity they will have to formally present their projects to an audience.

Note: For logistics and classroom management reasons, choose the Option below that best describes your Envision student participation and follow its set of directions.

Classroom Presentations Option A:
A minority of the class is participating in Envision

6A.1 When students arrive at school on Classroom Presentation day, have them place their materials in a safe location. This may be on a table, on the floor to the side of the room or at any other location that you specify.

6A.2 Just before you are ready to begin the presentations, gather a pen and the Teacher Assessments that you copied in Step 5.

Note: This will be your only opportunity to assess the presentations. However, you will have more time later to assess the exhibits.

6A.3 Set a table in the front of the room.

6A.4 Ask all students to sit at their regular classroom seats and face the front of the room.

6A.5 Sit in a location that will not be distracting to the presenter or the audience, yet will allow you to assess each presentation and each exhibit item clearly. The side of the room near the front usually works well.

6A.6 **The First Presenter:** Ask for a volunteer or select a student to begin presenting. The student who will present should carry her portfolio and exhibit components to the front of the room and set them on the table. (Enlist another student to help if necessary.)

6A.7 Record the presenting student's name on a Teacher Assessment.

6A.8 Ask the student to stand next to her project and begin her presentation.

6A.9 Assess the student's presentation using a Teacher Assessment.

IMPORTANT!

This will be your only opportunity to assess the presentation.

6A.10 Use any extra time during the presentation to begin assessing the student's exhibit components.

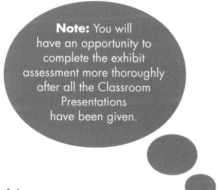

Note: You will have an opportunity to complete the exhibit assessment more thoroughly after all the Classroom Presentations have been given.

6A.11 Allow peers to ask questions of the presenter.

6A.12 **Transitioning Between Presenters:**
When the first presenter concludes her presentation and everyone has finished applauding, ask for the next volunteer or call the next student's name. As the next student is gathering his materials, the first student can remove hers and set them back where they had been placed earlier. Allow a minute or two for transitioning. Continue this process until all of your Envision students have presented.

6A.13 Conclude the presentations by thanking your Envision students for all of their hard work and by thanking all students for their attention.

Classroom Presentations Option B:
A majority or all of the class is participating in Envision

6B.1 When students arrive at school on Classroom Presentation day, have them place their materials in a safe location. This may be on a table, on the floor to the side of the room or at any other location that you specify.

6B.2 Just before you are ready to begin the presentations, gather a pen, the Teacher Assessments (copied in Step 5) and a clipboard or other writing surface to carry with you.

TEACHER INSTRUCTION GUIDE

6B.3 Instruct all Envision students to set up their portfolios and exhibits at their desks. This should take just a few minutes.

6B.4 **The First Presenter:** Ask for a volunteer or select a student to begin presenting.

6B.5 Record the presenting student's name on an assessment, using your clipboard for writing support.

6B.6 Have the student remain at her seat and stand to the side of her project. Ask all other students to quietly gather in front of her.

6B.7 Stand in a location that will not be distracting to the presenter or the audience, yet will allow you to assess each presentation and each exhibit item clearly. The side of the group near the front usually works well.

6B.8 Allow the student to begin her presentation.

6B.9 Assess the student's presentation using a Teacher Assessment.

IMPORTANT!
This will be your only opportunity to assess the presentation.

6B.10 Use any extra time during the presentation to begin assessing her exhibit components.

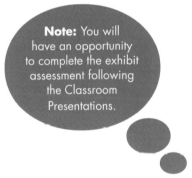

Note: You will have an opportunity to complete the exhibit assessment following the Classroom Presentations.

6B.11 **Transitioning Between Presenters:** When the first presenter concludes her presentation and everyone has finished applauding, ask for the next volunteer or call the next student's name. Direct everyone to quietly move to that student's exhibit. Continue this process until all of your Envision students have presented.

6B.12 Conclude the presentations by thanking your Envision students for all of their hard work and by thanking all students for their attention. Keep all projects set up as you will now be conducting the Classroom Expo.

STEP 7

Classroom Expo & Student Self-Assessment

The Classroom Expo is a time where classroom peers have a chance to walk around and view the projects. Each Envision student will stand with his project and answer any questions that his peers may have. This will now be your opportunity to further assess the exhibit components. Again, for logistics and classroom management reasons, choose the option below that best describes your Envision student participation and follow its set of directions.

Classroom Expo and Student Self-Assessment
Option A: A minority of the class is participating in Envision

7A.1 Just before you are ready to begin the Classroom Expo, gather a pen, the Teacher Assessments (copied in Step 5) and a clipboard or other writing surface to carry with you.

7A.2 Direct your non-Envision students to remain seated at their desks.

7A.3 Have your Envision students quietly set up their portfolios and exhibits. This can be done at a single large table, on a counter space or at each student's desk.

7A.4 Have each Envision student stand beside her exhibit.

7A.5 Instruct the rest of the class to put away their work materials and begin visiting each Envision exhibit. Encourage them to ask questions about the projects. Tell them the approximate amount of time they will have to visit all the exhibits.

7A.6 While students are enjoying the Classroom Expo, walk around the room and assess each student's exhibit components using your clipboard, pen and Teacher Assessments.

IMPORTANT!

Students will be leaving their exhibits in the classroom until they set up for the Project Expo. Therefore, if you need more time to assess the exhibits, you may continue the assessments at another time prior to the expo.

7A.7 At the Classroom Expo conclusion, ask non-Envision students to return to their desks. Allow your Envision students a few minutes to take down their exhibits and return them to a safe location.

7A.8 Have Envision students return to their desks.

7A.9 Distribute the Student Self-Assessments (copied in Step 5) to Envision students and ask the students privately complete them, including adding the total points for each component. Instruct the students to hand them in to you when they are finished.

TEACHER INSTRUCTION GUIDE

Classroom Expo and Student Self-Assessment
Option B: A majority or all of the class is participating in Envision

7B.1 Continue to carry your clipboard, pen and Teacher Assessments to use during the Classroom Expo.

7B.2 Direct half of your Envision students to stand beside their exhibits.

7B.3 Instruct the rest of the class to begin visiting each Envision exhibit. Encourage them to ask questions about the projects. Tell them the approximate amount of time they will have to visit all the exhibits.

7B.4 While students are enjoying the Classroom Expo, walk around the room and assess the vacant student exhibits using your clipboard, pen and Teacher Assessments.

7B.5 When you are ready to move on to the second set of exhibits, direct your students to switch roles. Any non-Envision students can continue visiting exhibits they have not yet been to.

7B.6 Again, proceed with the Classroom Expo remembering to tell students the approximate amount of time they will have to visit the remaining exhibits.

7B.7 During this time, walk around the room and assess the remaining student exhibits.

IMPORTANT!

Students will be leaving their exhibits in the classroom until they set up for the Project Expo. Therefore, if you need more time to assess the exhibits, you may continue the assessments at another time prior to the expo.

7B.8 At the Classroom Expo conclusion, ask students to help one another take down their exhibits and return them to a safe location. Non-Envision students can help with this as well.

7B.9 Have all students return to their desks.

7B.10 Distribute the Student Self-Assessments (copied in Step 5) to Envision students and ask the students privately complete them, including adding the total points for each component. Instruct the students to hand them in to you when they are finished.

STEP 8

Final Preparation for the Project Expo

Students take immense pride in sharing the fruits of their hard work with relatives and friends at the Project Expo. The expo offers a fun, festive environment where family and friends have the opportunity to meet all the Envision students and see their projects. It is also a forum for Envision students to share their project experiences and educational growth with guests.

Final Preparation for the Project Expo:

8.1 Ensure that tables, desks, chairs, refreshments and any special equipment are in place. Refer to your Teacher Forms Checklist for any special equipment needed.

8.2 Prepare and set aside a camera, and video recorder if desired, for your use at the expo.

8.3 Assign each student a location for exhibit setup.

8.4 Place the appropriate Student Name Sign (prepared in Step 5) at each student's exhibit area.

8.5 Allow small groups of students to take their project components to their designated exhibit areas.

8.6 Hang the Envision Poster at the entrance of the expo location building.

8.7 Hang the Expo Arrow Signs (prepared in Step 5) along the route from the entrance of the location building to the specific expo location itself.

8.8 Hang the Project Poster at the entrance to the Project Expo location.

8.9 Have the Student Certificates (prepared in Step 5) ready to present to the students at the expo.

8.10 Explain to students that they should be on their best behavior at the expo. Also explain that each student should remain at his or her exhibit for the majority of the expo to answer guests' project questions.

welcome

TRAVE

envision®

An inspirational real-world program for

TRAVEL PASSPORT

CAREER ASPIRATION

FINANCIAL ADVENTURE

KNOWLEDGE QUEST

STEP 9

The Project Expo:

9.1 Greet the students and guests as they enter the expo location. Ask students to go directly to their exhibits. Invite guests to explore and ask questions at each exhibit.

9.2 Be sure to take photos, and video if desired, of the expo. Obtain at least one photo of each student with his exhibit to post later on your project bulletin board. Also, the photos may come in handy if you need to double-check anything during your final project assessment.

9.3 After everyone has had time to view the projects, gather them together and formally present the Student Certificates to the Envision students. Thank everyone for attending and for supporting the hard work of the students. Ask the Envision students to take home all of their project components except for the portfolios. You will need to assess these, and you will return them with each student's final Teacher Assessment.

9.4 Collect the portfolios so that you can complete the Teacher Assessment for each project.

STEP 10

Conclusion, Teacher Assessment and Student Review

Conclusion and Teacher Assessment:

10.1 Develop all expo photos.

10.2 Hang the Envision Bulletin Board Banner on a bulletin board in a high-traffic area.

10.3 Pick up the Envision photos and arrange them on the bulletin board. This will show the students your pride in their work.

10.4 Referring to student portfolios, complete the "Teacher Points" column for the "Component 1: Building Your Project Portfolio" section of the Teacher Assessments.

10.5 Add all columns on each Teacher Assessment, recording the "Total Points" for each component along with the "Total Project Points" at the end of the assessment.

10.6 Average the amount of each "Total Points" section from each student's Student Self-Assessment with the corresponding "Total Points" amount for each component section on his or her Teacher Assessment.

10.7 Record each component's average amount in the "Average Points" column of the Teacher Assessment for each student.

10.8 For each student, record the "Total Project Points" in your personal record book. Staple each student's Student Self-Assessment to their Teacher Assessment. Copy these packets for your records.

Student Review:

10.9 Return each student's portfolio and completed assessment packet.

10.10 Allow the students time to review their assessment packets and ask questions if they wish.

APPENDIX 1:
TRAVEL PASSPORT FORMS
AND RESOURCE CARDS

Levels From Lowest to Highest:
KNOWLEDGE • COMPREHENSION • APPLICATION • ANALYSIS • EVALUATION • SYNTHESIS

Below you will find each Travel Passport requirement, along with its corresponding level of Bloom's Taxonomy.

> **IMPORTANT!**
>
> The levels listed above are cumulative. For example, the highest level of thinking, Synthesis, incorporates all other levels of thinking: Knowledge, Comprehension, Application, Analysis and Evaluation.

COMPONENT 1

Building Your Project Portfolio Total Possible Portfolio Points: 66 out of 100 total possible for project

1. Questions (3 points each):

• What is your specific travel destination (city, state/province, country)? **KNOWLEDGE** What is its absolute location (latitude and longitude) and relative location (refer to surroundings, such as nearby cities, geographical features or landmarks)? **COMPREHENSION** Why is this destination of interest to you? **EVALUATION**

• When will you take your trip (time, day, month, year)? **KNOWLEDGE** How long will you stay? **KNOWLEDGE** How do costs, seasonal patterns and the destination itself affect or determine your choices about when to travel and how long to stay? **ANALYSIS**

• Will you travel alone or with a companion? **KNOWLEDGE** What are the possible benefits and drawbacks of traveling alone, with a friend or with a family member? **ANALYSIS**

• What modes of transportation (car, plane, bicycle, train, boat) will you use for each stage of your trip? **KNOWLEDGE** How do cost and timing affect or determine your choices of transportation? **ANALYSIS**

• Where will you stay while traveling (hotel, resort, campground)? **KNOWLEDGE** Will you stay in one place or move around? **KNOWLEDGE** How do cost and location affect your choices of accommodations? **ANALYSIS**

• What specific attractions or sites will you visit? **KNOWLEDGE** What specific events or activities might you attend or partake in at each? **KNOWLEDGE** How do cost, timing and location affect your choices? **ANALYSIS**

• Where will you eat while on your trip (restaurants, fast food, vendors, at your place of accommodation)? **KNOWLEDGE** How do cost, timing and location affect your dining choices? **ANALYSIS**

• What clothes, special gear or special documents will you need for your trip? **KNOWLEDGE** What arrangements need to be made to obtain these items? **ANALYSIS**

• What souvenirs or keepsakes will you purchase while on your trip? **KNOWLEDGE** How does your budget affect your choices? **ANALYSIS**

• Will your trip cause you to miss any commitments at home? **ANALYSIS** What responsibilities – such as chores or caring for a pet – do you have that will be taken care of by someone else while you are away? **ANALYSIS** What arrangements have you made for these commitments and responsibilities while you are away? **SYNTHESIS** How does your budget affect your arrangements? **ANALYSIS**

2. Daily Itinerary (3 points): Organize a detailed daily itinerary for your trip beginning with the day you depart and concluding with the day of your return. Be sure to account for every part of each day. **SYNTHESIS**

3. Expense Chart (8 points): Create an expense chart showing every good or service you have purchased or plan to purchase for or during your trip. Be sure to include taxes, tips and a total for each expense. Also, show your grand total for all your travel expenses. Be sure that you do not go over your budget. If you are under budget, explain what you will do with any leftover money. **SYNTHESIS**

4. Computer-Generated Graph (8 points): Using a computer, create a graph that shows data relevant to your trip. The type of graph you choose (pictograph, pie graph, bar graph or line graph) should be suitable to the data you are presenting. Be sure to give your graph a title and provide a key. **SYNTHESIS**

5. Travel Memoir (8 points): Compose a travel memoir based on your trip. Imagine that you have gone away and that you have returned safely home. Use this memoir to reflect creatively on one significant event, place or activity from your trip. It must be in the first person and in the past tense. A memoir is not merely a record of events; it also includes your impressions, thoughts and insights. Consider, among other things, how expectations for your trip compared with "actual" experiences of the trip itself. Your memoir should be at least a page or two in length, but you are free to write several pages if you so choose. **SYNTHESIS**

6. Table of Contents (2 points): Write a table of contents that lists all the sections of your portfolio along with their corresponding page numbers. **COMPREHENSION**

7. Cover Page (1 point): Create an eye-catching cover page for your portfolio that includes an original title for your project as well as your name and the Classroom Presentation date. **SYNTHESIS**

8. Portfolio (1 point): Organize all of your materials in a three-ring binder. The table of contents should come first, followed by your responses to the ten sets of questions in the order presented in this guide. Next should be your itinerary, expense chart, graph and memoir. Your cover page should be placed on the front of the portfolio. **SYNTHESIS**

COMPONENT 2

Creating Your Project Exhibit Total Possible Exhibit Points: 24 (out of 100 total possible for project)

1. Route Map (3 points): Find or create one or more maps that show your entire round-trip journey. Mark the map or maps to show the routes you took and the approximate total miles you traveled. You might also want to mark where you stayed and what sites you visited. It might be desirable to use or create a combination of maps of different scale and type. **SYNTHESIS**

2. Collection of Informational Materials (3 points): Collect brochures, photos, articles, music or other materials having to do with your travel destination. Classify and arrange them in an effective and pleasing manner. Hint: Consult the Internet, a tourist center, the chamber of commerce local to your trip or a travel agent for help. **SYNTHESIS**

3. Postcard (4 points): Design and create an original post card that has to do with your trip. Be creative! Use three-dimensional materials if you like. On the front should be a scene from your trip. On the back should be the name and address (can be fictional) of a friend or relative, a stamp designed by you with the correct postage and a personal note from you. Refer to your itinerary and memoir for postcard ideas.

4. Three-Dimensional Visual (5 points): Construct a three-dimensional visual saying something about your trip that the other exhibit items do not address directly or fully. Your three-dimensional visual, like the other items, should complement the entire exhibit. **SYNTHESIS**

5. Display Board (5 points): Use a large two- or three-panel display board to create an "advertisement" for your trip. It must include your project's title and your name. You may then choose to add any of the required items or any additional materials that you wish. **SYNTHESIS**

6. Exhibit (4 points): Arrange your exhibit items, your portfolio and any additional materials you wish to include in an appealing and informative way. **SYNTHESIS**

COMPONENT 3:

Giving Your Classroom Presentation

Total Possible Classroom Presentation Points: 10 (out of 100 total possible for project)

1. What to Include in Your Presentation:

- Destination (1 point): Share your trip destination, a description of it and why you chose to go there. **EVALUATION**

- Location (2 points): Point to your trip destination on your map or maps. **KNOWLEDGE**

- Events (1 point): Explain some of the main events of your trip, pointing to any relevant informational materials on your display board. **COMPREHENSION**

- Portfolio and Graph (2 points): Show your portfolio and explain the graph you made. **COMPREHENSION**

- Postcard (1 point): Show both sides of your postcard and explain what its scene shows. **COMPREHENSION**

- Three-Dimensional Visual (2 points): Show your three-dimensional visual and explain how it adds to your exhibit. **EVALUATION**

2. Attire (1 point): Dress in clothing that relates to your trip. **SYNTHESIS**

Step Number	Form Title	Number of Copies
1.1	Teacher Planning Guide	1 only
2.1-2.3	Parent Envision Introduction Letter Parent Travel Passport Introduction Letter Student Travel Passport Introduction Letter Student Instruction Guide	1 completed, then 1 per student 1 completed, then 1 per student 1 completed only 1 only
3.1-3.4	Teacher Forms Checklist Student Commitment Contract	1 completed only 1 completed, then 1 per student
3.5	Student Travel Passport Introduction Letter* Student Instruction Guide* Travel Passport Resource Card Appendix Pages* (optional)	1 completed, then one per student 1 per student 1 per student
4.1-4.2	Student Checkpoint Organizer Teacher Checkpoint Record	1 per student 1 completed only
5.1-5.2	Student Expo Invitation	1 completed, then one per student
5.9-5.11	Student Certificate Student Name Sign (optional) Left Arrow Sign Right Arrow Sign	1 per student, then each completed 1 per student, then each completed Amount needed Amount needed
5.12-5.13	Teacher Assessment Student Self-Assessment	1 per student 1 per student

* Staple these items into a packet for each student

Events scheduled with the class are in black.

Week	Event (Step Numbers)	Day and Date	Time
1	Planning and Preparing for the Quarter (1.1-1.2)		
	Prepare for Travel Passport Introduction (2.1-2.3)		
	Travel Passport Introduction (2.4-2.7)		
	Preparation for Travel Passport Implementation (3.1-3.6)		
	Travel Passport Implementation (3.7-3.17)		
3	Preparation for the Checkpoint Meetings (4.1-4.2)		
	Distribute Checkpoint Organizers (4.3-4.6)		
	Checkpoint Meetings (4.7-4.12)		
5	Preparation for the Checkpoint Meetings (4.1-4.2)		
	Distribute Checkpoint Organizers (4.3-4.6)		
	Checkpoint Meetings (4.7-4.12)		
7	Preparation for the Checkpoint Meetings (4.1-4.2)		
	Distribute Checkpoint Organizers (4.3-4.6)		
	Checkpoint Meetings (4.7-4.12)		
8	Preparation for the Travel Passport Expo (5.1-5.2)		
	Invite Families to the Travel Passport Expo (5.3-5.4)		
	Preparation for the Travel Passport Expo Ctd. (5.5-5.11)		
9	Preparation for Classroom Presentations and the Travel Passport Expo (5.12-5.15)		
	Classroom Presentations (6A.1-6A.13 or 6B.1-6B.12)		
	Classroom Expo and Student Self-Assessment (7A.1-7A.9 or 7B.1-7B.10)		
10	Final Preparation for the Travel Passport Expo (8.1-8.10)		
	Travel Passport Expo (9.1-9.4)		
	Conclusion and Teacher Assessment (10.1-10.8)		
	Student Review (10.9-10.10)		

Maximum Travel Passport budget amount: $_____ • Minimum Travel Passport budget amount: $_____

 introduction letter

Dear Parent(s),

I am happy to inform you that your child has been invited to participate in an advanced academic program called Envision. I am sending you this letter to explain the program and ask for your permission to include your child in this special opportunity.

Envision is an exciting, yearlong program designed for students who are not sufficiently challenged by the standard grade-level curriculum. The focus of the program is on developing high-level critical thinking and creativity, and encourages students to *envision* how they might achieve their goals for the future. Envision guides students through four real-world-based projects, one for each quarter of the school year.

In chronological order, the four projects are: Travel Passport, Career Aspiration, Financial Adventure and Knowledge Quest. Travel Passport allows students to choose a destination and fully plan and coordinate an imaginary trip. Career Aspiration engages students in thinking concretely about possible academic and career choices they will face later in life. The third project, Financial Adventure, helps students discover the realities of personal finance, from housing expenses and paying bills, to making purchases and saving and investing for the future. Finally, Knowledge Quest allows students to research, in depth, any topic they are interested in and want to know more about. Each project introduces new ideas, new vocabulary, new technology and new challenges.

Students will work on Envision during class time, free time and at home.

To give permission for your child to participate in Envision, simply sign the Envision Permission Form at the bottom of this letter, detach it and return the form to me. If you want your child to participate in Envision, please read the attached Parent Travel Passport Introduction Letter. The letter introduces you to the first project, informs you of important dates and requests permission for your child's continued participation. You will receive a Parent Project Introduction Letter at the beginning of each quarter with the start of each new project.

Envision promises to be a wonderful learning opportunity for your child. I look forward to hearing from you. Please feel free to contact me if you have any questions.

Sincerely,

_____

_____

- -

 permission form

Please fill out this section, detach and return as soon as possible.   Date: _____

❑ I have read the Parent Envision Introduction Letter and give my child permission to participate in the Envision program.

❑ I have read the Parent Envision Introduction Letter and do not give my child permission to participate in the Envision program.

Child's Name:_____   Parent's Signature: _____

parent travel passport introduction letter

Dear Parent(s),

Welcome to Travel Passport, an Envision project that will challenge and inspire your child. Travel Passport gives your child an imaginary allowance to "travel" anywhere in the world. The challenge is that your child will plan, budget and document every aspect of the trip.

For this project, your child will conduct research on his or her travel destination and then make numerous informed decisions regarding concerns such as where, when and how to travel; where to stay; what to visit; and how to prepare for his or her absence from home. Your child will then create a daily itinerary, a travel-expense chart, a computer-generated graph of travel-related facts or statistics and a fictional travel memoir regarding his or her travel "experiences." Lastly, your child will build an exhibit that presents key aspects of his or her travels, and will give a brief formal presentation to the class.

A Student Instruction Guide will be provided to guide your child, step by step, through this process. The Instruction Guide is a comprehensive list of project requirements and is designed to engage higher-level thinking. The guide also refers to helpful Resource Cards, that provide additional explanations, ideas, tips and directions. There will be a set of these cards to which your child can refer in our classroom.

Travel Passport is designed to be worked on independently during class time, free time and at home. By scheduling several Checkpoint Meeting dates throughout the quarter, I will be able to monitor each student's progress. On these dates, I will meet with each student to discuss accomplishments and plan goals for the next checkpoint. I will also address any difficulties students might be having.

Travel Passport will conclude with a Project Expo. The expo will be your child's opportunity to share his or her finished project with family, friends and other guests. You will receive a detailed invitation to the Project Expo later in the quarter.

Dates to Remember:

Checkpoint 1: _____

Checkpoint 2: _____

Checkpoint 3: _____

Classroom Presentation: _____

Travel Passport Expo: _____ , _____

Sincerely,

_____

_____

TRAVEL PASSPORT

student travel passport introduction letter

Dear Student,

Welcome to Travel Passport! This is the first project you will embark on as part of the Envision Program experience. Travel Passport is about taking a journey – a journey of the imagination. It is also a very real journey of discovery, research and creativity.

The project begins with your receiving an imaginary travel budget of $____. You will be required to spend at least $____. Keeping these amounts in mind, you will choose a real travel destination, one that you can reach and enjoy within your budget. Your destination should be a place of special interest to you.

This project contains four components. The first will be to research and write about your destination and your trip. You will organize this information in a project portfolio. The second will be to create an exhibit of your trip as if you had already gone and come home. The third will be to share your completed portfolio and exhibit with your classmates. To do this, you will give a brief formal presentation. During your presentation, you will explain key aspects of your trip. Fourth is the Project Expo, an event that celebrates your hard work and achievements. This final component allows you the opportunity to invite family and friends to share in your success.

You will work on Travel Passport throughout the school day and also during your free time and at home. Generally, you will be expected to work on your own. You will consult with me periodically at Checkpoint Meetings to discuss your progress and receive guidance. Between the checkpoints, feel free to discuss your project with other Envision students.

The attached Student Instruction Guide contains all the information you will need to complete the required Travel Passport Project successfully. The Instruction Guide will challenge you to be resourceful, organized and to think at a higher level.

Dates to Remember:

Checkpoint 1: _____

Checkpoint 2: _____

Checkpoint 3: _____

Classroom Presentation: _____

Travel Passport Expo: _____ , _____

After reading this introduction, you are now ready to begin thinking about your travel destination and planning your adventure. Good luck and have fun!

Sincerely,

_____

_____

Building Your Project Portfolio • Creating Your Project Exhibit
Presenting Your Project • Attending the Expo

CREATIVITY IS HIGHLY ENCOURAGED!

IMPORTANT!

Available resource cards are denoted by a Travel Passport icon [icon]. When you see one of these icons, you will know that there is a corresponding numbered resource card available that gives additional helpful information and depicts visual examples for your reference. Also, be sure to visit mindvinepress.com, other trustworthy Internet sites, library reference materials and (if you like) a travel agent, for additional resources and examples.

COMPONENT 1

Building Your Project Portfolio Total Possible Portfolio Points: 66 out of 100 total possible for project

Get ready! It is now time to plan and make decisions about the trip of your dreams. This will be a wonderful experience and opportunity to engage your intellectual abilities as well as your imagination. Complete the numbered requirements below, in order, as they build upon one another and will guide you smoothly through the process. Bon voyage!

1. [icon] **Questions** (3 points each): Compose a paragraph or more for each bullet-pointed set of questions below. Write each paragraph on its own separate page. Title each page.

Note: You may write about yourself as if you were an adult, old enough to drive a car and rent a hotel room. You may "take along" a traveling companion, but the extra expenses must come out of your total travel budget.

- What is your specific travel destination (city, state/province, country)? What is its absolute location (latitude and longitude) and relative location (refer to surroundings, such as nearby cities, geographical features or landmarks)? Why is this destination of interest to you?

- When will you take your trip (time, day, month, year)? How long will you stay? How do costs, seasonal patterns and the destination itself affect or determine your choices about when to travel and how long to stay?

- Will you travel alone or with a companion? What are the possible benefits and drawbacks of traveling alone, with a friend or with a family member? Remember that your traveling companion's expenses will come out of your total travel budget.

- What modes of transportation (car, plane, bicycle, train, boat) will you use for each stage of your trip? How do cost and timing affect or determine your choices of transportation?

- Where will you stay while traveling (hotel, resort, campground)? Will you stay in one place or move around? How do cost and location affect your choices of accommodations?

- What specific attractions or sites will you visit? What specific events or activities might you attend or partake in at each? How do cost, timing and location affect your choices?

- Where will you eat while on your trip (restaurants, fast food, vendors, at your place of accommodation)? How do cost, timing and location affect your dining choices?

- What clothes, special gear or special documents will you need for your trip? What arrangements need to be made to obtain these items?

- What souvenirs or keepsakes will you purchase while on your trip? How does your budget affect your choices?

- Will your trip cause you to miss any commitments at home? What responsibilities – such as chores or caring for a pet – do you have that will be taken care of by someone else while you are away? What arrangements have you made for these commitments and responsibilities while you are away? How does your budget affect your arrangements?

2. ✈ **Daily Itinerary** (5 points): Organize a detailed daily itinerary for your trip beginning with the day you depart and concluding with the day of your return. Be sure to account for every part of each day.

3. ✈ **Expense Chart** (8 points): Create an expense chart showing every good or service you have purchased or plan to purchase for or during your trip. Be sure to include taxes, tips and a total for each expense. Also, show your grand total for all your travel expenses. Be sure that you do not go over your budget. If you are under budget, explain what you will do with any leftover money.

4. ✈ **Computer-Generated Graph** (8 points): Using a computer, create a graph that shows data relevant to your trip. The type of graph you choose (pictograph, pie graph, bar graph or line graph) should be suitable to the data you are presenting. Be sure to give your graph a title and provide a key.

5. ✈ **Travel Memoir** (8 points): Compose a travel memoir based on your trip. Imagine that you have gone away and that you have returned safely home. Use this memoir to reflect creatively on one significant event, place or activity from your trip. It must be in the first person and in the past tense. A memoir is not merely a record of events; it also includes your impressions, thoughts and insights. Consider, among other things, how expectations for your trip compared with "actual" experiences of the trip itself. Your memoir should be at least a page or two in length, but you are free to write several pages if you so choose.

6. ✈ **Table of Contents** (3 points): Write a table of contents that lists all the sections of your portfolio along with their corresponding page numbers.

7. ✈ **Cover Page** (2 points): Create an eye-catching cover page for your portfolio that includes an original title for your project as well as your name and the Classroom Presentation date.

8. ✈ **Portfolio** (2 points): Organize all of your materials in a three-ring binder. The table of contents should come first, followed by your responses to the ten sets of questions in the order presented in this guide. Next should be your itinerary, expense chart, graph and memoir. Your cover page should be placed on the front of the portfolio.

You have completed Component 1 of the Travel Passport Project. By completing your portfolio, you have created an important resource that will help you work on Components 2 and 3. Though several worthy challenges lie ahead, you are now prepared to meet each of them, knowing that you have laid the necessary groundwork that will increase your chances for success. Good luck as you move on to creating your project exhibit items.

STUDENT INSTRUCTION GUIDE

COMPONENT 2

Creating Your Project Exhibit Total Possible Exhibit Points: 24 out of 100 total possible for project

Having "returned" from your trip, it is now time to design and create an informative and appealing visual exhibit of your destination and experiences. The items you complete will be viewed by your classmates on the day of your Classroom Presentation and also by everyone who attends the Travel Passport Expo at the end of the term. As always, put your best work into designing, creating and integrating your exhibit items.

> **Note:**
> Keep in mind that each item is only one part of the overall exhibit. In other words, no single item has to say everything about your destination or your trip. Decide upon a purpose for each item. Consider how best to arrange your exhibit for the greatest effect.

1. Route Map (3 points): Find or create one or more maps that show your entire round-trip journey. Mark the map or maps to show the routes you took and the approximate total miles you traveled. You might also want to mark where you stayed and what sites you visited. It might be desirable to use or create a combination of maps of different scale and type.

2. Collection of Informational Materials (3 points): Collect brochures, photos, articles, music or other materials having to do with your travel destination. Classify and arrange them in an effective and pleasing manner. Hint: Consult the Internet, a tourist center, the chamber of commerce (local to your trip) or a travel agent for help.

3. Postcard (4 points): Design and create an original postcard that has to do with your trip. Be creative! Use three-dimensional materials if you like. On the front should be a scene from your trip. On the back should be the name and address (can be fictional) of a friend or relative, a stamp designed by you with the correct postage and a personal note from you. Refer to your itinerary and memoir for postcard ideas.

4. Three-Dimensional Visual (5 points): Construct a three-dimensional visual saying something about your trip that the other exhibit items do not address directly or fully. Your three-dimensional visual, like the other items, should complement the entire exhibit.

5. Display Board (5 points): Use a large two- or three-panel display board to create an "advertisement" for your trip. It must include your project's title and your name. You may then choose to add any of the required items or any additional materials that you wish.

6. Exhibit (4 points): Arrange your exhibit items, your portfolio and any additional materials you wish to include in an appealing and informative way.

You have now completed Component 2 of the Travel Passport Project, an important exhibit that creatively displays your trip. Now that you have finished your portfolio and exhibit, you are ready to confidently prepare for your Classroom Presentation (Component 3). Enjoy sharing your exciting project with your peers and teacher!

COMPONENT 3:

Giving Your Classroom Presentation
Total Possible Classroom Presentation Points: 10 out of 100 total possible for project

Now that you have planned, "returned from" and reflected on your trip, it is time to share your experiences with others. Your Classroom Presentation is an opportunity to formally present some highlights from your trip and to share some of your hard work. Your portfolio and exhibit contain all the information you will need to refer to for the presentation, so relax and have fun with it.

1. ✈ **What to Include in Your Presentation:**

- **Destination (1 point):** Share your trip destination, a description of it and why you chose to go there.
- **Location (2 points):** Point to your trip destination on your map or maps.
- **Events (1 point):** Explain some of the main events of your trip, pointing to any relevant informational materials on your display board.
- **Portfolio and Graph (2 points):** Show your portfolio and explain the graph you made.
- **Postcard (1 point):** Show both sides of your postcard and explain what its scene shows.
- **Three-Dimensional Visual (2 points):** Show your three-dimensional visual and explain how it adds to your exhibit.

Note: Your presentation should last between 3-4 minutes and should be rehearsed, but not memorized. If you forget to include information from one of the bullet points, your teacher will ask you the question so that you have a chance to answer it.

2. Attire (1 point): Dress in clothing that relates to your trip.

Bring to the Classroom Presentation: All of your exhibit items and anything extra that you would like to enhance your exhibit. Remember to dress in clothing that reflects your trip.

You are now finished with Components 1, 2 and 3 – all of the assessed portions of your project. The final Component, Attending the Travel Passport Expo, provides a festive closure to the Travel Passport Project.

COMPONENT 4:

Attending the Travel Passport Expo (The expo does not involve any points.)

Now that you have completed your project and presented it to your peers, it's time to share your work with family and friends at the Travel Passport Expo. The expo is an event that recognizes and celebrates the hard work you have done on your Travel Passport Project. At the expo, you will set up and stand by your exhibit as invited guests walk around informally and view the projects. Guests may ask you friendly questions about your project as they visit your exhibit, so have fun sharing your Travel Passport experiences with them.

Bring to the Expo: all of your exhibit items and anything extra that you would like to enhance your exhibit. Remember to dress in clothing that reflects your trip.

CONGRATULATIONS ON YOUR COMPLETED TRAVEL PASSPORT PROJECT!

TEACHER FORMS CHECKLIST

use this checklist to record forms submitted by the students

student name	envision permission form	student commitment contract	student checkpoint organizer 1	student checkpoint organizer 2	student checkpoint organizer 3	expo invitation response number attending special equip. needed
1.						
2.						
3.						
4.						
5.						
6.						
7.						
8.						
9.						
10.						
11.						
12.						
13.						
14.						
15.						
16.						
17.						
18.						
19.						
20.						
21.						
22.						
23.						
24.						
25.						

STUDENT COMMITMENT CONTRACT

expectations

project work time

I agree to:

- be responsible for following my Student Instruction Guide to do my work.
- keep track of all my project materials.
- work hard on Envision without disturbing others.
- save my unanswered questions until my teacher is free to talk.

checkpoint meetings

I will come prepared with:

- my Student Instruction Guide.
- my completed Student Checkpoint Organizer.
- all of my project materials.

important dates and times

Checkpoint 1: _____

Checkpoint 2: _____

Checkpoint 3: _____

Classroom Presentation: _____

Travel Passport Expo: _____

_____

signatures

I agree to:

- meet expectations on the dates listed above.
- complete each of the Travel Passport requirements to the best of my ability.
- bring my project work to school each day so that I can work on it during extra time.
- take my project work from school each night so that I can work on it at home.

I understand that the Envision Travel Passport Project is a special opportunity, and that if I do not meet the above expectations, I may be asked to return to normal classroom activities.

Student Signature: _____ Date: _____

Parent Signature: _____ Date: _____

Please return this contract by: _____

STUDENT CHECKPOINT ORGANIZER

Student Name: _____ Checkpoint Date: _____

Travel Destination: _____

directions

1. Using your Student Instruction Guide check off any requirements that you have completed up to this point.

2. Bring the following items to the Checkpoint Meeting:

• your Student Instruction Guide.

• your completed Student Checkpoint Organizer.

• all of your project materials.

questions

1. Which requirements have you completed up to this point?

_____

_____

2. Is there anything you need help with?

_____

_____

3. Is there anything else about your project that you would like to discuss?

_____

_____

4. List at least three goals you expect to accomplish by the next checkpoint.

_____

_____

TEACHER CHECKPOINT RECORD

student name	travel destination	checkpoint 1 notes	checkpoint 2 notes	checkpoint 3 notes
1.				
2.				
3.				
4.				
5.				
6.				
7.				
8.				
9.				
10.				

YOU'RE INVITED!

TRAVEL PASSPORT

EXPO INVITATION RESPONSE

Please fill out and return by: _____

Student Name: _____

Student Attending? ☐ Yes ☐ No

Number of Student Guests Attending: _____

Will your child need any special school equipment for the expo (i.e., a computer or TV)? Please List: _____

_____

Thank you.

We look forward to seeing you at this special event!

TRAVEL PASSPORT

PLEASE JOIN US FOR OUR ENVISION TRAVEL PASSPORT EXPO!

Why? _____

Who? _____

Where? _____

When? _____

Remember to bring your camera!

TRAVEL PASSPORT

CERTIFICATE OF ACHIEVEMENT

AWARDED TO

DATE

SIGNATURE

envision

TRAVEL PASSPORT

TRAVEL PASSPORT PROJECT

STUDENT

envision®

TRAVEL PASSPORT

travel passport expo

envision®

TEACHER ASSESSMENT

Component 1: Building Your Project Portfolio
Total Possible Portfolio Points: 66 out of 100 total possible for project

Requirements	Possible Points	Teacher Points	Average Points
1. Questions			
What is your specific travel destination (city, state/province, country)? What is its absolute location (latitude and longitude) and relative location (refer to surroundings, such as nearby cities, geographical features or landmarks)? Why is this destination of interest to you?	3		
When will you take your trip (time, day, month, year)? How long will you stay? How do costs, seasonal patterns and the destination itself affect or determine your choices about when to travel and how long to stay?	3		
Will you travel alone or with a companion? What are the possible benefits and drawbacks of traveling alone, with a friend or with a family member? Remember that your traveling companion's expenses will come out of your total travel budget.	3		
What modes of transportation (car, plane, bicycle, train, boat) will you use for each stage of your trip? How do cost and timing affect or determine your choices of transportation?	3		
Where will you stay while traveling (hotel, resort, campground)? Will you stay in one place or move around? How do cost and location affect your choices of accommodations?	3		
What specific attractions or sites will you visit? What specific events or activities might you attend or partake in at each? How do cost, timing and location affect your choices?	3		
Where will you eat while on your trip (restaurants, fast food, vendors, at your place of accommodation)? How do cost, timing and location affect your dining choices?	3		
What clothes, special gear or special documents will you need for your trip? What arrangements need to be made to obtain these items?	3		
What souvenirs or keepsakes will you purchase while on your trip? How does your budget affect your choices?	3		
Will your trip cause you to miss any commitments at home? What responsibilities – such as chores or caring for a pet – do you have that will be taken care of by someone else while you are away? What arrangements have you made for these commitments and responsibilities while you are away? How does your budget affect your arrangements?	3		
2. Daily Itinerary: Organize a detailed daily itinerary for your trip beginning with the day you depart and concluding with the day of your return. Be sure to account for every part of each day.	5		
3. Expense Chart: Create an expense chart showing every good or service you have purchased or plan to purchase for or on your trip. Be sure to include taxes, tips and a total for each expense. Also, show your grand total for all your travel expenses. Be sure that you do not go over your budget. If you are under budget, explain what you will do with any leftover money.	8		

4. Computer-Generated Graph: Using a computer, create a graph that shows data relevant to your trip. The type of graph you choose (pictograph, pie graph, bar graph or line graph) should be suitable to the data you are presenting. Be sure to give your graph a title and provide a key.	8		
5. Travel Memoir: Compose a travel memoir based on your trip. Imagine that you have gone away and that you have returned safely home. Use this memoir to reflect creatively on one significant event, place or activity from your trip. It must be in the first person and in the past tense. A memoir is not merely a record of events; it also includes your impressions, thoughts and insights. Consider, among other things, how expectations for your trip compared with "actual" experiences of the trip itself. Your memoir should be at least a page or two in length, but you are free to write several pages if you so choose.	8		
6. Table of Contents: Write a table of contents that lists all the sections of your portfolio along with their corresponding page numbers.	3		
7. Cover Page: Create an eye-catching cover page for your portfolio that includes an original title for your project as well as your name and the Classroom Presentation date.	2		
8. Portfolio: Organize all of your materials in a three-ring binder. The table of contents should come first, followed by your responses to the ten sets of questions in the order presented in this guide. Next should be your itinerary, expense chart, graph and memoir. Your cover page should be placed on the front of the portfolio.	2		
TOTAL PORTFOLIO POINTS	**66**		

Component 2: Creating the Project Exhibit
Total Possible Exhibit Points: 24 out of 100 total possible for project

1. Route Map: Find or create one or more maps that show your entire round-trip journey. Mark the map or maps to show the routes you took and the approximate total miles you traveled. You might also want to mark where you stayed and what sites you visited. It might be desirable to use or create a combination of maps of different scale and type.	3		
2. Collection of Informational Materials: Collect brochures, photos, articles, music or other materials having to do with your travel destination. Classify and arrange them in an effective and pleasing manner. Hint: Consult the Internet, a tourist center, the chamber of commerce (local to your trip) or a travel agent for help.	3		
3. Postcard: Design and create an original postcard that has to do with your trip. Be creative! Use three-dimensional materials if you like. On the front should be a scene from your trip. On the back should be the name and address (can be fictional) of a friend or relative, a stamp designed by you with the correct postage and a personal note from you. Refer to your itinerary and memoir for postcard ideas.	4		

4. Three-Dimensional Visual: Construct a three-dimensional visual saying something about your trip that the other exhibit items do not address directly or fully. Your three-dimensional visual, like the other items, should complement the entire exhibit.	5		
5. Display Board: Use a large two- or three-panel display board to create an "advertisement" for your trip. It must include your project's title and your name. You may then choose to add any of the required items or any additional materials that you wish.	5		
6. Exhibit: Arrange your exhibit items, your portfolio and any additional materials you wish to include in an appealing and informative way.	4		
TOTAL EXHIBIT POINTS	**24**		
Component 3: Giving Your Classroom Presentation Total Possible Classroom Presentation Points: 10 out of 100 total possible for project			
1. What to Include in Your Presentation:			
Destination: Share your trip destination, a description of it and why you chose to go there.	1		
Location: Point to your trip destination on your map or maps	2		
Events: Explain some of the main events of your trip, pointing to any relevant informational materials on your display board.	1		
Portfolio and Graph: Show your portfolio and explain the graph you made.	2		
Postcard: Show both sides of your postcard and explain what its scene shows.	1		
Three-Dimensional Visual: Show your three-dimensional visual and explain how it adds to your exhibit.	2		
2. Attire: Dress in clothing that relates to your trip.	1		
TOTAL CLASSROOM PRESENTATION POINTS	**10**		
TOTAL PROJECT POINTS	**100**		

Component 1: Building Your Project Portfolio
Total Possible Portfolio Points: 66 out of 100 total possible for project

Requirements	Possible Points	Student Points
1. Questions		
What is your specific travel destination (city, state/province, country)? What is its absolute location (latitude and longitude) and relative location (refer to surroundings, such as nearby cities, geographical features or landmarks)? Why is this destination of interest to you?	3	
When will you take your trip (time, day, month, year)? How long will you stay? How do costs, seasonal patterns and the destination itself affect or determine your choices about when to travel and how long to stay?	3	
Will you travel alone or with a companion? What are the possible benefits and drawbacks of traveling alone, with a friend or with a family member? Remember that your traveling companion's expenses will come out of your total travel budget.	3	
What modes of transportation (car, plane, bicycle, train, boat) will you use for each stage of your trip? How do cost and timing affect or determine your choices of transportation?	3	
Where will you stay while traveling (hotel, resort, campground)? Will you stay in one place or move around? How do cost and location affect your choices of accommodations?	3	
What specific attractions or sites will you visit? What specific events or activities might you attend or partake in at each? How do cost, timing and location affect your choices?	3	
Where will you eat while on your trip (restaurants, fast food, vendors, at your place of accommodation)? How do cost, timing and location affect your dining choices?	3	
What clothes, special gear or special documents will you need for your trip? What arrangements need to be made to obtain these items?	3	
What souvenirs or keepsakes will you purchase while on your trip? How does your budget affect your choices?	3	
Will your trip cause you to miss any commitments at home? What responsibilities – such as chores or caring for a pet – do you have that will be taken care of by someone else while you are away? What arrangements have you made for these commitments and responsibilities while you are away? How does your budget affect your arrangements?	3	
2. Daily Itinerary: Organize a detailed daily itinerary for your trip beginning with the day you depart and concluding with the day of your return. Be sure to account for every part of each day.	5	
3. Expense Chart: Create an expense chart showing every good or service you have purchased or plan to purchase for or during your trip. Be sure to include taxes, tips and a total for each expense. Also, show your grand total for all your travel expenses. Be sure that you do not go over your budget. If you are under budget, explain what you will do with any leftover money.	8	

4. Computer-Generated Graph: Using a computer, create a graph that shows data relevant to your trip. The type of graph you choose (pictograph, pie graph, bar graph or line graph) should be suitable to the data you are presenting. Be sure to give your graph a title and provide a key.	8	
5. Travel Memoir: Compose a travel memoir based on your trip. Imagine that you have gone away and that you have returned safely home. Use this memoir to reflect creatively on one significant event, place or activity from your trip. It must be in the first person and in the past tense. A memoir is not merely a record of events; it also includes your impressions, thoughts and insights. Consider, among other things, how expectations for your trip compared with "actual" experiences of the trip itself. Your memoir should be at least a page or two in length, but you are free to write several pages if you so choose.	8	
6. Table of Contents: Write a table of contents that lists all the sections of your portfolio along with their corresponding page numbers.	3	
7. Cover Page: Create an eye-catching cover page for your portfolio that includes an original title for your project as well as your name and the Classroom Presentation date.	2	
8. Portfolio: Organize all of your materials in a three-ring binder. The table of contents should come first, followed by your responses to the ten sets of questions in the order presented in this guide. Next should be your itinerary, expense chart, graph and memoir. Your cover page should be placed on the front of the portfolio.	2	
TOTAL PORTFOLIO POINTS	**66**	

Component 2: Creating the Project Exhibit
Total Possible Exhibit Points: 24 out of 100 total possible for project

1. Route Map: Find or create one or more maps that show your entire round-trip journey. Mark the map or maps to show the routes you took and the approximate total miles you traveled. You might also want to mark where you stayed and what sites you visited. It might be desirable to use or create a combination of maps of different scale and type.	3	
2. Collection of Informational Materials: Collect brochures, photos, articles, music or other materials having to do with your travel destination. Classify and arrange them in an effective and pleasing manner. Hint: Consult the Internet, a tourist center, the chamber of commerce (local to your trip) or a travel agent for help.	3	
3. Postcard: Design and create an original postcard that has to do with your trip. Be creative! Use three-dimensional materials if you like. On the front should be a scene from your trip. On the back should be the name and address (can be fictional) of a friend or relative, a stamp designed by you with the correct postage and a personal note from you. Refer to your itinerary and memoir for postcard ideas.	4	

4. Three-Dimensional Visual: Construct a three-dimensional visual saying something about your trip that the other exhibit items do not address directly or fully. Your three-dimensional visual, like the other items, should complement the entire exhibit.	5	
5. Display Board: Use a large two- or three-panel display board to create an "advertisement" for your trip. It must include your project's title and your name. You may then choose to add any of the required items or any additional materials that you wish.	5	
6. Exhibit: Arrange your exhibit items, your portfolio and any additional materials you wish to include in an appealing and informative way.	4	
TOTAL EXHIBIT POINTS	**24**	

Component 3: Giving Your Classroom Presentation Total Possible Classroom Presentation Points: 10 out of 100 total possible for project		
1. What to Include in Your Presentation:		
Destination: Share your trip destination, a description of it and why you chose to go there.	1	
Location: Point to your trip destination on your map or maps.	2	
Events: Explain some of the main events of your trip, pointing to any relevant informational materials on your display board.	1	
Portfolio and Graph: Show your portfolio and explain the graph you made.	2	
Postcard: Show both sides of your postcard and explain what its scene shows.	1	
Three-Dimensional Visual: Show your three-dimensional visual and explain how it adds to your exhibit.	2	
2. Attire: Dress in clothing that relates to your trip.	1	
TOTAL CLASSROOM PRESENTATION POINTS	**10**	
TOTAL PROJECT POINTS	**100**	

SPANISH TRANSLATIONS OF PARENT FORMS AND STUDENT INSTRUCTION GUIDE

carta de introducción

Estimados Padres,

Tengo el placer de informarles que su hijo/a ha sido seleccionado para participar en un programa para niños destacados llamado "Envision". El motivo de la presente es para explicarles el programa y para solicitar su permiso para que su hijo/a pueda participar en esta oportunidad tan especial.

"Envision" es un programa extraordinario diseñado para aquellos estudiantes cuyas habilidades no están siendo satisfechas con el programa común de su nivel académico. Este programa se enfoca en el desarrollo del pensamiento crítico y la creatividad; y motiva a los estudiantes a descubrir como pueden alcanzar sus metas en el futuro. "Envision" guía a los estudiantes a través de cuatro proyectos basados en la vida real, uno para cada trimestre del año escolar.

En orden cronológico, los proyectos son: "Pasaporte para Viajar", "Aspiración a una Carrera", "Aventura Financiera" y "Búsqueda de Conocimiento". "Pasaporte para Viajar" permite a los estudiantes elegir un destino, planificar cada detalle, y coordinar un viaje imaginario. "Aspiración a una Carrera" involucra a los estudiantes en el pensamiento concreto acerca de las posibilidades académicas y profesionales que enfrentará en el futuro. El tercer proyecto, "Aventura Financiera", ayuda a los estudiantes a descubrir la realidad de las finanzas personales, desde los gastos del hogar, hasta cómo manejar compras necesarias, y ahorrar e invertir para el futuro. Finalmente, "Búsqueda de Conocimiento" permite a los estudiantes investigar profundamente sobre un tema en el cual ellos tengan un interés. Cada proyecto presenta ideas nuevas, vocabulario nuevo, tecnología nueva y retos nuevos.

Los estudiantes trabajarán con "Envision" durante el tiempo en el salón de clase, su tiempo libre y en la casa.

Para que su hijo/a pueda participar en "Envision" por favor llene el Formulario de Participación de "Envision" al final de esta carta y mándelo de vuelta al salón de clase. Si a usted le gustaría que su hijo/a participe en "Envision", por favor lea la Carta para Padres del Proyecto "Pasaporte para Viajar" que se adjunta. Esta carta le presenta el primer proyecto, le informa de las fechas importantes, y solicita su permiso para la participación de su hijo/a. Usted recibirá una Carta para Padres de Presentación de Proyecto al inicio de cada trimestre y al comienzo de cada nuevo proyecto.

"Envision" será una oportunidad de aprendizaje estupenda para su hijo/a. Espero que su hijo/a participe en este programa, y si tiene preguntas por favor no dude en ponerse en contacto conmigo.

Sinceramente,

_____

_____

- -

envision formulario de participación

Por favor llene este formulario y envíelo de vuelta lo antes posible. Fecha: _____

❑ He leído la Carta para Padres de "Envision" y le doy permiso a mi hijo/a para que participe en este programa.

❑ He leído la Carta para Padres de "Envision" y no le doy permiso a mi hijo/a para que participe en este programa.

Nombre del Estudiante:_____ Firma del Padre: _____

carta de introducción para padres del proyecto pasaporte para viajar

Estimados Padres,

Bienvenidos a "Pasaporte para Viajar", un proyecto de "Envision" que inspirará y mantendrá la atención educativa de su hijo/a. "Pasaporte para Viajar" le dará a su hijo/a una cantidad de dinero ficticio para viajar a cualquier lugar del mundo. El reto de este proyecto es que el estudiante tendrá que diseñar un plan, mantener un presupuesto, y por último tendrá que documentar cada aspecto de su viaje.

Para este proyecto el alumno realizará investigaciones acerca de su destino y hará varias decisiones basadas en la información obtenida. Tendrá que decidir adonde, cuando y como viajará a su destino. Además el alumno decidirá hospedaje, lugares de exploración, y como planear para su ausencia de casa. El alumno creará un itinerario diario, una gráfica de gastos para su viaje, una gráfica generada por computadora de los hechos o estadísticas relacionadas con su viaje y un sumario de las "experiencias" de su viaje ficticio. Finalmente, su hijo/a diseñará un modelo que demuestra los aspectos claves de su viaje y dará una breve presentación a sus compañeros de clase.

Una Guía Estudiantil será proveída para orientar al estudiante paso por paso y guiarlo por este proceso. La Guía Estudiantil es una lista completa que indica los requisitos de este proyecto y está diseñada para guiar al alumno a que comience a pensar usando un nivel superior. La guía también menciona las Tarjetas de Recursos que proveen explicaciones adicionales, ideas, consejos, y otra información. Estas tarjetas también estarán disponibles en el salón de su hijo/a para el uso de él/ella.

El proyecto "Pasaporte para Viajar" está diseñado para que el alumno pueda trabajar independientemente en su salón, durante su tiempo libre y en casa. Las "Juntas de Revisión" están programadas durante el proyecto para que yo esté al pendiente del progreso del estudiante. En las fechas indicadas, el estudiante y yo nos reuniremos para discutir sus logros y para planear nuevas metas para la siguiente junta. También, veremos si el estudiante ha tenido dificultades o si tiene algunas preguntas.

"Pasaporte para Viajar" se terminará en una "Exposición de Proyectos". Esta Exposición dará una oportunidad al estudiante a que comparta su trabajo y sus experiencias con su familia, amigos, e invitados. Usted recibirá una invitación para la "Exposición de Proyectos" más adelante en el trimestre.

Fechas para recordar:

Revisión 1: _____

Revisión 2: _____

Revisión 3: _____

Presentación en el Salón de Clase: _____

Exposición de "Pasaporte para Viajar": _____ , _____

Sinceramente,

_____

_____

expectativas

tiempo de proyecto

Acepto:

- seguir los pasos indicados en mi guía estudiantil mientras que hago mi trabajo.
- mantener en orden mis materiales de proyecto.
- trabajar duro en Envision sin molestar a otros.
- mantener mis preguntas para mi mismo, hasta que mi maestro/a esté libre para hablar.

juntas de revisión

Vendré preparado con:

- mi Guía Estudiantil.
- mi Organizador Estudiantil.
- todos los materiales necesarios para el proyecto.

fechas importantes

Revisión: _____

Revisión: _____

Revisión: _____

Presentación en el Salón de Clase: _____

Exposición Pasaporte para Viajar: _____

_____

firmas

Acepto:

- cumplir con las expectativas en las fechas citadas anteriormente.
- utilizaré mis mejores habilidades y conocimientos para completar los requisitos de Pasaporte para Viajar.
- traer mi proyecto a la escuela todos los días, así podré trabajar en él durante mi tiempo libre.
- llevar mi proyecto a la casa todos los días, así podré trabajar en casa.

Entiendo que el proyecto Pasaporte para Viajar de "Envision" es una oportunidad especial, y si no cumplo con las expectativas mencionadas existe la posibilidad de que tenga que regresar a las actividades normales de mi salón.

Firma del Estudiante: _____ Fecha: _____

Firma del Padre: _____ Fecha: _____

Por favor devuelva este contrato antes de: _____

Construyendo el Portafolio de Tu Proyecto • Creando la Exibición de tu Proyecto • Presentación de tu Proyecto • Asistiendo a la Exposición

Te recomendamos mucho que uses tu creatividad!

Importante!

Las tarjetas de recursos disponibles están señaladas por el símbolo de Pasaporte para Viajar. Cuando veas este símbolo, sabrás que hay una tarjeta numerada de recurso disponible que te dará información adicional útil, así como ejemplos para tu referencia. Además, no dejes de visitar mindvinepress.com, otros sitios confiables de internet, usar materiales de referencia de la biblioteca y (si tu quieres) un agente de viajes como recursos adicionales.

COMPONENTE 1

Construyendo el Portafolio de Tu Proyecto Total de Puntos Posibles por el Portafolio: 66 de un total de 100 por el proyecto

Prepárate! Ahora es el momento de tomar decisiones sobre el viaje de tus sueños. Esta será una oportunidad y experiencia maravillosa en la cual podrás hacer uso de tus habilidades intelectuales así como de tu imaginación. Completa los siguientes requisitos enumerados, siguiendo el orden en el que se encuentran ya que depende el uno del otro, y te guiará sin problemas a través del proceso. Bon voyage!

1. ✈ **Preguntas** (3 puntos c/u): Escribe un párrafo o más por cada punto señalado en el grupo de preguntas que están a continuación. Usa una hoja de papel para cada párrafo y ponle un título a cada hoja.

Nota: Debes escribir acerca de ti como si fueras un adulto con edad suficiente para rentar un carro y cuarto de hotel. Puedes "llevar" un compañero de viaje. Pero los gastos adicionales deben salir del total de tu presupuesto de viaje.

- ¿Cuál es específicamente tu destino (ciudad, estado/provincia, país)? ¿Cuál es su localización exacta (latitud y longitud) y su ubicación relativa (considera el entorno, como ciudades cercanas, características geográficas o puntos de referencia)? ¿Por qué tienes interés en este lugar?

- ¿Cuándo harás tu viaje (hora, día, mes, año)? ¿Cuánto tiempo te quedarás? ¿Cómo los precios en las diferentes temporadas y el lugar a donde quieres ir afecta tu decisión de cuándo viajar y cuánto tiempo permanecer?

- ¿Vas a viajar solo o acompañado? ¿Cuáles serían las posibles ventajas o desventajas de viajar solo, con un amigo o miembro de la familia? Recuerda que los gastos de tu acompañante saldrán de tu presupuesto de viaje.

- ¿Qué medio de transporte (carro, avión, bicicleta, tren, barco) vas a utilizar para cada etapa de tu viaje? ¿Cómo el costo y tiempo determinan tus opciones de transportación?

- ¿Dónde te alojarás durante tu viaje (hotel, centro de turistas, acampando) ¿Te quedarás en un solo lugar o visitarás varios? ¿Cómo los costos y el lugar afectan tus opciones de alojamiento?

- Cuáles lugares de interés o sitios específicos visitarás? ¿A cuáles eventos o en qué actividades participarás en cada uno de ellos? ¿Cómo influyen los costos, tiempo y ubicación en tus elecciones?

- ¿Dónde vas a comer durante tu viaje (restaurantes, comida rápida, vendedores, o en tu hotel)? ¿Cómo es que el costo, tiempo y lugar afectan tus opciones de dónde vas a cenar?

- ¿Qué clase de ropa, equipo especial o documentos necesitas para tu viaje? ¿Qué arreglos tienes que hacer para obtener estas cosas?

- ¿Qué recuerdos/souvenirs comprarías durante tu viaje? ¿Cómo podría tú presupuesto afectar tus opciones de compra?

- ¿Tu viaje causará que faltes a algún tipo de compromiso en casa? ¿Qué tipo de responsabilidades como labores domésticas o el cuidado de una mascota puedes tener de los cuales alguien más tenga que tomar cuidado mientras estás fuera? ¿Cuáles arreglos has hecho para tomar cuidado de esto mientras estás fuera? ¿Cómo afecta tu presupuesto el tipo de arreglo que puedes hacer?

2. ✈ **Itinerario Diario** (5 puntos): Organiza un itinerario detallado por día de tu viaje empezando con el día de tu partida y terminando con el día de tu regreso. Asegúrate de detallar cada parte del día.

3. ✈ **Gráfica de Gastos** (8 puntos): Haz una gráfica/tabla que muestre todos los gastos de bienes o servicios que has hecho o planeas hacer durante tu viaje. Asegúrate de incluir los impuestos, propinas y de hacer un total para cada gasto. Además muestra tu total final de todos los gastos de tu viaje. Cerciórate de no sobre pasar tu presupuesto. Si tienes un sobrante en tu presupuesto, explica que harás con el dinero.

4. ✈ **Gráfica Computarizada** (8 puntos): Usando una computadora, crea una gráfica que muestre datos importantes de tu viaje. El tipo de gráfica que elijas (pictográfica, gráfica circular, gráfica de barras o gráfica lineal) deberá adaptarse o ser conveniente a los datos/información que estás presentando. Asegúrate que tu gráfica tiene un título y la clave de símbolos.

5. ✈ **Memorias del Viaje** (8 puntos): Escribe las memorias del viaje basadas en tu viaje. Imagínate que te has ido de viaje y que ya has regresado a salvo a tu casa. Utiliza estas memorias para reflexionar creativamente acerca de un evento significativo, lugar o actividad durante tu viaje. Debes escribir en primera persona y en tiempo pasado. Una memoria no es meramente un registro de eventos; también incluye tus impresiones, pensamientos y reflexiones. Considera, entre otras cosas, cómo las expectativas de tu viaje se comparan con las experiencias "reales" del viaje. Tus memorias deben ser de al menos una o dos páginas, pero eres libre de escribir más páginas si así lo decides.

6. ✈ **Tabla de Contenido o Índice** (3 puntos): Escribe una tabla de contenido o índice que lista todas las secciones así como sus números correspondientes.

7. ✈ **Cubierta o Portada** (2 puntos): Crea una página cubierta o portada llamativa para tu portafolio que incluya un título original para tu proyecto así como tu nombre y la fecha de Presentación en el Salón de Clase.

8. ✈ **Portafolio** (2 puntos): Organiza todos tus materiales en una carpeta de tres argollas. La tabla de contenido o índice debe estar primero, seguida de tus respuestas a los diez grupos de preguntas en el orden en que se presentaron en esta guía. Después deben ir tu itinerario, la tabla de gastos, la gráfica y las memorias. Tu página cubierta o portada deberá ir al frente de tu portafolio.

Has terminado el Componente numero1 de tu Proyecto Pasaporte para Viajar. Al completar tu portafolio has creado un importante recurso que te ayudará en tu trabajo en los Componentes 2 y 3. Aun cuando quedan importantes retos por delante, tú estás ahora preparado para llevar a cabo cada uno de ellos, sabiendo que has puesto los fundamentos que aumentarán tus oportunidades de tener éxito. Buena suerte en tanto avanzas en la creación de las cosas y el material que vas a exhibir en tu proyecto.

COMPONENTE 2

Creando la Exhibición de Tu Proyecto Total de Puntos por la Exhibición: 24 de un total de 100 por el proyecto

Habiendo "regresado" de tu viaje, ahora es tiempo de diseñar y crear una atractiva e informativa exhibición visual del lugar que visitaste y tus experiencias. Las cosas que prepares serán vistas por tus compañeros de clase el día de la Presentación en el Salón de Clase y también por las personas que asistan a la Exposición Pasaporte para Viajar al final del término. Como siempre, pon tu mejor esfuerzo para diseñar, crear e integrar las cosas que vas a exhibir.

> **Nota:**
> Recuerda que cada elemento es solo una parte de tu exhibición. En otras palabras, un solo elemento no tiene que decir todo acerca del lugar al que viajaste o de tu viaje. Decide acerca del propósito de cada elemento. Considera cual es la mejor manera de organizar tu exhibición para lograr el mayor efecto.

1. Mapa de Ruta (3 puntos): Encuentra o crea uno o más mapas que muestren tu viaje de ida y vuelta. Marca el mapa o mapas para mostrar las rutas que tomaste y un aproximado del total de millas que viajaste. Puedes también querer marcar los lugares donde te quedaste y que sitios visitaste. Puede ser deseable usar o crear una combinación de mapas de diferentes escalas y tipos.

2. Colección de Materiales Informativos (3 puntos): Colecta folletos, fotos, artículos, música u otros materiales que tengan que ver con tu viaje. Clasifícalos y organízalos de manera efectiva y agradable. Sugerencia: Consulta el Internet, un centro turístico, la cámara de comercio (de la localidad a donde viajaste) o una agencia de viajes para que te ayude.

3. Tarjeta Postal (4 puntos): Diseña y crea una tarjeta postal original que tenga relación con el lugar al que viajaste. Se creativo! Si lo deseas utiliza materiales tridimensionales. En la parte de enfrente debe de haber una imagen o escena de tu viaje. En la parte de atrás deberá estar el nombre y la dirección (puede ser ficticio/inventado) de un amigo o familiar, una estampilla postal diseñada por ti con el valor correcto y una nota personal que tu escribas. Usa tu itinerario y tus memorias para ayudarte a tener ideas para tu tarjeta postal.

4. Visual Tridimensional (5 puntos): Construye un visual tridimensional diciendo algo acerca de tu viaje que los demás materiales de tu exhibición no mencionen directamente o completamente. Tu visual tridimensional, como las demás cosas o materiales deberá complementar la exhibición total.

5. Tablero de Exhibición (5 puntos): Utiliza un tablero de exhibición de dos o tres páneles (secciones) para crear un "anuncio" de tu viaje. Tu tablero de exhibición deberá incluir el título de tu proyecto y tu nombre. Puedes añadir el material adicional que tú desees.

6. Exhibición (4 puntos): Organiza y ordena las cosas que vas a exhibir, tu portafolio y todos los materiales adicionales que hayas querido incluir en una manera informativa y atractiva.

Has completado el componente 2 de tu Proyecto Pasaporte Para Viajar, una importante exhibición que de una manera creativa muestra tu viaje. Ahora que has terminado tu portafolio y tu exhibición, estás listo para prepararte con confianza para tu Presentación en el Salón de Clase (Componente 3). Disfruta compartiendo tu proyecto con tus compañeros y maestro!

COMPONENTE 3:

Dando Tu Presentación en el Salón de Clase
Total de Puntos Posibles por tu Presentación en el Salón de Clase: 10 de un total de 100 por el proyecto

Ahora que ya planeaste, "regresaste de" y reflexionaste acerca de tu viaje, es tiempo de compartir tus experiencias con otros. La Presentación en el Salón de Clase es una oportunidad para formalmente presentar algunos puntos destacados de tu viaje y algo de tu arduo trabajo. Tu portafolio y exhibición contienen toda la información que necesitas para tu presentación, así que relájate y disfrútala.

1. ✈ Que Incluir en Tu Presentación:

- Lugar al que Viajaste (1 punto): Comparte acerca del lugar a donde viajaste, una descripción del mismo y por qué lo elegiste para ir.

- Localización (2 puntos): Señala en un mapa o mapas el lugar al que viajaste.

- Eventos (1 punto): Explica algunos de los principales eventos durante tu viaje, señalando cualquier material informativo relevante en tu tablero de exhibición.

- Portafolio y Gráfica (2 puntos): Muestra tu portafolio y explica las gráficas que hiciste.

- Tarjeta Postal (1 punto): Muestra ambos lados de tu tarjeta postal y explica lo que aparece en la escena o imagen.

- Visual Tridimensional (2 puntos): Muestra tu visual tridimensional y explica cómo se añade a tu exhibición.

> **Nota:** Tu presentación deberá durar de 3-4 minutos y deberá ser ensayada, pero no memorizada. Si olvidas incluir información de alguno de los puntos, tu maestro te hará una pregunta relacionada para que tengas la oportunidad de incluirla.

2. Atuendo o Vestimenta (1 punto): Viste con ropa que se relacione con tu viaje.

Que Traer a la Presentación del Salón de Clase: Todas las cosas de tu exhibición y cualquier cosa extra que tu quieras que te pueda ayudar a ampliar y mejorar tu exhibición. Además, recuerda vestir ropa que se relacione con tu viaje.

Has terminado los Componentes 1, 2 y 3 – todas las porciones que serán evaluadas de tu proyecto. El Componente Final, Asistiendo a la Exposición de Pasaporte para Viajar, te da un cierre o final maravilloso para tu Proyecto de Pasaporte para Viajar.

COMPONENTE 4:

Asistiendo a la Exposición Pasaporte para Viajar (La exposición no te da puntos.)

Ahora que has terminado tu proyecto y lo has presentado a tus compañeros, es tiempo de compartir tu trabajo con tu familia y amigos en la Exposición Pasaporte para Viajar. La exposición es un evento que reconoce y celebra el duro trabajo que has hecho para hacer tu Proyecto de Pasaporte para Viajar. En la exposición, tú colocarás tu exhibición y permanecerás al lado de tu exhibición mientras los invitados caminan y observan los proyectos. Los invitados pueden hacer algunas preguntas acerca de tu proyecto mientras ellos visitan tu exhibición, así que disfruta y diviértete compartiendo las experiencias de tu Pasaporte para Viajar con ellos.

Que Traer a la Exposición: Todas las cosas de tu exhibición y cualquier cosa extra que tu quieras que te pueda ayudar a ampliar y mejorar tu exhibición. Además, recuerda vestir ropa que se relacione con tu viaje.

FELICITACIONES POR HABER TERMINADO TU PROYECTO DE PASAPORTE PARA VIAJAR!

TRAVEL PASSPORT

¡ESTA INVITADO!

RESPUESTA A LA "EXPO"

Por favor complete y regrese antes de: _____

Nombre del estudiante: _____

¿El estudiante estará presente? ☐ Sí ☐ No

¿Número de invitados?: _____

¿El estudiante necesitará equipo especial para su "expo" (p. ej. una Tele)? Por favor escriba lo necesario:

_____

Gracias.

Esperamos contar con su presencia durante este evento especial.

TRAVEL PASSPORT

¡POR FAVOR VENGAN A VISITARNOS A LA EXPO PASAPORTE PARA VIAJAR!

¿Por qué? _____

¿Quién?_____

¿Dónde? _____

¿Cuándo? _____

Recuerde de traer su cámara!

TRAVEL PASSPORT

TRAVEL PASSPORT RESOURCE CARDS FOR STUDENTS

QUESTIONS

Each bulleted question for Component 1 should be answered on a separate sheet of paper. Each answer should be a paragraph or more in length. The question should be written clearly at the top of the page. Your answer should be well explained and include your thought process and reasoning. When you have completed your answer, you may have extra white space on the page. Use this white space to demonstrate your creativity with art, borders or other finishing touches.

EXAMPLE

WHAT IS MY SPECIFIC TRAVEL DESTINATION?

I am going to Toronto! It is the capitol of the Canadian province of Ontario. Its relative location is 223.5 miles northeast of my home in Harrison Township, Michigan. It is on the north shore of Lake Ontario. Its absolute location is 43° 40′ North and 79° 22′ West.

I was debating whether to visit Toronto or the city of Calgary, located in the province of Alberta. I chose Toronto because it is much closer to my home, which makes the trip more affordable. It also has a tremendous variety of activities and is beautiful during the holiday season. Another great thing about Toronto is that things are close together and easy to get to. I won't waste a lot of time and money on day trips. Some interesting facts I found out about Toronto while researching are…

DAILY ITINERARY

An itinerary is a plan of how you will spend your time each day. It should be well thought-out and organized. It should also include as much detail as possible. An itinerary is not set in stone, but is an estimated plan. It will help save you decision-making time while you are on your trip. Your itinerary can be in a chart form, timeline form or other layout that works for you. The example below shows only portions of one layout of an itinerary.

EXAMPLE

GRAND CANYON AREA ITINERARY: DAY 1

Date	Time	Plan of Action
9/10/XX	5:00 am	Leave my house and drive to the airport. Eat a snack breakfast while waiting for my flight.
	8:07 am	Depart Metro Airport.
	11:29 am	Arrive in Flagstaff, Arizona. Rent a car, eat lunch at Salsa Salsa (local Mexican restaurant) and drive to the hotel.
	4:00 pm	Check into the hotel, unpack, take a rest and freshen up.
	6:30 pm	Have dinner at Best Dining Room located in the hotel (casually elegant dining).
	8:30 pm	Go shopping at the local trading posts.
	10:00 pm	Return to hotel, relax, review tomorrow's activities, go to sleep.

EXPENSE CHART

An expense chart displays all of the goods and services you purchased on or for your trip. It should be detailed, organized and complete. Remember to include all taxes and tips. Show your grand total along with what you will do with any leftover money. The example below shows only portions of an expense chart and does not, therefore, display all expenses involved in the grand total shown.

EXAMPLE

Expenses for Washington D.C. Trip			
Date	Name	Type of Good or Service	Total Cost (including taxes and tips)
5/10/XX	Food Mart	Snack food and beverages purchased ahead to bring along	$51.06
5/11/XX	Transportation	Gasoline for trip (1375.6 miles total ÷ 22 mpg x $3.00 p/gallon)	$187.58
5/11-5/15/XX	Bed and Breakfast	Accommodation + Breakfast	$866.81 (for 7 nights)
Grand Total			$2977.85
I will put my leftover $22.15 into my savings account to help pay for college.			

COMPUTER-GENERATED GRAPH

A graph is a visual representation of data. It allows you to display data quickly and easily. Your graph should be accurate, complete and professional looking. You may choose to create a pictograph, pie graph, bar graph or line graph. You are responsible for collecting the data and creating an original graph. Remember to title your graph and include a key.

EXAMPLE

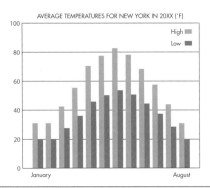

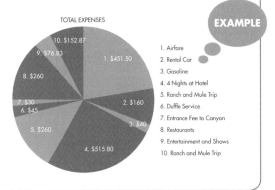

TRAVEL MEMOIR

A memoir is a narrative written in first person (uses the words I, me, myself). It usually focuses on one event and incorporates vivid description and detail. Your memoir should be about one specific event that "happened" on your trip and should, therefore, be written in the past tense. It should have a complete beginning, middle and end. Remember to include your personal impressions, thoughts and insights. It should be one to two pages or more in length.

EXAMPLE

MEMOIR OF A MORNING IN GREECE

The day started better than I ever imagined. Here I was in the most beautiful place on Earth: Greece. I had arrived late the night before, and it was my first day of waking up in the villa. I strolled out onto my balcony where the sun was shining so brightly it made the water below sparkle like a million jewels. The air was sweet, crisp, fresh and cool on my face. I had dreamed that this would be a beautiful place to visit, but I didn't realize how rejuvenating it would feel just simply being there.

After enjoying the morning and getting ready for my fist day, I decided to take a walk through the city. As I was wandering through the open-air market, I noticed a small shop where a weathered little lady was sitting in a rocking chair quietly singing and selling her wares. I walked over to her and said, "Hello."

She only nodded to me, smiled and gestured to her shop. I couldn't believe my eyes when I looked inside...

TABLE OF CONTENTS

Your table of contents should be the first page in your portfolio, although you write it after you finish all of the pages on the inside. Writing it after finishing the contents allows you to be accurate with your page numbers and titles in case you make any last minute changes. Your table of contents should list each section and the page it begins on. It should be neat and well organized, but feel free to be creative with your own layout.

EXAMPLE

TABLE OF CONTENTS

Page Number	Section Title
1	What is my specific travel destination?
2	When will I take my trip?
11	Daily Itinerary
12	Expense Chart
18-21	Extra Internet Information
22-26	Extra Brochures

COVER PAGE AND PORTFOLIO

The cover page of your portfolio should entice people to read about your project. It should include an original title, your name and the Classroom Presentation date. Your portfolio is used to organize most of your paper items. A one- to two-inch binder with a clear cover works well. Arrange your papers in the order listed in your Student Instruction Guide. You may choose to add tab dividers, page protectors and creative touches.

FRONT COVER   SPINE   BACK COVER

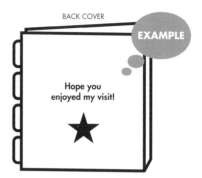

EXAMPLE

ROUTE MAP

Obtain a map (or maps) that includes your entire round-trip route. Highlight the route you traveled, from start to finish. The entire route should be highlighted whether you change forms of transportation during your travels or not. Calculate your total mileage and record it on the map. Feel free to include more than one map to show detail of various areas. Also, be creative in showing specific places you stayed at and visited while on your trip.

EXAMPLE

Round-Trip Mileage: 4,172 miles

COLLECTION OF INFORMATIONAL MATERIALS

Collecting, classifying and arranging various pieces of media, such as pictures, maps and brochures, is an excellent way to show different aspects of your travels to others. When you have collected your informational materials, classify them into main groups. Then arrange them on your display board or in your exhibit area – or even in a scrapbook! Be sure to create titles for each of your groupings. Hint: The Internet, chambers of commerce, tourist centers and travel agents are wonderful resources for finding materials. The examples below show three methods of classifying. Feel free to arrange your materials as you see fit.

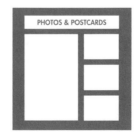
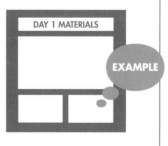

EXAMPLE

POSTCARD

A postcard is a brief informal note written to someone, usually while you are on a trip. Most vacation areas sell postcards with pictures of their attractions on one side of the card. On the opposite side of the card is where you write your note, address the card and place your postage.

You should create your postcard on a 5x8" card. On one side, design an attraction or scene from your trip. Be creative! You don't have to do this on the computer. You may even make it three-dimensional if you like. On the reverse, you should write your note, address it and design the postage stamp. Remember to follow proper letter format (date, salutation, letter body, closing and signature).

DISPLAY BOARD AND EXHIBIT

The purpose of your display board and exhibit is to draw people's attention to your project. It should be neat, colorful and creative. You should include the items listed in your Student Instruction Guide and any additional materials you wish to bring. The example below is to be used only as a guide; feel free to rearrange. Tip: Two- or three-panel display boards can be purchased at most craft or office stores. If you prefer to make one, you can ask an adult to help construct one from a large cardboard box.

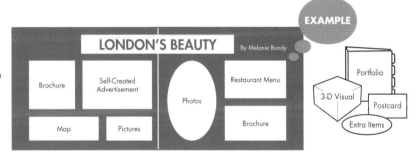

WHAT TO INCLUDE IN YOUR PRESENTATION

Your presentation will be a talk on what you learned, collected and produced for your project. You should practice until you are comfortable with what you will say, but do not memorize a speech. Your presentation should be three to four minutes long and address the bulleted information listed in Component 3 your Student Instruction Guide. Also, remember to dress in clothing that reflects your trip.

REMEMBER TO:

- Take a deep breath, relax and enjoy sharing.
- Greet your audience and introduce yourself.
- Speak at a natural pace, clearly and loudly enough so everyone can hear you.
- Stand still and calm; don't fidget.
- Point to and show various visuals as you speak about them.
- Make eye contact with your audience, looking around the room naturally.
- Thank your audience when you are finished.

APPENDIX 2:
CAREER ASPIRATION FORMS
AND RESOURCE CARDS

Levels From Lowest to Highest:
KNOWLEDGE • COMPREHENSION • APPLICATION • ANALYSIS • EVALUATION • SYNTHESIS

Below you will find each Career Aspiration's requirement, along with its corresponding level of Bloom's Taxonomy.

> **IMPORTANT!**
> The levels listed above are cumulative. For example, the highest level of thinking, Synthesis, incorporates all other levels of thinking: Knowledge, Comprehension, Application, Analysis and Evaluation.

COMPONENT 1
Building Your Project Portfolio
Total Possible Portfolio Points: 81 out of 100 total possible for project

Portfolio Section 1: Choosing Your Career

1. Career Interest Inventory (3 points): Using the Internet, take a career interest inventory and print your results. **ANALYSIS**

2. Career Choice Questions (2 points each): Consider the results of your career interest inventory as well as your own personal wishes, and choose a career that you would like to pursue after high school. Gather information about your chosen career by consulting knowledgeable persons and by referring to reliable Internet and library sources. **COMPREHENSION**

- How do you feel about the results of your career interest inventory? **EVALUATION** How do these results affect your choice of career? **SYNTHESIS**

- What career did you choose? **KNOWLEDGE** What aspects of the career especially appeal to you and why? **EVALUATION**

- What will be your approximate starting salary? **KNOWLEDGE** How important was salary to you when you chose your career? **SYNTHESIS**

- What personal and professional qualifications will you need for this career? Explain them. **COMPREHENSION**

- What will be your basic day-to-day duties in this career? Be sure to consider all aspects of the work. Explain them. **COMPREHENSION**

- What will be the general conditions of your work environment? (Where will you work? With whom will you work? What will your work schedule be like?) Explain. **COMPREHENSION** What benefits or drawbacks are there to these conditions? **EVALUATION**

- What are two or three aspects of the career that you think will challenge you most? Explain. **EVALUATION**

- How will you meet these challenges? **APPLICATION**

- What is the current job outlook for people starting out in this career? **COMPREHENSION** What will you do if there is a shortage of available jobs when you are ready to enter the workforce? **APPLICATION** What other careers or occupations might you be qualified for with your background and training? **APPLICATION**

- How might this career affect your personal life outside of work, especially regarding the time you will have for family, social activities, recreation and other pursuits? **SYNTHESIS**

- How will having this career allow you to contribute to your community, directly or indirectly? **SYNTHESIS**

3. Career Choice Interview (4 points): With the help of your parents, arrange to interview someone involved in the career you have chosen or in a related field. Be sure the person understands the purpose of the interview. Before the interview, prepare ten to fifteen career-related questions to ask the interviewee. Write your questions down, leaving enough room to record the responses. Try to write questions that require more than a simple "Yes" or "No" response. During the interview, feel free to ask additional questions and take care to record all responses accurately. If a one-on-one interview is not possible, conduct the interview over the phone or arrange to mail or email your questions to the interviewee. Be sure to thank the interviewee when you are finished. **SYNTHESIS**

Portfolio Section 2: Education and Training

1. High School Experience (3 points): Contact the high school you are most likely to attend. Explain the project you are working on, and ask for information regarding the school's academic courses and extra-curricular activities, such as sports and clubs. Review the materials carefully and choose one course or activity that you think might help prepare you, directly or indirectly, for your chosen career. Write a paragraph or more in which you explain how the course or activity you have chosen might help you. **SYNTHESIS**

2. Customized Career Path Flow Chart (4 points): Just as there are many different careers, there are also many different career paths. A career path includes the education or training a person receives on the way to achieve his or her desired career. Some career paths involve several months of occupational or on-the-job training. Others involve years of university or college education. Still others include a combination of training, higher education and one or more internships. Follow the steps below to create a customized flow chart showing the stages of education or training for your chosen career.

Step 1: Consult your parents, high school guidance counselors, teachers, people working in your chosen field and reliable Internet and library sources to learn about the education or training you will need to prepare for your career. **COMPREHENSION**

Step 2: Decide how many stages of education or training you will need. For example, if your chosen career is visual art, the first stage of your education and training might be three years of art school; the second stage might be a year of study abroad; the third stage might be two years of graduate study. Record each stage, in chronological order, across the top of a plain sheet of paper. **ANALYSIS**

Step 3: If you have more than one stage written at the top of your paper, draw a vertical line or lines to separate the stages. When you finish this step, you should have one or more columns, each with a heading that names a stage of the education or training you will need. **KNOWLEDGE**

Step 4: For each stage on your flow chart, consult reliable sources to compile a list of places such as schools, universities and training centers, where you might like to go to receive training. Skip a line space below each column heading and transfer each list to the appropriate column. Leave room for one final choice at the bottom of each column. **SYNTHESIS**

Step 5: From your list of choices in each column, choose the one school or institution you think will best suit your plans, desires and interests for that particular stage of your education or training. Leave a line space, and then write the name of your choice at the bottom of each column. **EVALUATION**

3. Informational Materials About Your Chosen Schools (2 points): Refer to your customized career path and contact the appropriate person at each school or training center. Explain your project and ask him or her to mail you all the materials normally sent to someone interested in applying for admission. Most schools and training centers will have a website where such materials can be viewed and downloaded. However, you should still call and ask for information to be mailed. Often, you may receive more than what you find on the website. **COMPREHENSION**

4. Education and Training Questions (2 points each):

- While customizing your career path flow chart, what was one major decision you made when choosing from among your education or training options? Explain the reasons for your decision. **EVALUATION**

- What prerequisites, prior knowledge or experience, will you need in order to begin your education or training? **KNOWLEDGE**

- What stages of your education or training are you most looking forward to? Explain. **EVALUATION**

- What additional activities might you get involved in to better prepare you for your career? Explain. **EVALUATION**

- How long do you think it will take you to complete your education or training? **COMPREHENSION** What type of certification or degree do you hope to receive at the end of your education or training? **COMPREHENSION**

- What additional, non-required activities or training might you pursue to better prepare you for your career? **EVALUATION**

5. First-Year Expense Charts (3 points): Create an expense chart for the first year of each stage in your education or training. Each chart should show all the expenses you would be likely to incur over the course of a year. Estimate a total for each category listed that would apply to your situation: rent, food, tuition, books, supplies and transportation. Show a total for each kind of expense, and then show a grand total for all expenses. Be sure to include taxes. **SYNTHESIS**

6. Total Career Path Expenses and Funding (3 points): Use your first-year expense charts to calculate the total amount you will spend during the entire time of your education or training. To accomplish this, multiply each first-year total by the number of years required for that stage of your education. Think about and research different funding options that could help finance your education. **APPLICATION** What options will be available to you? Which do you think you would choose? Explain why. **EVALUATION**

7. Computer-Generated Pie Graph (3 points): Referring to your first-year expense charts, create a computer-generated pie graph showing all expenses (grouped by category of expense) that you will incur over the entire time of your education or training. Be sure to give your pie graph a title and provide a key. **SYNTHESIS**

8. Applying to Your School or Training Center (2 points): Review the informational materials you have gathered and locate the application form for the first school you would attend. Complete this form as you would if you were actually applying for admission. If you are asked to provide additional materials such as a personal essay, letters of recommendation or samples of your work, be creative. Do not include your real social security number on the application. **SYNTHESIS**

9. Computer-Generated Brochure (3 points): Choose the school or training center you are most looking forward to attending. Using the computer, design an original and authentic-looking brochure that "advertises" various aspects of that school. Refer to the materials you have gathered for information and ideas, but make your brochure original. **SYNTHESIS**

Portfolio Section 3: Applying for the Job

1. Prospective Employers List (2 points): Make a list of prospective employers you might apply to after completing your education or training. Gather information about these employers and write a brief description of each. If your career path leads to only one obvious prospective employer (the United States Coast Guard, for example) consider some reasonable alternatives, or simply do a more extensive description for that one employer. **SYNTHESIS**

2. Job Posting (2 points): Consult trade journals, the Internet and newspapers to find listings of available jobs in your career field. Choose the posting that most appeals to you and attach it to a piece of paper. On this same paper, explain why this job appeals to you over other jobs. **EVALUATION**

3. Professional Cover Letter (3 points): Write a professional, one-page cover letter stating your background, qualifications and interest in the job you have chosen. Address your letter as indicated by the job listing you chose. A cover letter is a standard part of most formal job applications. However, if the application for the job you chose does not require a cover letter, compose one in order to explore and express your career interests. **SYNTHESIS**

4. Professional Resume (4 points): Write a professional resume outlining your education, experience, professional goals and other relevant information. Refer to the job listing you have chosen to know what specific details to include. There are many different ways to format a resume. Be sure to look at many examples and choose the one that is most appropriate for your situation. Like a real-life cover letter, a real-life resume is a standard part of most formal job applications. However, if the application for the job you chose does not require a resume, create one for your own benefit. **SYNTHESIS**

5. Post-Interview Thank-You Letter (3 points): Write a professional thank-you letter to a prospective employer as if you have interviewed for a job. Be positive and write in a tone that reflects the qualities the prospective employer is seeking. **SYNTHESIS**

Remaining Portfolio Materials

1. Table of Contents (1 point): Write a table of contents that lists all the sections of your portfolio along with their corresponding page numbers. **COMPREHENSION**

2. Cover Page (1 point): Create an eye-catching cover page for your portfolio that includes an original title for your project as well as your name and the Classroom Presentation date. **SYNTHESIS**

3. Portfolio (1 point): Organize all of your materials in a three-ring binder. The table of contents should come first, followed by your work from Portfolio Sections 1, 2 and 3 above in the order presented. Your cover page should be placed on the front of the portfolio. **SYNTHESIS**

COMPONENT 2
Creating Your Project Exhibit
Total Possible Exhibit Points: 10 out of 100 total possible for project

1. Route Map(s) (2 points): It is always a good idea to know where your plans will take you. Therefore, find or create one or more maps that show the location of your home and the location or locations of where you will go for your education or training. Mark all the routes you will travel and indicate the total miles and type of transportation you will use. **SYNTHESIS**

2. Arrangement of Your Informational Materials (2 points): Gather the informational materials about your career and career training. Classify and arrange them in an effective and pleasing manner. **SYNTHESIS**

3. Display Board (3 points): Use a large two- or three-panel exhibit board to create an "advertisement" for your career and customized career path. Use half of your board to showcase your career. Use the other half to showcase your customized career path. Your display board should include your project's title and your name. You may then choose to post your route map, certain informational materials and any additional materials on your board. **SYNTHESIS**

4. Exhibit (3 points): Arrange all of the above exhibit items, your portfolio and any additional materials you wish to include, to create an appealing and informative overall exhibit. **SYNTHESIS**

COMPONENT 3:
Giving Your Classroom Presentation
Total Possible Classroom Presentation Points: 9 out of 100 total possible for project

1. What to Include in Your Presentation:

* Career Choice and Display Board (2 points): Share your career choice, explain why you chose that career and provide a basic description of what your day-to-day duties are likely to be, pointing to any relevant informational materials on your display board. **EVALUATION**

* Career and Your Personal Life (2 points): Explain one way your career will affect your life outside of work. **SYNTHESIS**

* Career Path (2 points): Share a description of your career path and two to three aspects that you are most looking forward to. **EVALUATION**

* Portfolio, Career Path Expenses and Funding (2 points): Show your portfolio and share your expense charts and computer-generated pie graph. Discuss your total career path cost and some funding options you might choose. **COMPREHENSION**

2. Attire (1 point): Dress in clothing that relates to your career. **SYNTHESIS**

TEACHER COPY CHART

Step Number	Form Title	Number of Copies
1.1	Teacher Planning Guide	1 only
2.1-2.3	Parent Career Aspiration Introduction Letter Student Career Aspiration Introduction Letter Student Instruction Guide	1 completed, then 1 per student 1 completed only 1 only
3.1-3.4	Teacher Forms Checklist Student Commitment Contract	1 completed only 1 completed, then 1 per student
3.5	Student Career Aspiration Introduction Letter* Student Instruction Guide* Career Aspiration Resource Card Appendix Pages* (optional)	1 completed, then one per student 1 per student 1 per student
4.1-4.2	Student Checkpoint Organizer Teacher Checkpoint Record	1 per student 1 completed only
5.1-5.2	Student Expo Invitation	1 completed, then one per student
5.9-5.11	Student Certificate Student Name Sign (optional) Left Arrow Sign Right Arrow Sign	1 per student, then each completed 1 per student, then each completed Amount needed Amount needed
5.12-5.13	Teacher Assessment Student Self-Assessment	1 per student 1 per student

* Staple these items into a packet for each student

*Events scheduled with the class are in black.

Week	Event (Step Numbers)	Day and Date	Time
1	Planning and Preparing for the Quarter (1.1-1.2)		
	Prepare for Career Aspiration Introduction (2.1-2.3)		
	Career Aspiration Introduction (2.4-2.7)		
	Preparation for Career Aspiration Implementation (3.1-3.6)		
	Career Aspiration Implementation (3.7-3.17)		
3	Preparation for the Checkpoint Meetings (4.1-4.2)		
	Distribute Checkpoint Organizers (4.3-4.6)		
	Checkpoint Meetings (4.7-4.12)		
5	Preparation for the Checkpoint Meetings (4.1-4.2)		
	Distribute Checkpoint Organizers (4.3-4.6)		
	Checkpoint Meetings (4.7-4.12)		
7	Preparation for the Checkpoint Meetings (4.1-4.2)		
	Distribute Checkpoint Organizers (4.3-4.6)		
	Checkpoint Meetings (4.7-4.12)		
8	Preparation for the Career Aspiration Expo (5.1-5.2)		
	Invite Families to the Career Aspiration Expo (5.3-5.4)		
	Preparation for the Career Aspiration Expo Ctd. (5.5-5.11)		
9	Preparation for Classroom Presentations and the Career Aspiration Expo (5.12-5.15)		
	Classroom Presentations (6A.1-6A.13 or 6B.1-6B.12)		
	Classroom Expo and Student Self-Assessment (7A.1-7A.9 or 7B.1-7B.10)		
10	Final Preparation for the Career Aspiration Expo (8.1-8.10)		
	Career Aspiration Expo (9.1-9.4)		
	Conclusion and Teacher Assessment (10.1-10.8)		
	Student Review (10.9-10.10)		

parent career aspiration introduction letter

Dear Parent(s),

Welcome to Career Aspiration, an Envision project that will challenge and inspire your child. Career Aspiration is designed to enlighten your child about where education can lead in life. Your child will have the opportunity to take a career interest inventory, chose a potential career, research their chosen career and not only select, but investigate the education or training needed to reach this major life goal. Your child will also research and choose a potential school for continued education.

For the project portfolio, your child will investigate numerous aspects of his or her chosen career path, interview someone in that field, create career-related expense charts and graphs, fill out an application to a school, create a brochure, create a professional cover letter and resume, and much more. Lastly, your child will build an exhibit that presents key aspects of his or her career path and give a brief formal presentation to the class.

A Student Instruction Guide will be provided to guide your child, step by step, through this process. The Instruction Guide is a comprehensive list of project requirements and is designed to engage higher-level thinking. The guide also references helpful Resource Cards, which provide additional explanations, ideas, tips and directions. There will be a set of these cards in our classroom to which your child may refer.

Career Aspiration is designed to be worked on independently during class time, free time and at home. By scheduling several Checkpoint Meeting dates throughout the quarter, I will be able to monitor each student's progress. On these dates, I will meet with each student to discuss accomplishments and plan goals for the next checkpoint. I will also address any difficulties students might be having.

Career Aspiration will conclude with a Project Expo. The expo will be your child's opportunity to share his or her finished project with family, friends and other guests. You will receive a detailed invitation to the Project Expo later in the quarter.

Dates to Remember:

Checkpoint 1: _____

Checkpoint 2: _____

Checkpoint 3: _____

Classroom Presentation: _____

Career Aspiration Expo: _____ , _____

Sincerely,

_____

_____

student career aspiration introduction letter

Dear Student,

Welcome to Career Aspiration, one of the Envision Program projects. This project is an exercise in choosing and planning for your potential career. It will be a personal voyage of discovery and an opportunity to explore a major life goal.

To begin, you will take a career interest inventory, which is a questionnaire designed to help you identify careers you might be interested in and suited for. You will then choose a career to research and plan for. Career Aspiration is divided into four components. The first component involves researching your career path and organizing that research in a project portfolio. For the second component, you will create an exhibit that presents key information and aspects about your chosen career path. The third component is a classroom presentation, given to an audience of your peers. The fourth and final component is the project expo, at which you will share you completed project with family, friends and invited guests.

You will work on Career Aspiration throughout the school day, during your free time and at home. Generally, you will be expected to work on your own. You will consult with me periodically at Checkpoint Meetings to discuss your progress and receive guidance. Between the checkpoints, feel free to discuss your project with other Envision students.

The attached Student Instruction Guide contains all the information you will need to complete the required Career Aspiration Project successfully. The Instruction Guide will challenge you to be resourceful, organized and to think at a higher level.

Dates to Remember:

Checkpoint 1: _____

Checkpoint 2: _____

Checkpoint 3: _____

Classroom Presentation: _____

Career Aspiration Expo: _____ , _____

After reading this introduction, you are now ready to begin thinking about your future career. Good luck and have fun!

Sincerely,

_____

_____

Building Your Project Portfolio • Creating Your Project Exhibit
Presenting Your Project • Attending the Expo

BE CREATIVE!

IMPORTANT!

Resource cards are denoted by a Career Aspiration icon ![icon]. When you see one of these icons, you will know that there is a corresponding resource card available that gives additional helpful information and examples. Also, be sure to visit www.mindvinepress.com, other trustworthy Internet sites and library reference materials for helpful resources and examples. Warning: Never fill out any forms while logged onto the Internet. If you find a form you need, print it and fill out the hard copy. Also, never supply any identifying personal information while online, such as your name, address, email address, phone number or social security number, even if a site asks you for it. Lastly, each time you see the Mind Vine Press icon ![icon] in this instruction guide, go to www.mindvinepress.com to find helpful links for that requirement.

COMPONENT 1

Building Your Project Portfolio Total Possible Portfolio Points: 81 out of 100 total possible for project

For this project, you will research and set goals for potential choices for a career and career path. The term career path refers to all the stages of development and experience a person encounters after choosing a profession or occupation. The path begins with choosing a career. The next steps along the path usually involve some kind of education or training, and the path ends with retirement or a move to a different career. For this project, we will focus on the beginning two steps. Complete the numbered requirements below, in order, as they build upon one another and will guide you smoothly through this planning process.

Note: "Component 1: Building Your Career Aspiration Portfolio" is separated into three sections: "Portfolio Section 1: Choosing Your Career", "Portfolio Section 2: Education and Training" and "Portfolio Section 3: Applying for the Job".

STUDENT INSTRUCTION GUIDE

Portfolio Section 1: Choosing Your Career

1. **Career Interest Inventory** (3 points): Using the Internet, take a career interest inventory and print your results. There are many inventory websites available, so find a site that does not ask you to provide any personal information, such as your name, address, email address, telephone number or social security number.

2. **Career Choice Questions** (2 points each): Consider the results of your career interest inventory as well as your own personal wishes, and choose a career that you would like to pursue after high school. Gather information about your chosen career by consulting knowledgeable persons and by referring to reliable Internet and library sources. Use the sets of questions below to help guide your research and answer them according to these guidelines: compose a paragraph or more for your response to each set of questions; use a separate sheet of paper for each set of responses; and record the first question for each set of questions at the top of each sheet.

- How do you feel about the results of your career interest inventory? How do these results affect your choice of career?

- What career did you choose? What aspects of the career especially appeal to you and why?

- What will be your approximate starting salary? How important was salary to you when you chose your career?

- What personal and professional qualifications will you need for this career? Explain them.

- What will be your basic day-to-day duties in this career? Be sure to consider all aspects of the work. Explain them.

- What will be the general conditions of your work environment? (Where will you work? With whom will you work? What will your work schedule be like? Explain. What benefits or drawbacks are there to these conditions?

- What are two or three aspects of the career that you think will challenge you most? Explain.

- How will you meet these challenges?

- What is the current job outlook for people starting out in this career? What will you do if there is a shortage of available jobs when you are ready to enter the workforce? What other careers or occupations might you be qualified for with your background and training?

- How might this career affect your personal life outside of work, especially regarding the time you will have for family, social activities, recreation and other pursuits?

- How will having this career allow you to contribute to your community, directly or indirectly?

3. **Career Choice Interview** (4 points): With the help of your parents, arrange to interview someone involved in the career you have chosen or in a related field. Be sure the person understands the purpose of the interview. Before the interview, prepare ten to fifteen career-related questions to ask the interviewee. Write your questions down, leaving enough room to record the responses. Try to write questions that require more than a simple "Yes" or "No" response. During the interview, feel free to ask additional questions, and take care to record all responses accurately. If a one-on-one interview is not possible, conduct the interview over the phone, or arrange to mail or email your questions to the interviewee. Be sure to thank the interviewee when you are finished.

Portfolio Section 2: Education and Training

Note: This project assumes that the serious pursuit of a career begins after high school. However, because a high school education is so important, and because some career paths begin in high school, the first requirement below deals with how high school can help you in your chosen career. The remaining requirements ask you to identify and write about the various stages of education and training particular to the path you might follow as you pursue your chosen career.

1. High School Experience (3 points): Contact the high school you are most likely to attend. Explain the project you are working on, and ask for information regarding the school's academic courses and extra-curricular activities, such as sports and clubs. Review the materials carefully and choose one course or activity that you think might help prepare you, directly or indirectly, for your chosen career. Write a paragraph or more in which you explain how the course or activity you have chosen might help you.

2. Customized Career Path Flow Chart (4 points): Just as there are many different careers, there are also many different career paths. A career path includes the education or training a person receives on the way to achieve his or her desired career. Some career paths involve several months of occupational or on-the-job training. Others involve years of university or college education. Still others include a combination of training, higher education and one or more internships. Follow the steps below to create a customized flow chart showing the stages of education or training for your chosen career.

Step 1: Consult your parents, high school guidance counselors, teachers, people working in your chosen field and reliable Internet and library sources to learn about the education or training you will need to prepare for your career.

Step 2: Decide how many stages of education or training you will need. For example, if your chosen career is visual art, the first stage of your education and training might be three years of art school; the second stage might be a year of study abroad; the third stage might be two years of graduate study. Record each stage, in chronological order, across the top of a plain sheet of paper.

Step 3: If you have more than one stage written at the top of your paper, draw a vertical line or lines to separate the stages. When you finish this step, you should have one or more columns, each with a heading that names a stage of the education or training you will need.

Step 4: For each stage on your flow chart, consult reliable sources to compile a list of places such as schools, universities and training centers where you might like to go to receive training. Skip a line space below each column heading and transfer each list to the appropriate column. Leave room for one final choice at the bottom of each column.

Step 5: From your list of choices in each column, choose the one school or institution you think will best suit your plans, desires and interests for that particular stage of your education or training. Leave a line space, and then write the name of your choice at the bottom of each column.

3. Informational Materials About Your Chosen Schools (2 points): Refer to your customized career path and contact the appropriate person at each school or training center. Explain your project and ask him or her to mail you all the materials normally sent to someone interested in applying for admission. Most schools and training centers will have a website where such materials can be viewed and downloaded. However, you should still call and ask for information to be mailed. Often, you may receive more than what you find on the website.

4. Education and Training Questions (2 points each): Use your customized career path flow chart and the information you have gathered to answer the sets of questions below.

- While customizing your career path flow chart, what was one major decision you made when choosing from among your education or training options? Explain the reasons for your decision.

- What prerequisites, prior knowledge or experience, will you need in order to begin your education or training?

- What stages of your education or training are you most looking forward to? Explain.

- What additional activities might you get involved in to better prepare you for your career? Explain.

- How long do you think it will take you to complete your education or training? What type of certification or degree do you hope to receive at the end of your education or training?

- What additional, non-required activities or training might you pursue to better prepare you for your career?

5. **First-Year Expense Charts** (3 points): Create an expense chart for the first year of each stage in your education or training. Each chart should show all the expenses you would be likely to incur over the course of a year. Estimate a total for each category listed that would apply to your situation: rent, food, tuition, books, supplies and transportation. Show a total for each kind of expense, and then show a grand total for all expenses. Be sure to include taxes.

6. Total Career Path Expenses and Funding (3 points): Use your first-year expense charts to calculate the total amount you will spend during the entire time of your education or training. To accomplish this, multiply each first-year total by the number of years required for that stage of your education. Think about and research different funding options that could help finance your education. What options will be available to you? Which do you think you would choose? Explain why.

7. **Computer-Generated Pie Graph** (3 points): Referring to your first-year expense charts, create a computer-generated pie graph showing all expenses (grouped by category of expense) that you will incur over the entire time of your education or training. Be sure to give your pie graph a title and provide a key.

8. Applying to Your School or Training Center (2 points): Review the informational materials you have gathered and locate the application form for the first school you would attend. Complete this form as you would if you were actually applying for admission. If you are asked to provide additional materials such as a personal essay, letters of recommendation or samples of your work, be creative. Do not include your real social security number on the application.

> Important: For this fictional application, you may creatively invent certain information. However, real-life applications must be thoroughly accurate.

9. **Computer-Generated Brochure** (3 points): Choose the school or training center you are most looking forward to attending. Using the computer, design an original and authentic-looking brochure that "advertises" various aspects of that school. Refer to the materials you have gathered for information and ideas, but make your brochure original.

Portfolio Section 3: Applying for the Job

1. Prospective Employers List (2 points): Make a list of prospective employers you might apply to after completing your education or training. Gather information about these employers and write a brief description of each. If your career path leads to only one obvious prospective employer (the United States Coast Guard, for example) consider some reasonable alternatives, or simply do a more extensive description for that one employer.

2. Job Posting (2 points): Consult trade journals, the Internet and newspapers to find listings of available jobs in your career field. Choose the posting that most appeals to you and attach it to a piece of paper. On this same paper, explain why this job appeals to you over other jobs.

3. Professional Cover Letter (3 points): Write a professional, one-page cover letter stating your background, qualifications and interest in the job you have chosen. Address your letter as indicated by the job listing you chose. A cover letter is a standard part of most formal job applications. However, if the application for the job you chose does not require a cover letter, compose one in order to explore and express your career interests.

> Important: For this fictional cover letter, you may creatively invent certain information. However, real-life cover letters must be thoroughly accurate.

4. Professional Resume (4 points): Write a professional resume outlining your education, experience, professional goals and other relevant information. Refer to the job listing you have chosen to know what specific details to include. There are many different ways to format a resume. Be sure to look at many examples and choose the one that is most appropriate for your situation. Like a real-life cover letter, a real-life resume is a standard part of most formal job applications. However, if the application for the job you chose does not require a resume, create one for your own benefit.

> Important: For this fictional resume, you may creatively invent certain information. However, real-life resumes must be thoroughly accurate.

5. Post-Interview Thank-You Letter (3 points): Write a professional thank-you letter to a prospective employer as if you have interviewed for a job. Be positive and write in a tone that reflects the qualities the prospective employer is seeking.

Remaining Portfolio Materials

1. Table of Contents (1 point): Write a table of contents that lists all the sections of your portfolio along with their corresponding page numbers.

2. Cover Page (1 point): Create an eye-catching cover page for your portfolio that includes an original title for your project as well as your name and the Classroom Presentation date.

3. Portfolio (1 point): Organize all of your materials in a three-ring binder. The table of contents should come first, followed by your work from Portfolio Sections 1, 2 and 3 above in the order presented. Your cover page should be placed on the front of the portfolio.

You have completed Component 1 of the Career Aspiration Project. By completing your portfolio, you have created an important resource that will help you work on Components 2 and 3. Though several worthy challenges lie ahead, you are now prepared to meet each of them, knowing that you have laid the necessary groundwork that will increase your chances for success. Good luck as you move on to creating your project exhibit items.

COMPONENT 2
Creating Your Career Aspiration Exhibit
Total Possible Exhibit Points: 10 out of 100 total possible for project

Having researched and chosen your career, and charted the beginning of your career path, it is now time to design and create an informative and appealing exhibit of your work. The items you complete will be viewed by your classmates on the day of your Classroom Presentation and also by everyone who attends the Career Aspiration Expo at the end of the term. As always, put your best work into designing, creating and integrating your exhibit items.

Note:
Keep in mind that each item is only one part of the overall exhibit. In other words, no single item has to say everything about your project. Decide upon a purpose for each item. Consider how best to arrange your exhibit for the greatest effect.

1. Route Map(s) (2 points): It is always a good idea to know where your plans will take you. Therefore, find or create one or more maps that show the location of your home and the location or locations of where you will go for your education or training. Mark all the routes you will travel and indicate the total miles and type of transportation you will use.

2. Arrangement of Your Informational Materials (2 points): Gather the informational materials about your career and career training. Classify and arrange them in an effective and pleasing manner.

3. Display Board (3 points): Use a large two- or three-panel exhibit board to create an "advertisement" for your career and customized career path. Use half of your board to showcase your career. Use the other half to showcase your customized career path. Your display board should include your project's title and your name. You may then choose to post your route map, certain informational materials and any additional materials on your board.

4. Exhibit (3 points): Arrange all of the above exhibit items, your portfolio and any additional materials you wish to include, to create an appealing and informative overall exhibit.

You have now completed Component 2 of the Career Aspiration Project, giving you an important exhibit that creatively displays your career and customized career path. Now that you have finished your portfolio and exhibit, you are ready to prepare for your Classroom Presentation (Component 3), during which you will share your project with your peers and teacher.

COMPONENT 3:

Giving Your Classroom Presentation

Total Possible Classroom Presentation Points: 9 out of 100 total possible for project

Now that you have researched, chosen and made plans for your career and education, it is time to share your aspirations with others. The Classroom Presentation is an opportunity to formally present your goals and to share your hard work with your classmates and teacher. Your portfolio and exhibit contain all the information you will need to prepare for the presentation, so relax and have fun.

1. What to Include in Your Presentation:

- Career Choice and Display Board (2 points): Share your career choice, explain why you chose that career and provide a basic description of what your day-to-day duties are likely to be, pointing to any relevant informational materials on your display board.

- Career and Your Personal Life (2 points): Explain one way your career will affect your life outside of work.

- Career Path (2 points): Share a description of your career path and two to three aspects that you are most looking forward to.

- Portfolio, Career Path Expenses and Funding (2 points): Show your portfolio and share your expense charts and computer-generated pie graph. Discuss your total career path cost and some funding options you might choose.

Note: Your presentation should last between 3-4 minutes and should be rehearsed, but not memorized. If you forget to include information from one of the bullet points, your teacher will ask you the question so that you have a chance to answer it.

2. **Attire** (1 point): Dress in clothing that relates to your career.

Bring to the Classroom Presentation:
All of your exhibit items and anything extra that you would like to enhance your exhibit. Remember to dress in clothing that reflects your career.

You are now finished with Components 1, 2 and 3 – all of the assessed portions of your project. The final component, Attending the Career Aspiration Expo, provides a festive closure to the Career Aspiration Project.

COMPONENT 4:

Attending the Career Aspiration Expo (The expo does not involve any points.)

Now that you have completed your project and presented it to your peers, it is time to share your work with family and friends at the Career Aspiration Expo. The expo is an event that recognizes and celebrates the hard work you have done on your Career Aspiration Project. At the expo, you will set up and stand by your exhibit as invited guests walk around informally and view the projects. Guests may ask you friendly questions about your project as they visit your exhibit, so have fun sharing your and any additional materials onto your board.

Bring to the Expo: all of your exhibit items and anything extra that you think will enhance your exhibit. Remember to dress in clothing that reflects your career.

CONGRATULATIONS ON YOUR COMPLETED CAREER ASPIRATION PROJECT!

TEACHER FORMS CHECKLIST

use this checklist to record forms submitted by the students

student name	student commitment contract	student checkpoint organizer 1	student checkpoint organizer 2	student checkpoint organizer 3	expo invitation response number attending	special equip. needed
1.						
2.						
3.						
4.						
5.						
6.						
7.						
8.						
9.						
10.						
11.						
12.						
13.						
14.						
15.						
16.						
17.						
18.						
19.						
20.						
21.						
22.						
23.						
24.						
25.						

STUDENT COMMITMENT CONTRACT

expectations

project work time

I agree to:

- be responsible for following my Student Instruction Guide to do my work.
- keep track of all my project materials.
- work hard on Envision without disturbing others.
- save my unanswered questions until my teacher is free to talk.

checkpoint meetings

I will come prepared with:

- my Student Instruction Guide.
- my completed Student Checkpoint Organizer.
- all of my project materials.

important dates and times

Checkpoint 1: _____

Checkpoint 2: _____

Checkpoint 3: _____

Classroom Presentation: _____

Career Aspiration Expo: _____

_____

signatures

I agree to:

- meet expectations on the dates listed above.
- complete each of the Career Aspiration requirements to the best of my ability.
- bring my project work to school each day so that I can work on it during extra time.
- take my project work from school each night so that I can work on it at home.

I understand that the Envision Career Aspiration Project is a special opportunity, and that if I do not meet the above expectations, I may be asked to return to normal classroom activities.

Student Signature: _____ Date: _____

Parent Signature: _____ Date: _____

Please return this contract by: _____

Student Name: _____ Checkpoint Date: _____

Career Choice: _____

Training Choice(s): _____

directions

1. Using your Student Instruction Guide, check off any requirements that you have completed up to this point.

2. Bring the following items to the Checkpoint Meeting:

• your Student Instruction Guide.

• your completed Student Checkpoint Organizer.

• all of your project materials.

questions

1. Which requirements have you completed up to this point?

_____

_____

2. Is there anything you need help with?

_____

_____

3. Is there anything else about your project that you would like to discuss?

_____

_____

4. List at least three goals you expect to accomplish by the next checkpoint.

_____

_____

TEACHER CHECKPOINT RECORD

student name	career and training choice	checkpoint 1 notes	checkpoint 2 notes	checkpoint 3 notes
1.				
2.				
3.				
4.				
5.				
6.				
7.				
8.				
9.				
10.				

CAREER ASPIRATION

YOU'RE INVITED!

EXPO INVITATION RESPONSE

Please fill out and return by: _____

Student Name: _____

Student Attending? ☐ Yes ☐ No

Number of Student Guests Attending: _____

Will your child need any special school equipment for the expo (i.e., computer or TV)? Please List: _____
_____

Thank you.

We look forward to seeing you at this special event!

PLEASE JOIN US FOR OUR ENVISION CAREER ASPIRATION EXPO!

Why? _____

Who? _____

Where? _____

When? _____

Remember to bring your camera!

CAREER ASPIRATION

CERTIFICATE OF ACHIEVEMENT

CAREER ASPIRATION

AWARDED TO

DATE

SIGNATURE

envision®

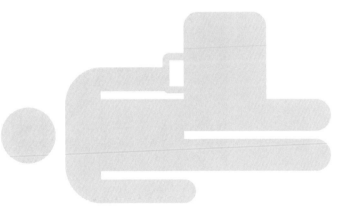

CAREER ASPIRATION PROJECT

STUDENT

envision®

CAREER ASPIRATION

career aspiration expo

envision®

career aspiration expo

envision®

TEACHER ASSESSMENT

Component 1: Building Your Career Aspiration Portfolio
Total Possible Portfolio Points: 81 out of 100 total possible for project

Requirements	Possible Points	Teacher Points	Average Points
Portfolio Section 1: Choosing your Career			
1. Career Interest Inventory: Using the Internet, take a career interest inventory and print your results. There are many inventory websites available, so find a site that does not ask you to provide any personal information, such as your name, address, email address, telephone number or social security number.	3		
2. Career Choice Questions:			
• How do you feel about the results of your career interest inventory? How do these results affect your choice of career?	2		
• What career did you choose? What aspects of the career especially appeal to you and why?	2		
• What will be your approximate starting salary? How important was salary to you when you chose your career?	2		
• What personal and professional qualifications will you need for this career? Explain them.	2		
• What will be your basic day-to-day duties in this career? Be sure to consider all aspects of the work. Explain them.	2		
• What will be the general conditions of your work environment? (Where will you work? With whom will you work? What will your work schedule be like?) Explain. What benefits or drawbacks are there to these conditions?	2		
• What are two or three aspects of the career that you think will challenge you most? Explain.	2		
• How will you meet these challenges?	2		
• What is the current job outlook for people starting out in this career? What will you do if there is a shortage of available jobs when you are ready to enter the workforce? What other careers or occupations might you be qualified for with your background and training?	2		
• How might this career affect your personal life outside of work, especially regarding the time you will have for family, social activities, recreation and other pursuits?	2		
• How will having this career allow you to contribute to your community, directly or indirectly?	2		
3. Career Choice Interview: With the help of your parents, arrange to interview someone involved in the career you have chosen or in a related field. Be sure the person understands the purpose of the interview. Before the interview, prepare ten to fifteen career-related questions to ask the interviewee. Write your questions down, leaving enough room to record the responses. Try to write questions that require more than a simple "Yes" or "No" response. During the interview, feel free to ask additional questions, and take care to record all responses accurately. If a one-on-one interview is not possible, conduct the interview over the phone, or arrange to mail or email your questions to the interviewee. Be sure to thank the interviewee when you are finished.	4		

Portfolio Section 2: Education and Training

1. High School Experience: Contact the high school you are most likely to attend. Review the materials carefully and choose one course or activity that you think might help prepare you, directly or indirectly, for your chosen career. Write a paragraph or more in which you explain how the course or activity you have chosen might help you.	3		
2. Customized Career Path Flow Chart: Just as there are many different careers, there are also many different career paths. Follow the steps below to create a customized flow chart showing the stages of education or training for your chosen career.	4		
3. Informational Materials About Your Chosen Schools: Refer to your customized career path and contact the appropriate person at each school or training center. Explain your project and ask him or her to mail you all the materials normally sent to someone interested in applying for admission.	2		
4. Education and Training Questions:			
• While customizing your career path flow chart, what was one major decision you made when choosing from among your education or training options? Explain the reasons for your decision.	2		
• What prerequisites, prior knowledge or experience, will you need in order to begin your education or training?	2		
• What stages of your education or training are you most looking forward to? Explain.	2		
• What additional activities might you get involved in to better prepare you for your career? Explain.	2		
• How long do you think it will take you to complete your education or training? What type of certification or degree do you hope to receive at the end of your education or training?	2		
• What additional, non-required activities or training might you pursue to better prepare you for your career?	2		
5. First-Year Expense Charts: Create an expense chart for the first year of each stage in your education or training. Each chart should show all the expenses you would be likely to incur over the course of a year. Estimate a total for each category listed that would apply to your situation: rent, food, tuition, books, supplies and transportation. Show a total for each kind of expense, and then show a grand total for all expenses. Be sure to include taxes.	3		
6. Total Career Path Expenses and Funding: Use your first-year expense charts to calculate the total amount you will spend during the entire time of your education or training. To accomplish this, multiply each first-year total by the number of years required for that stage of your education. Think about and research different funding options that could help finance your education. What options will be available to you? Which do you think you would choose? Explain why.	3		
7. Computer-Generated Pie Graph: Referring to your first-year expense charts, create a computer-generated pie graph showing all expenses (grouped by category of expense) that you will incur over the entire time of your education or training. Be sure to give your pie graph a title and provide a key.	3		

8. Applying to Your School or Training Center: Review the informational materials you have gathered and locate the application form for the first school you would attend. Complete this form as you would if you were actually applying for admission. If you are asked to provide additional materials such as a personal essay, letters of recommendation or samples of your work, be creative. Do not include your real social security number on the application.	2		
9. Computer-Generated Brochure: Choose the school or training center you are most looking forward to attending. Using the computer, design an original and authentic-looking brochure that "advertises" various aspects of that school. Refer to the materials you have gathered for information and ideas, but make your brochure original.	3		
Portfolio Section 3: Applying for the Job			
1. Prospective Employers List: Make a list of prospective employers you might apply to after completing your education or training. Gather information about these employers and write a brief description of each. If your career path leads to only one obvious prospective employer (the United States Coast Guard, for example) consider some reasonable alternatives, or simply do a more extensive description for that one employer.	2		
2. Job Posting: Consult trade journals, the Internet and newspapers to find listings of available jobs in your career field. Choose the posting that most appeals to you and attach it to a piece of paper. On this same paper, explain why this job appeals to you over other jobs.	2		
3. Professional Cover Letter: Write a professional, one-page cover letter stating your background, qualifications and interest in the job you have chosen. Address your letter as indicated by the job listing you chose.	3		
4. Professional Resume: Write a professional resume outlining your education, experience, professional goals and other relevant information. There are many different ways to format a resume. Be sure to look at many examples and choose the one that is most appropriate for your situation.	4		
5. Post-Interview Thank-You Letter: Write a professional thank-you letter to a prospective employer as if you have interviewed for a job. Be positive and write in a tone that reflects the qualities the prospective employer is seeking.	3		
Remaining Portfolio Materials			
1. Table of Contents: Write a table of contents that lists all the sections of your portfolio along with their corresponding page numbers.	1		
2. Cover Page: Create an eye-catching cover page for your portfolio that includes an original title for your project as well as your name and the Classroom Presentation date.	1		
3. Portfolio: Organize all of your materials in a three-ring binder. The table of contents should come first, followed by your work from Portfolio Sections 1, 2 and 3 above in the order presented. Your cover page should be placed onto the front of the portfolio.	1		
TOTAL PORTFOLIO POINTS	**81**		

TEACHER ASSESSMENT

Component 2: Creating Your Career Aspiration Exhibit
Total Possible Exhibit Points: 10 out of 100 total possible for project

1. Route Map: It is always a good idea to know where your plans will take you. Therefore, find or create one or more maps that show the location of your home and the location or locations of where you will go for your education or training. Mark all the routes you will travel and indicate the total miles and type of transportation you will use.	2		
2. Arrangement of Your Informational Materials: Gather the informational materials about your career and career training. Classify and arrange them in an effective and pleasing manner.	2		
3. Display Board: Use a large two- or three-panel exhibit board to create an "advertisement" for your career and customized career path. Use half of your board to showcase your career. Use the other half to showcase your customized career path. Your display board should include your project's title and your name. You may then choose to post your route map, certain informational materials and any additional materials on your board.	3		
4. Exhibit: Arrange all of the above exhibit items, your portfolio and any additional materials you wish to include, to create an appealing and informative overall exhibit	3		
TOTAL EXHIBIT POINTS	**10**		

Component 3: Giving Your Classroom Presentation
Total Possible Classroom Presentation Points: 9 out of 100 total possible for project

1. What to Include in Your Presentation:			
• Career Choice and Display Board: Share your career choice, explain why you chose that career and provide a basic description of what your day-to-day duties are likely to be, pointing to any relevant informational materials on your display board.	2		
• Career and Your Personal Life: Explain one way your career will affect your life outside of work.	2		
• Career Path: Share a description of your career path and two to three aspects that you are most looking forward to.	2		
• Portfolio, Career Path Expenses and Funding: Show your portfolio and share your expense charts and computer-generated pie graph. Discuss your total career path cost and some funding options you might choose.	2		
2. Attire: Dress in clothing that relates to your career.	1		
TOTAL CLASSROOM PRESENTATION POINTS	**9**		
TOTAL PROJECT POINTS	**100**		

STUDENT SELF-ASSESSMENT

Component 1: Building Your Career Aspiration Portfolio
Total Possible Portfolio Points: 81 out of 100 total possible for project

Requirements	Possible Points	Student Points
Portfolio Section 1: Choosing your Career		
1. Career Interest Inventory: Using the Internet, take a career interest inventory and print your results. There are many inventory websites available, so find a site that does not ask you to provide any personal information, such as your name, address, email address, telephone number or social security number.	3	
2. Career Choice Questions:		
• How do you feel about the results of your career interest inventory? How do these results affect your choice of career?	2	
• What career did you choose? What aspects of the career especially appeal to you and why?	2	
• What will be your approximate starting salary? How important was salary to you when you chose your career?	2	
• What personal and professional qualifications will you need for this career? Explain them.	2	
• What will be your basic day-to-day duties in this career? Be sure to consider all aspects of the work. Explain them.	2	
• What will be the general conditions of your work environment? (Where will you work? With whom will you work? What will your work schedule be like?) Explain. What benefits or drawbacks are there to these conditions?	2	
• What are two or three aspects of the career that you think will challenge you most? Explain.	2	
• How will you meet these challenges?	2	
• What is the current job outlook for people starting out in this career? What will you do if there is a shortage of available jobs when you are ready to enter the workforce? What other careers or occupations might you be qualified for with your background and training?	2	
• How might this career affect your personal life outside of work, especially regarding the time you will have for family, social activities, recreation and other pursuits?	2	
• How will having this career allow you to contribute to your community, directly or indirectly?	2	
3. Career Choice Interview: With the help of your parents, arrange to interview someone involved in the career you have chosen or in a related field. Be sure the person understands the purpose of the interview. Before the interview, prepare ten to fifteen career-related questions to ask the interviewee. Write your questions down, leaving enough room to record the responses. Try to write questions that require more than a simple "Yes" or "No" response. During the interview, feel free to ask additional questions, and take care to record all responses accurately. If a one-on-one interview is not possible, conduct the interview over the phone, or arrange to mail or email your questions to the interviewee. Be sure to thank the interviewee when you are finished.	4	

Portfolio Section 2: Education and Training

1. High School Experience: Contact the high school you are most likely to attend. Review the materials carefully and choose one course or activity that you think might help prepare you, directly or indirectly, for your chosen career. Write a paragraph or more in which you explain how the course or activity you have chosen might help you.	3	
2. Customized Career Path Flow Chart: Just as there are many different careers, there are also many different career paths. Follow the steps below to create a customized flow chart showing the stages of education or training for your chosen career.	4	
3. Informational Materials About Your Chosen Schools: Refer to your customized career path and contact the appropriate person at each school or training center. Explain your project and ask him or her to mail you all the materials normally sent to someone interested in applying for admission.	2	
4. Education and Training Questions:		
• While customizing your career path flow chart, what was one major decision you made when choosing from among your education or training options? Explain the reasons for your decision.	2	
• What prerequisites, prior knowledge or experience, will you need in order to begin your education or training?	2	
• What stages of your education or training are you most looking forward to? Explain.	2	
• What additional activities might you get involved in to better prepare you for your career? Explain.	2	
• How long do you think it will take you to complete your education or training? What type of certification or degree do you hope to receive at the end of your education or training?	2	
• What additional, non-required activities or training might you pursue to better prepare you for your career?	2	
5. First-Year Expense Charts: Create an expense chart for the first year of each stage in your education or training. Each chart should show all the expenses you would be likely to incur over the course of a year. Estimate a total for each category listed that would apply to your situation: rent, food, tuition, books, supplies and transportation. Show a total for each kind of expense, and then show a grand total for all expenses. Be sure to include taxes.	3	
6. Total Career Path Expenses and Funding: Use your first-year expense charts to calculate the total amount you will spend during the entire time of your education or training. To accomplish this, multiply each first-year total by the number of years required for that stage of your education. Think about and research different funding options that could help finance your education. What options will be available to you? Which do you think you would choose? Explain why.	3	
7. Computer-Generated Pie Graph: Referring to your first-year expense charts, create a computer-generated pie graph showing all expenses (grouped by category of expense) that you will incur over the entire time of your education or training. Be sure to give your pie graph a title and provide a key.	3	

8. Applying to Your School or Training Center: Review the informational materials you have gathered and locate the application form for the first school you would attend. Complete this form as you would if you were actually applying for admission. If you are asked to provide additional materials such as a personal essay, letters of recommendation or samples of your work, be creative. Do not include your real social security number on the application.	2	
9. Computer-Generated Brochure: Choose the school or training center you are most looking forward to attending. Using the computer, design an original and authentic-looking brochure that "advertises" various aspects of that school. Refer to the materials you have gathered for information and ideas, but make your brochure original.	3	
Portfolio Section 3: Applying for the Job		
1. Prospective Employers List: Make a list of prospective employers you might apply to after completing your education or training. Gather information about these employers and write a brief description of each. If your career path leads to only one obvious prospective employer (the United States Coast Guard, for example) consider some reasonable alternatives, or simply do a more extensive description for that one employer.	2	
2. Job Posting: Consult trade journals, the Internet and newspapers to find listings of available jobs in your career field. Choose the posting that most appeals to you and attach it to a piece of paper. On this same paper, explain why this job appeals to you over other jobs.	2	
3. Professional Cover Letter: Write a professional, one-page cover letter stating your background, qualifications and interest in the job you have chosen. Address your letter as indicated by the job listing you chose.	3	
4. Professional Resume: Write a professional resume outlining your education, experience, professional goals and other relevant information. There are many different ways to format a resume. Be sure to look at many examples and choose the one that is most appropriate for your situation.	4	
5. Post-Interview Thank-You Letter: Write a professional thank-you letter to a prospective employer as if you have interviewed for a job. Be positive and write in a tone that reflects the qualities the prospective employer is seeking.	3	
Remaining Portfolio Materials		
1. Table of Contents: Write a table of contents that lists all the sections of your portfolio along with their corresponding page numbers.	1	
2. Cover Page: Create an eye-catching cover page for your portfolio that includes an original title for your project as well as your name and the Classroom Presentation date.	1	
3. Portfolio: Organize all of your materials in a three-ring binder. The table of contents should come first, followed by your work from Portfolio Sections 1, 2 and 3 above in the order presented. Your cover page should be placed onto the front of the portfolio.	1	
TOTAL PORTFOLIO POINTS	**81**	

Component 2: Creating Your Career Aspiration Exhibit
Total Possible Exhibit Points: 10 out of 100 total possible for project

1. Route Map: It is always a good idea to know where your plans will take you. Therefore, find or create one or more maps that show the location of your home and the location or locations of where you will go for your education or training. Mark all the routes you will travel and indicate the total miles and type of transportation you will use.	2	
2. Arrangement of Your Informational Materials: Gather the informational materials about your career and career training. Classify and arrange them in an effective and pleasing manner.	2	
3. Display Board: Use a large two- or three-panel exhibit board to create an "advertisement" for your career and customized career path. Use half of your board to showcase your career. Use the other half to showcase your customized career path. Your display board should include your project's title and your name. You may then choose to post your route map, certain informational materials and any additional materials on your board.	3	
4. Exhibit: Arrange all of the above exhibit items, your portfolio and any additional materials you wish to include, to create an appealing and informative overall exhibit.	3	
TOTAL EXHIBIT POINTS	**10**	

Component 3: Giving Your Classroom Presentation
Total Possible Classroom Presentation Points: 9 out of 100 total possible for project

1. What to Include in Your Presentation:		
• Career Choice and Display Board: Share your career choice, explain why you chose that career and provide a basic description of what your day-to-day duties are likely to be, pointing to any relevant informational materials on your display board.	2	
• Career and Your Personal Life: Explain one way your career will affect your life outside of work.	2	
• Career Path: Share a description of your career path and two to three aspects that you are most looking forward to.	2	
• Portfolio, Career Path Expenses and Funding: Show your portfolio and share your expense charts and computer-generated pie graph. Discuss your total career path cost and some funding options you might choose.	2	
2. Attire: Dress in clothing that relates to your career.	1	
TOTAL CLASSROOM PRESENTATION POINTS	**9**	
TOTAL PROJECT POINTS	**100**	

SPANISH TRANSLATIONS OF PARENT FORMS AND STUDENT INSTRUCTION GUIDE

carta de introducción para padres del proyecto aspiración a una carrera

Estimados Padres,

Bienvenidos a "Aspiración a una Carera", un proyecto de "Envision" que inspirará y mantendrá la atención educativa de su hijo/a. "Aspiración a una Carrera" está diseñado para informar a su hijo/a acerca de adonde lo puede guiar la educación en la vida. Su hijo/a tendrá la oportunidad de tomar un inventario de interés de profesión, elegir una profesión, investigar su carrera elegida, también tendrá que investigar la educación o capacitación necesaria para alcanzar esta meta tan importante. Su hijo/a también investigará y elegirá una universidad adonde quiera acudir para continuar su educación.

Para este proyecto el alumno investigará distintos aspectos de la carrera que elija, entrevistará a una persona en esa área, creará una tabla y una gráfica de los gastos relacionados con su carrera, llenará una aplicación para una escuela, creará un folleto, una carta de presentación y su curriculum profesional, y mucho más. Finalmente, su hijo/a construirá una exhibición que demuestra los aspectos claves de su carrera y dará una breve presentación a sus compañeros.

Una Guía Estudiantil será proveída para orientar al estudiante paso por paso y guiarlo por este proceso. La Guía Estudiantil es una lista completa que indica los requisitos de este proyecto y está diseñada para guiar al alumno a que comience a pensar usando un nivel superior. La guía también menciona las Tarjetas de Recursos que proveen explicaciones adicionales, ideas, consejos, y otra información. Estas tarjetas también estarán disponibles en el salón de su hijo/a para el uso de él/ella.

El proyecto "Aspiración a una Carrera" está diseñado para que el alumno pueda trabajar independientemente en su salón, durante su tiempo libre y en casa. "Juntas de Revisión" están programadas durante el proyecto para que yo esté al pendiente del progreso del estudiante. En las fechas indicadas, el estudiante y yo nos reuniremos para discutir sus logros y para planear nuevas metas para la siguiente junta. También, veremos si el estudiante ha tenido dificultades o si tiene algunas preguntas.

"Aspiración a una Carrera" se terminará en una "Exposición de Proyectos". Esta Exposición dará una oportunidad al estudiante a que comparta su trabajo y sus experiencias con su familia, amigos, e invitados. Usted recibirá una invitación para la "Exposición de Proyectos" más adelante en el trimestre.

Fechas para recordar:

Revisión 1: _____

Revisión 2: _____

Revisión 3: _____

Presentación en el Salón de Clase: _____

Exposición de "Aspiración a una Carrera": _____ , _____

Sinceramente,

_____

_____

CONTRATO DE COMPROMISO ESTUDIANTIL

expectativas

tiempo de proyecto

Acepto:

- seguir los pasos indicados en mi guía estudiantil mientras que hago mi trabajo.
- mantener en orden mis materiales de proyecto.
- trabajar duro en Envision sin molestar a otros.
- mantener mis preguntas para mi mismo, hasta que mi maestro/a esté libre para hablar.

juntas de revisión

Vendré preparado con:

- mi Guía Estudiantil.
- mi Organizador Estudiantil.
- todos los materiales necesarios para el proyecto.

fechas importantes

Revisión 1: _____

Revisión 2: _____

Revisión 3: _____

Presentación en el Salón de Clase: _____

Exposición de Aspiración a una Carrera: _____

_____

firmas

Acepto:

- cumplir con las expectativas en las fechas citadas anteriormente.
- utilizaré mis mejores habilidades y conocimientos para completar los requisitos de "Aspiración a una Carrera".
- traer mi proyecto a la escuela todos los días, así podré trabajar en él durante mi tiempo libre.
- llevar mi proyecto a la casa todos los días, así podré trabajar en casa.

Entiendo que el proyecto "Aspiración a una Carrera" de Envision es una oportunidad especial, y si no cumplo con las expectativas mencionadas existe la posibilidad de que tenga que regresar a las actividades normales de mi salón.

Firma del Estudiante: _____ Fecha: _____

Firma del Padre: _____ Fecha: _____

Por favor devuelva este contrato antes de: _____

GUÍA DE INSTRUCCIONES PARA EL ESTUDIANTE

Construyendo el Portafolio de Tu Proyecto • Creando la Exhibición de tu Proyecto • Presentación de tu Proyecto• Asistiendo a la Exposición

Se Creativo!

IMPORTANTE!

Las tarjetas de recursos están señaladas por el icono de Aspiración a una Carrera. Cuando veas uno de estos íconos, sabrás que hay una tarjeta correspondiente de recursos disponibles que te dará información y ejemplos adicionales que te serán de mucha ayuda. También asegúrate de visitar www.mindvinepress.com, así como otros sitios confiables de internet y usar materiales de referencias de la biblioteca para obtener más recursos y ejemplos. Advertencia: Nunca llenes una forma mientras estés conectado a la red de internet. Si encuentras una forma que necesites, imprímela y llena la forma que imprimiste. Tampoco des ninguna información personal de identificación mientras estás en línea, como: tu nombre, dirección, correo electrónico, número de teléfono o seguro social, aun cuando se te pregunte por ello. Por ultimo cada vez que veas el ícono de Mind Vine Press en esta guía de instrucciones ve a www.mindvinepress.com y encontrarás diferentes sitios de internet que te serán de valiosa ayuda para ese requisito.

COMPONENTE 1

Construyendo el Portafolio de Tu Proyecto Total de Puntos Posibles por el Portafolio: 81 de un total de 100 por el proyecto

Para este proyecto, deberás investigar y establecer metas de posibles opciones de carreras y su trayectoria profesional. El término trayectoria profesional se refiere a todas las etapas de desarrollo y a la experiencia que una persona encuentra después de haber elegido una profesión u ocupación. Esta trayectoria se inicia al elegir una carrera. Los siguientes pasos a lo largo de dicha trayectoria usualmente incluyen algún tipo de educación o entrenamiento, y el trayecto termina al momento de la jubilación o cambio de carrera. Para este proyecto, nos vamos a enfocar en los dos primeros pasos. Completa los requisitos que se encuentran a continuación en orden numérico. Es necesario seguir el orden en el que se encuentran, ya que dependen el uno del otro, esto te ayudará a terminar sin problema tu proceso de planificación.

Nota: "Componente 1: Construyendo el Portafolio de Aspiración a una Carrera" Se divide en tres secciones: "Portafolio Sección 1: Eligiendo tu Carrera", "Portafolio Sección 2: Educación y Entrenamiento" y "Portafolio Sección 3: Solicitando el Empleo".

Portafolio Sección 1: Eligiendo tu Carrera

1. 🔲 🔲 **Inventario de Interés Profesional** (3 puntos): Usando el internet, toma un inventario de interés profesional e imprime los resultados. Hay muchos sitios de interés que ofrecen este tipo de inventarios, así que busca uno que no te pida ningún tipo de información personal como: tu nombre, dirección, correo electrónico, número de teléfono o número de seguro social.

2. 🔲 **Preguntas Para Elegir una Carrera** (2 puntos cada una): Toma en consideración los resultados del inventario de interés profesional, así como tus preferencias personales, y elige la carrera que te gustaría continuar después de graduarte de preparatoria. Reúne información acerca de la carrera que seleccionaste preguntando a personas que sean expertas en ella, usando sitios confiables de internet y los recursos en la biblioteca. Utiliza la serie de preguntas a continuación como guía de investigación y contéstalas de acuerdo a las normas siguientes: redacta un párrafo o más para responder cada serie de preguntas; utiliza una hoja de papel para cada serie de respuestas; y escribe la primera pregunta de cada serie de preguntas en la parte superior de cada hoja.

- ¿Qué piensas acerca de los resultados de tu inventario de interés profesional? ¿Cómo estos resultados afectan la carrera que elegiste?

- ¿Qué carrera elegiste? ¿Qué aspectos de esta carrera tienen especial interés para ti y por qué?

- ¿Cuál sería aproximadamente tu sueldo inicial? ¿Qué tan importante fue para ti el sueldo al momento de escoger tu carrera?

- ¿Qué calificaciones personales y profesionales se necesitan para esta carrera? Explícalos.

- ¿Cuáles serian tus labores diarias en esta profesión? Asegúrate de considerar todos los aspectos del trabajo. Explícalos.

- ¿Cuáles serán en general las condiciones del ambiente de tu trabajo? ¿Dónde trabajarás? ¿Con quien vas a trabajar? ¿Cuál será tu horario de trabajo? Explica. ¿Cuáles son las ventajas o desventajas que hay en estas condiciones?

- ¿Cuáles son dos o tres aspectos de la carrera que piensas pueden ser un desafío para ti? Explícalo.

- ¿Cómo harías frente a dicho desafío?

- ¿Cuáles son las oportunidades laborales para las personas que empiezan en esta carrera? ¿Qué harías si existiera una escasez de puestos de trabajo cuando estés listo para empezar a trabajar? ¿En qué otra carrera o trabajo estarías calificado con tu experiencia y educación.

- ¿Cómo podría afectar esta profesión tu vida personal fuera del trabajo, especialmente en relación con el tiempo que tendrías para tu familia, actividades sociales, recreaciones u otras actividades?

- ¿Cómo te permitirá esta carrera contribuir a tu comunidad, directa o indirectamente?

3. 🔲 **Entrevista de la Carrera Seleccionada** (4 puntos): Con ayuda de tus padres, haz una entrevista a una persona que está relacionada con la carrera que escogiste o en un campo relacionado. Asegúrate de que la persona entienda el propósito de la entrevista. Antes de la entrevista, prepara de diez a quince preguntas para la persona que entrevistarás relacionadas con la carrera. Escribe tus preguntas dejando espacio suficiente para poder escribir tus respuestas. Trata de hacer preguntas que requieran más que un "Si o un No" como respuesta. Durante la entrevista no dudes en hacer más preguntas y anotar con exactitud todas las respuestas. Si no es posible que hagas la entrevista de manera personal, hazla por teléfono, o haz arreglos para enviar por correo o correo electrónico tus preguntas al entrevistado. No olvides dar las gracias a la persona entrevistada cuando hayas terminado.

Portafolio Sección 2: Educación y Entrenamiento

Nota: Este proyecto asume que la seriedad de seguir una carrera inicia después de terminar la preparatoria. Sin embargo debido a que la educación de preparatoria es muy importante, y porque algunas carreras comienzan en la preparatoria, el primer requisito a continuación trata de como la escuela preparatoria puede ayudarte con la carrera elegida. En los requisitos restantes se te pedirá que identifiques y escribas acerca de las diferentes etapas de educación y entrenamiento especial para la ruta que tú podrías seguir para lograr la carrera elegida.

1. Experiencia de Preparatoria (3 puntos): Ponte en contacto con la escuela preparatoria a la cual podrías asistir. Explícales el proyecto en el cual estás trabajando, y pídeles información acerca de los cursos académicos de la escuela, y de las actividades extracurriculares como, deportes y clubes. Revisa los materiales cuidadosamente y elige un curso o actividad que pienses te pueda ayudar en la preparación directa o indirecta de la carrera que hayas elegido. Escribe un párrafo o más en el que expliques como el curso o la actividad que elegiste te puede ayudar.

2. Diagrama Personalizado de Flujo de la Trayectoria Profesional (4 puntos): Así como hay diferentes carreras, también hay muchas rutas diferentes a seguir. Una trayectoria profesional incluye la educación y entrenamiento que una persona recibe durante el camino para lograr la carrera deseada. Algunas rutas profesionales implican meses de entrenamiento ocupacional en el puesto de trabajo. Otras, años de Universidad o de educación técnica. Algunas otras requieren una combinación de entrenamiento con años de educación superior y uno o más internados. Sigue los siguientes pasos para crear un diagrama de flujo personalizado que muestre las etapas de educación o entrenamiento que son necesarias para lograr la carrera que tú has elegido.

Paso 1: Consulta a tus padres, consejeros de la preparatoria, maestros, personas que trabajan en el campo de la carrera que tú elegiste, así como fuentes confiables de internet y recursos de la biblioteca para aprender acerca de la educación o entrenamiento que van a ser necesarios en la preparación de tu carrera.

Paso 2: Decide cuantas etapas de educación o entrenamiento son las que necesitas. Por ejemplo, si la carrera elegida es arte visual, la primera etapa de educación y entrenamiento podría ser de tres años en la escuela de arte; la segunda etapa podría ser de un año de estudios en el extranjero, y la tercera etapa podría ser de dos años de postgrado. Anota cada etapa en orden cronológico en la parte superior de una hoja de papel en blanco.

Paso 3: Si tienes más de una etapa escrita en la parte superior de tu hoja, dibuja una línea o líneas verticales para separar las etapas. Cuando termines este paso deberás tener una o más columnas, cada una con el nombre de la etapa de la educación o entrenamiento que vas a necesitar.

Paso 4: Para cada etapa de tu diagrama de flujo, consulta con fuentes confiables para hacer una lista de lugares tales como escuelas, universidades y centros de entrenamiento donde te gustaría asistir para recibir tu educación. Deja un renglón en blanco debajo del encabezado de cada columna y transfiere cada una de las listas a la columna que corresponde. Deja espacio para una última elección al final de cada columna.

Paso 5: De tu lista de opciones de cada columna, escoge una escuela o institución que pienses se adapte mejor a tus planes, deseos e intereses en esa etapa en particular de tu educación o entrenamiento. Deja un renglón en blanco, y escribe el nombre que elegiste en la parte inferior de cada columna.

3. Material Informativo de las Escuelas que Elegiste (2 puntos): Consulta tu ruta profesional personalizada y contacta a la persona adecuada en cada escuela o centro de entrenamiento. Explícales tu proyecto y pide que te envíen por correo todos los materiales de información que normalmente le mandan a una persona que está interesada en aplicar para ser admitida. La mayoría de las escuelas y centros de entrenamiento cuentan con sitios de internet donde puedes buscar dichos materiales y descargarlos. Sin embargo aun así tú debes llamar para pedir la información, a menudo vas a recibir más información que la que puedes encontrar en el sitio de internet.

4. Preguntas de Educación y Entrenamiento (2 puntos c/u): Usa el diagrama personalizado de flujo de tu carrera y la información que has reunido para responder el siguiente grupo de preguntas.

- ¿Cuál fue la principal decision que tuviste que tomar al tener que escoger entre las opciones de educación o entrenamiento, al estar elaborando tu diagrama personalizado de flujo de tu trayectoria profesional? Explica cuales fueron las razones para tomar tu decisión.

- ¿Cuáles fueron los pre-requisitos, conocimiento previo o experiencia que tu necesitarás para poder empezar tu educación o entrenamiento?

- ¿Qué etapas de tu educación o entrenamiento te interesan más? Explica.

- ¿Cuáles son las actividades adicionales en las que deberás estar involucrado para prepararte mejor para tu carrera? Explica.

- ¿Cuánto tiempo piensas que te va a tomar terminar tu carrera o entrenamiento? ¿Qué tipo de certificado o título esperas recibir al final de tu educación o entrenamiento?

- ¿En cuáles actividades adicionales no requeridas podrías involucrarte para prepararte mejor en tu carrera?

5. Tabla de Gastos del Primer Año (3 puntos): Haz una tabla de los gastos para el primer año por cada etapa de tu educación o entrenamiento. Cada tabla debe incluir todos los gastos probables de ese año. Evalúa el total por cada categoría que hay en la lista que se aplican a tu situación: renta, comida, colegiatura, libros, útiles y transportación. Saca el total de cada tipo de gasto, y luego deberás sacar un total de todos los gastos. No olvides incluir los impuestos.

6. Total de Gastos y Financiamiento de la Trayectoria Profesional (3 puntos): Utiliza la tabla de gastos del primer año para calcular la cantidad total que gastarás durante el tiempo que dure terminar tu educación o entrenamiento. Para poder hacer esto, multiplica el total del primer año por el número de años que necesitas para terminar tu carrera. Considera esto e investiga acerca de las diferentes opciones de financiamiento que podrían ayudarte a terminar tu educación. ¿Cuales son las opciones que estarán disponibles para ti? ¿Cuáles crees que tu escogerías? Explica por qué.

7. Gráfica Circular en la Computadora (3 puntos): Tomando como referencia tu tabla de gastos, crea una gráfica circular en tu computadora que muestre todos los gastos (agrúpalos por categorías de gastos) que tú harás durante el tiempo que dure tu educación. Asegúrate de ponerle nombre y clave a esta gráfica circular.

8. Aplicando a tu Escuela o Centro de Entrenamiento (2 puntos): Revisa los materiales de información que pudiste reunir y encuentra la forma de solicitud para entrar a la escuela a la que tú quieres ir. Llena la forma como si estuvieras haciendo la solicitud para entrar a esa escuela. Si se te pide que incluyas información adicional como un ensayo personal, cartas de recomendación, o ejemplos de tu trabajo, se creativo. No incluyas tu número verdadero de seguro social en esta solicitud.

> Importante: En esta solicitud ficticia, tú puedes inventar cierta información. Sin embargo en una solicitud real la información debe ser verdadera y exacta.

9. Folleto Creado en tu Computadora (3 puntos): Elige la escuela a la que más te gustaría asistir. Utiliza tu computadora y diseña un folleto de publicidad que sea original y auténtico donde se "promuevan" varios aspectos de esa escuela. Puedes consultar los materiales de información que has recolectado para darte ideas, pero asegúrate que tu folleto sea original.

Portafolio Sección 3: Solicitando el Empleo

1. Lista de Posibles Empleadores (2 puntos): Haz una lista de posibles empleadores donde después de terminar tu educación podrías solicitar empleo. Reúne información acerca de estos empleadores y escribe una breve descripción de cada uno de ellos. Si tu trayectoria profesional te lleva o conduce a un solo empleador (por ejemplo los Guardacostas de Los Estados Unidos) considera algunas alternativas razonables o simplemente haz una descripción más extensa de ese empleador.

2. Anuncios de Oferta de Trabajo (2 puntos): Para encontrar listas de empleos disponibles en tu campo profesional, puedes buscar en publicaciones especializadas, internet y periódicos. Selecciona el anuncio que más te atraiga y pégalo en una hoja de papel, en el mismo papel explica por qué este anuncio fue más atractivo para ti que los demás anuncios de trabajo.

3. Carta de Presentación Profesional (3 puntos): Escribe una carta de presentación profesional de una hoja que incluya tus antecedentes, educación, títulos e interés en el trabajo que has elegido. Envía tu carta a donde se te indica en el anuncio de trabajo que elegiste. Una carta de presentación profesional comúnmente forma parte de la mayoría de las solicitudes de empleo. Sin embargo si la solicitud de empleo que elegiste no requiere de una carta de presentación, escribe una para que expreses tu interés profesional.

> Importante: En esta carta ficticia tú puedes inventar alguna información, pero en la carta verdadera toda la información deberá ser real y exacta.

4. Currículo Vitae (4 puntos): Escribe tu currículo vitae (hoja de vida) en el cual detalles tu educación, experiencia, metas profesionales y otra información que pueda ser de importancia. Consulta la lista de empleos que has seleccionado para saber que detalles específicamente debes incluir. Hay muchas maneras de hacer tu currículo. Asegúrate de ver varios ejemplos y escoger el que sea más apropiado dependiendo de tu situación. Al igual que la carta de presentación, un currículo forma parte de la solicitud de empleo, sin embargo si la solicitud de empleo no requiere de un currículo, haz uno para tu propio beneficio.

> Importante: En este currículo ficticio tú puedes inventar alguna información, pero en el verdadero toda la información deberá ser real y exacta.

5. Carta de Agradecimiento después de la Entrevista (3 puntos): Escribe una carta de agradecimiento profesional dirigida a un posible empleador como si hubieras tenido una entrevista de trabajo. Se positivo y escríbela de manera que dejes ver las cualidades que el empleador está buscando.

Los Materiales restantes del Portafolio

1. Tabla de Contenido o Índice (1 punto): Escribe una tabla de contenido o índice donde enumeres todas las secciones de tu portafolio, así como el número de la página que le corresponde.

2. Página de Cubierta o Portada (1 punto): Haz una portada o página de cubierta que sea llamativa la cual debe incluir un titulo original para tu proyecto, así como tu nombre, y la fecha de Presentación en el Salón de Clase.

3. Portafolio (1 punto): Organiza todos tus materiales en una carpeta de argollas. El índice o tabla de contenido debe estar primero, luego deberá seguir tu trabajo de las secciones 1, 2 y 3 del portafolio en el orden indicado anteriormente. Tu página de cubierta o portada deberá ir en la parte de enfrente del portafolio.

Has completado el Componente 1 del proyecto Aspiración a una Carrera. Al completar tu portafolio, has creado una fuente importante de recursos que te ayudarán cuando trabajes en los componentes 2 y 3. Aunque encontrarás algunos desafíos mas adelante, ya estás preparado para enfrentar cada uno de ellos, sabiendo que has sentado las bases necesarias que aumentan tus posibilidades de tener éxito. Buena suerte conforme vayas avanzando en la creación del material para tu proyecto.

COMPONENTE 2
Creando la Exhibición de Tu proyecto Aspiración a una Carrera

Total de Puntos Posibles por la Exhibición: 10 de un total de 100 por el proyecto

Después de haber investigado y elegido tu carrera, y establecido el principio de tu trayectoria profesional, ha llegado el momento de crear el diseño de la exhibición de tu trabajo de una manera atractiva e informativa. Los componentes de tu trabajo serán vistos por tus compañeros de clase el día de tu presentación, así como por los asistentes que atiendan a la Exposición de Aspiración a una Carrera al final del término. Como siempre, pon todo tu empeño en la integración, el diseño y creación de los componentes de tu exhibición.

Nota:
Recuerda que cada elemento es solo una parte de toda la exhibición. En otras palabras, un solo elemento no tiene que decir todo acerca de tu proyecto. Decide cual es el propósito de cada elemento. Considera cual es la mejor manera de organizar tu exhibición para tener mayor efecto.

1. Mapa(s) de la Ruta (2 puntos): Siempre es bueno tener una idea de a donde te llevarán tus planes. Por lo tanto, busca o crea un mapa o mapas que muestren la localización de tu casa y el lugar o lugares a donde tú irás a recibir tu educación. Marca todas las rutas o caminos que tendrás que recorrer e indica el total de millas y tipo de transportación que usarás.

2. Arreglo de Tus Materiales de Información (2 puntos): Reúne todos los materiales de información acerca de tu carrera o entrenamiento profesional. Clasifícala y organízala de manera eficaz y agradable.

3. Tablero de Exhibición (3 puntos): Utiliza un tablero grande de dos o tres secciones para crear un anuncio de tu carrera y trayectoria profesional personalizada. Usa la mitad de tu tablero para exhibir tu carrera o profesión y la otra mitad para mostrar tu trayectoria profesional personalizada. Tu tablero de exhibición deberá incluir el título de tu proyecto y tu nombre. Después debes decidir también si incluyes el mapa de la ruta, así como materiales de información adicional.

4. Exhibición (3 puntos): Organiza y ordena las cosas que vas a exhibir, tu portafolio y todos los materiales adicionales que hayas querido incluir en una manera informativa y atractiva.

Ya has completado el Componente 2 del Proyecto Aspiración a una Carrera, dándote una exhibición importante que muestra de forma creativa tu carrera y la trayectoria profesional personalizada. Ahora que has terminado tu portafolio y exhibición, debes empezar a prepararte para tu Presentación en el Salón de Clase (Componente 3), en la cual compartirás tu proyecto con tus compañeros y maestro.

COMPONENTE 3:
Dando Tu Presentación en el Salón de Clase
Total de Puntos Posibles por la Presentación en el Salón de Clase: 9 de un total de 100 por el proyecto

Ahora que ya has investigado, elegido y hecho planes para tu carrera y educación, es tiempo de que compartas tus aspiraciones con otros. La Presentación en el Salón de Clase es una oportunidad para presentar formalmente tus metas y compartir tu arduo trabajo con tus compañeros y maestro. Tu portafolio y material de exhibición es todo lo que necesitas para dar tu presentación, así que relájate y diviértete.

1. 🛄 Que Incluir en Tu Presentación:

- Opciones de Carreras y Tablero de Exhibición (2 puntos): Comparte las opciones de carrera que tuviste, explica por qué elegiste esa profesión y proporciona una descripción básica de lo que va a ser tu trabajo todos los días, señalando cualquier información importante que esté en los materiales de información que hay en tu tablero de exhibición.

- Tu Vida Personal y Tu Carrera (2 puntos): Explica una manera en la cual tu profesión afectará tu vida fuera del trabajo.

- Trayectoria Profesional (2 puntos): Comparte una descripción de tu trayectoria profesional y dos o tres aspectos importantes que tu esperas.

- Portafolio, Gastos de la trayectoria profesional y Financiamiento (2 puntos): Muestra tu portafolio y comparte la tabla de tus gastos, así como la gráfica circular que hiciste en tu computadora. Haz comentarios acerca del costo total de tu carrera y las opciones de financiamiento que tú elegirías.

Nota: Tu presentación solo debe durar de 3-4 minutos y debe ser ensayada pero no memorizada. Si olvidas incluir información de alguno de los puntos, tu maestro te hará una pregunta para que tu tengas oportunidad de incluirla.

2. Atuendo (1 punto): Viste ropa relacionada con tu carrera.

Que Traer a la Presentación en el Salón de Clase:
Todos los componentes de tu exhibición y cualquier cosa extra que te ayude en ella. Recuerda vestir de acuerdo a tu carrera.

Ya has terminado con los Componentes 1, 2 y 3 – y todas las partes que se requirieron para tu proyecto. El Componente final será asistir a la Exposición Aspiración a una Carrera, donde habrá una celebración para clausurar este proyecto.

COMPONENTE 4:
Asistiendo a la Exposición Aspiración a una Carrera (La Exposición no te dará puntos.)

Ahora que has terminado con tu proyecto y lo has compartido con tus compañeros, ha llegado el momento de presentar tu trabajo a tu familia y amigos en la Exposición Aspiración a una Carrera. Esta feria es un evento que reconoce y celebra el arduo trabajo que has realizado a lo largo de tu proyecto. Durante la exposición tú estarás a un lado de tu exhibición, mientras los invitados caminan de una manera informal para ver los diferentes proyectos. Algún invitado puede hacer una pregunta amistosa acerca de tu proyecto cuando vea tu exhibición, así que diviértete compartiendo los materiales adicionales que hay en tu tablero.

Que Traer a la Exposición: Todos los componentes de tu exhibición y cualquier cosa extra que te ayude en ella. Recuerda vestir de acuerdo a tu profesión.

¡ESTA INVITADO!

RESPUESTA A LA "EXPO"

Por favor complete y regrese antes de: _____

Nombre del estudiante: _____

¿El estudiante estará presente? ☐ Si ☐ No

¿Número de invitados?: _____

¿El estudiante necesitará equipo especial para su "expo" (p. ej. una Tele)? Por favor escriba lo necesario:
_____

Gracias.

Esperamos contar con su presencia durante este evento especial.

¡POR FAVOR VENGAN A VISITARNOS A LA EXPO ASPIRACION A UNA CARRERA!

¿Por qué? _____

¿Quién?_____

¿Dónde? _____

¿Cuándo? _____

Recuerde de traer su cámara!

CAREER ASPIRATION
RESOURCE CARDS
FOR STUDENTS

CAREER INTEREST INVENTORY

A career interest inventory is a questionnaire designed to help you identify a career that best suits your personality. When taking the inventory, it is important that you answer every question, even if you are not entirely sure of your answer. When you finish, read and print out your results. Use the results as a guide in choosing a potential career. You are not required to choose a career suggested by the inventory. It is merely a guide.

CAREER CHOICE QUESTIONS

Respond to each career choice question for Portfolio Section 1 on a separate sheet of paper. Write the first question for each set of questions at the top of each sheet. Your responses should be a paragraph or more in length. They should also be well explained and include your thought process and reasoning. Once you have completed your response, you may have extra white space on the page. Use this white space to demonstrate your creativity with art, borders or other finishing touches.

EXAMPLE

HOW DO I FEEL ABOUT THE RESULTS OF MY CAREER INTEREST INVENTORY?

After taking two career interest inventories, I found that I scored highest in the investigative and social categories. The terms in the investigative category that best describe me are scientific, observant, curious and independent. The terms in the social category that best describe me are friendly, helpful, kind and patient.

Scoring high in these categories made me feel confident in my career choice as a pediatrician. I have always wanted to work with children. Knowing that I am friendly, helpful, kind and patient helps me know that I will be able to work with children successfully. I have also always loved trying to figure things out. As a pediatrician, I will be able to use my investigative and scientific skills to help sick children be well again.

CAREER CHOICE INTERVIEW

An interview is a series of questions that you ask someone. You need to interview someone who is in the career field that you are choosing or a related career field. Whether you are going to conduct your interview in person, on the phone, or by mail, you need to prepare your questions ahead of time so that you are organized and can gather the information that is most important to you. Your interview should consist of approximately ten to fifteen questions. As you ask the questions, record the responses you receive. During the interview, feel free to ask additional questions as they arise.

EXAMPLE

INTERVIEW WITH A TEACHER

1. How difficult were your teacher preparation courses? The teacher preparation courses I took throughout my college career were very time consuming. They took a lot of creativity and organization, but I wouldn't say that they were difficult. As long as I worked hard and used what I learned, I completed my work successfully.

2. How long did you have to student teach and what was it like? Student-teaching requirements vary from college to college. For the college I attended, I was required to student-teach for one year. It was during the last year of…

CUSTOMIZED CAREER PATH FLOW CHART

A flow chart shows a sequence of movement within a system. In this case, your flow chart will show the stages of education or training you identified, the options for education you considered, and the final choices you made. The example below shows three stages of education. Under each stage are the possible options, and below each list of options is the final choice for that stage.

CAREER PATH FLOW CHART

EXAMPLE

2 Years of Community College	2 Years at a University	3 Years for Graduate School (Includes Clinical Research and Education)
↓	↓	↓
Valley Community College Mountain Community College River Community College	University of State Physical Therapy University	University of State Physical Therapy University Southern University
↓	↓	↓
Mountain Community College	University of State	University of State

FIRST-YEAR EXPENSE CHARTS

Your first-year expense charts should show all the expenses you would incur during the first year at each school or training center you would attend. In order to calculate these totals, refer to the materials you have gathered. These materials should include figures for tuition along with books and supplies. Read the information carefully. It may give you amounts per month, semester or year. If it is per month or semester, multiply the amount by the number of months or semesters in one school year. You may or may not find figures on rent, food or other figures. This will partially depend on whether or not you will commute to the school or live there. To estimate the general costs of figures not supplied by your materials, consult your parents or other adult. Once you have gathered the figures for each chart, show all categories and amounts, add them together and show the grand total for your first year at each school.

EXAMPLE

FIRST YEAR OF COMMUNITY COLLEGE

Tuition	$5,703
Books & Supplies	$910
Food	$2000
Transportation	$800
Other	$1,800
TOTAL	**$11,213**

FIRST YEAR AT THE UNIVERSITY

Tuition	$8,935
Books & Supplies	$940
Rent & Food	$7,102
Transportation	$200
Other	$1,800
TOTAL	**$18,977**

COMPUTER-GENERATED PIE GRAPH

Referring to your first-year expense charts, create a computer-generated pie graph showing all expenses, grouped by type of expense, that you will incur for your entire career path. Be sure to give your graph a title and provide a key. Most word processing programs have a simple option for creating graphs.

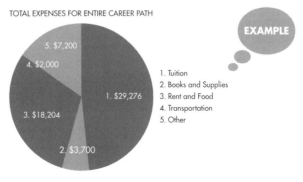

TOTAL EXPENSES FOR ENTIRE CAREER PATH

EXAMPLE

5. $7,200
4. $2,000
3. $18,204
2. $3,700
1. $29,276

1. Tuition
2. Books and Supplies
3. Rent and Food
4. Transportation
5. Other

TOTAL EXPENSE AMOUNT: $60,380

COMPUTER-GENERATED BROCHURE

Educational institutions publish brochures to attract potential students to their facilities. Choose the school training center you are most looking forward to attending and design a brochure that highlights one or more interesting aspects of that school. Your brochure should be original, attractive and informative. Use the informational materials you have received for data and ideas. Cite your sources.

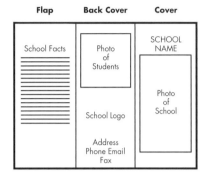

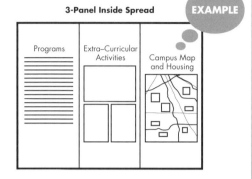

EXAMPLE

PROFESSIONAL COVER LETTER

The purpose of a cover letter is to introduce yourself to prospective employers. It should make prospective employers interested in reading your resume. It needs to be organized and professional. It should also be typed in a business font such as Times New Roman and should have a character size of 10 or 12. The following example shows only a portion of a cover letter.

EXAMPLE

Your Name
Your Address
Your Phone Number

Date

Full Name of Addressee
Title of Addressee
Address of Company

Dear Dr. Star:
I am a hard working, energetic self-starter who is excited to apply for a position as a pediatrician with your staff. This opportunity to use my talent with children was brought to my attention by Dr. Beverly Smith. Dr. Smith supervised my residency this past spring. I am happy to share my background with you, and I am sincerely interested in being part of your team…

PROFESSIONAL RESUME

The purpose of a resume is to highlight your qualifications and accomplishments as a prospective employee. It should make prospective employers interested in interviewing you. There are many different ways to format a resume. Be sure to look at many examples and choose the one that is most appropriate for your situation. It needs to be neat, organized and professional. It should also be typed in a business font such as Times New Roman and should have a character size of 10 or 12.

EXAMPLE

ELIZABETH A. JONES
45441 Yellow Street, Lawton, MI, 48291
(586) 231-7676

OBJECTIVE
Seeking an elementary school teaching position where an enthusiastic, adaptable and organized professional is needed to creatively provide quality student-centered education in all subject areas.

EDUCATION
Teacher University, 2007: Bachelor's of Science in Elementary Education; Elementary Education Certificate, K-5 All Subjects/K-8 Self Contained CC; Language Arts' Major, Physical Science Minor; Graduated Cum Laude, 3.73 GPA.

POST-INTERVIEW THANK-YOU LETTER

After an interview it is customary to send a thank-you letter to the prospective employer who interviewed you. A thank-you letter allows you to thank the interviewer for his or her time, to reaffirm your interest in the position and to briefly mention anything you were unable to talk about during the interview. It must be formal, organized and professional. It should also be typed in a business font such as Times New Roman and should have a character size of 10-12.

Your Name
Your Address
Your Phone Number

Date

Full Name of Addressee
Title of Addressee
Address of Company

Dear Dr. Bloom:
Thank you for taking the time to interview me for a design team position yesterday. It was a pleasure to discuss my qualifications with you. I am very interested in being a team member at Embark Industries…

TABLE OF CONTENTS

Your table of contents should be the first page in your portfolio, although you write it after you finish all of the other pages. Writing it after finishing the inside allows you to be accurate with your page numbers and titles in case you make any last minute changes. Your table of contents should list each section and the page it begins on. It should be neat and well organized, but feel free to be creative with your own layout.

PORTFOLIO TABLE OF CONTENTS

EXAMPLE

Page Number	Section Title
1	Career Interest Inventory
2	How do I feel about the results of my career interest inventory?
3	What career did I choose and why?
4	What will be my approximate starting salary?
5	What personal and professional qualifications will I need for this career?
6	What will be my basic day-to-day duties in this career?

COVER PAGE AND PORTFOLIO

The cover page of your portfolio should entice people to read about your project. It should include an original title, your name and the Classroom Presentation date. Your portfolio is used to organize most of your paper items. A one- to two-inch binder with a clear cover works well. Arrange your papers in the order listed in your Student Instruction Guide. You may choose to add tab dividers, page protectors and creative touches.

FRONT COVER   SPINE   BACK COVER

ROUTE MAP

Maps are an excellent way to see where locations are in relation to one another. Find or create one or more maps that show the location of your home and the location or locations of where you will go for your education or training. Mark all the routes you will travel and indicate the total miles and type of transportation you will use.

Map From My House to the Places on my Career Path

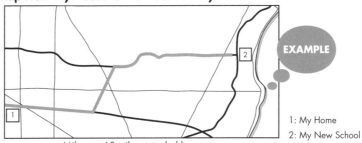

EXAMPLE

1: My Home
2: My New School

Mileage: 65 miles, traveled by car

ARRANGEMENT OF YOUR INFORMATIONAL MATERIALS

Arranging the information you received about your career and career path is an excellent way to show different aspects of your aspirations to others. Classify your materials into main groups then arrange them on your display board or in your exhibit area – even in a scrapbook! Be sure to create titles for each of your groupings. Feel free to arrange your materials however you see fit.

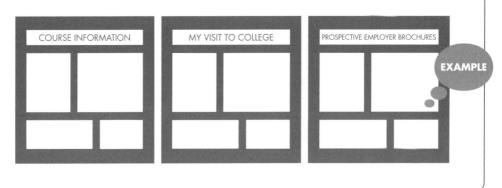

COURSE INFORMATION

MY VISIT TO COLLEGE

PROSPECTIVE EMPLOYER BROCHURES

EXAMPLE

DISPLAY BOARD AND EXHIBIT

The purpose of your display board and exhibit is to draw people's attention to your project. It should be neat, colorful and creative. You should include the items listed in your Student Instruction Guide and any additional materials you wish to bring. The example below is to be used only as a guide; feel free to rearrange. Tip: Two- or three-panel display boards can be purchased at most craft or office stores. If you prefer to make one, you can ask an adult to help construct one from a large cardboard box.

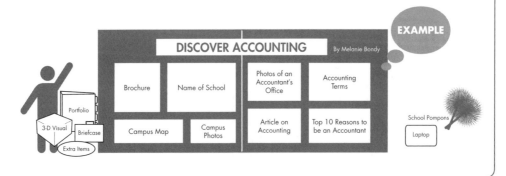

EXAMPLE

DISCOVER ACCOUNTING By Melanie Bondy

Brochure | Name of School | Photos of an Accountant's Office | Accounting Terms

Campus Map | Campus Photos | Article on Accounting | Top 10 Reasons to be an Accountant

Portfolio

3-D Visual | Briefcase

Extra Items

School Pompons

Laptop

WHAT TO INCLUDE IN YOUR PRESENTATION

Your presentation is a formal delivery of what you learned and produced for your project. It should be practiced until you are comfortable with the things you will say (not a memorized speech). It should fit into the 3-4 minute time frame and include the bulleted information listed on your Student Instruction Guide. Remember to dress in clothing that reflects your career. The additional suggestions below may help you prepare.

REMEMBER TO:

- Take a deep breath, relax and enjoy sharing.
- Greet your audience and introduce yourself.
- Speak clearly, loudly enough so everyone can hear you, and at a natural pace.
- Stand still and calm; don't fidget.
- Point to and show various visuals as you speak about them.
- Have fun while presenting. Show your excitement about your experiences.
- Make eye contact with your audience, looking around the room naturally.
- Thank your audience when you are finished.

APPENDIX 3:
FINANCIAL ADVENTURE FORMS
AND RESOURCE CARDS

Levels From Lowest to Highest:
KNOWLEDGE • COMPREHENSION • APPLICATION • ANALYSIS • EVALUATION • SYNTHESIS

Below you will find each Financial Adventure requirement, along with its corresponding level of Bloom's Taxonomy.

> **IMPORTANT!**
>
> The levels listed above are cumulative. For example, the highest level of thinking, Synthesis, incorporates all other levels of thinking: Knowledge, Comprehension, Application, Analysis and Evaluation.

COMPONENT 1
Building Your Financial Adventure Portfolio
Total Possible Portfolio Points: 74 out of 100 total possible for project

Portfolio Section 1: Accepting a Job and Charting Your Salary

1. Job-Offer Acceptance Letter (5 points): Imagine that you have been offered the job you applied for in the Career Aspiration Project. Write a professional job-offer acceptance letter stating your acceptance of the position, your understanding of the job's terms and your enthusiasm for the company. Visit www.mindvinepress.com for helpful links and more information. **SYNTHESIS**

2. Salary Chart (2 points): Create a computer-generated salary chart that displays your gross annual income* and net annual income*. On the chart, also show your net annual income in its monthly, biweekly, weekly, daily and hourly amounts. Your gross annual income should be based on the starting salary for the position you accepted. **COMPREHENSION**

Portfolio Section 2: Budgeting Your Monthly Expenses

1. Housing and Roommate Decision (1 point): The requirements below ask you to create a budget for your living expenses. Before beginning, consider having one of your Envision classmates as a roommate to help share costs. If you choose to have a roommate, choose a place of residence together and plan to share only rent and utility expenses. Each roommate will work on his or her project independently, creating his or her own portfolio and exhibit, and presenting independently to the class. In order to be roommates, you must complete a Roommate Questionnaire and a Roommate Discussion Guide. If you decide to live alone, choose a specific home to rent or purchase. Write a paragraph explaining the rationale for your roommate and housing decisions and include it in your portfolio. **EVALUATION**

2. Fixed Necessities Chart and Pie Graph (5 points): Create a computer-generated chart showing how much money you will spend on fixed necessities* in one month. Your chart should include: (1) a list of your fixed necessities for one month; (2) the amount of money you will spend on each fixed necessity in one month; (3) the amount of money you will set aside biweekly for each fixed necessity; (4) the total amount of money you will spend on fixed necessities in one month; and (5) the total amount of money you will set aside biweekly for fixed necessities. Next, create a computer-generated pie graph showing the amount of money you will spend on each fixed necessity in one month. Include a title and key with your pie graph. **SYNTHESIS**

3. Variable Necessities Chart and Pie Graph (5 points): Create a computer-generated chart showing how much money you will spend on variable necessities* in one month. Your chart should include: (1) a list of your variable necessities for one month; (2) the amount of money you will spend on each variable necessity in one month; (3) the amount of money you will set aside biweekly for each variable necessity; (4) the total amount of money you will spend on variable necessities in one month; and (5) the total amount of money you will set aside biweekly for variable necessities. Next, create a computer-generated pie graph showing the amount of money you will spend on each variable necessity in one month. Include a title and key with your pie graph. **SYNTHESIS**

4. Savings and Investing Chart and Pie Graph (5 points): Create a computer-generated chart showing how much money you will contribute to savings* and financial investments* each month. Your chart should include: (1) a list of the savings accounts and investments you will contribute to each month; (2) the amount of money you will put into each account and investment each month; (3) the amount of money you will set aside biweekly for each account and investment; (4) the combined total amount of money you will contribute to savings accounts and investments each month; and (5) the total amount of money you will set aside biweekly for savings and investments. Next, create a computer-generated pie graph showing the amount of money you will contribute to each savings account and investment each month. Include a title and key with your pie graph. **SYNTHESIS**

5. Budget Opportunity Costs (4 points): Describe at least five opportunity costs* for the decisions that you made in budgeting for your necessities, savings and investments. **EVALUATION**

6. Fixed Discretionary Items Chart and Pie Graph (5 points): Create a computer-generated chart showing how much money you will spend on fixed discretionary items* in one month. Your chart should include: (1) a list of your fixed discretionary items for one month; (2) the amount of money you will spend on each fixed discretionary item in one month; (3) the amount of money you will set aside biweekly for each fixed discretionary item; (4) the total amount of money you will spend on fixed discretionary items in one month; and (5) the total amount of money you will set aside biweekly for fixed discretionary items. Next, create a computer-generated pie graph showing the amount of money you will spend on each fixed discretionary item in one month. Include a title and key with your pie graph. **SYNTHESIS**

7. Variable Discretionary Items Chart and Pie Graph (5 points): Create a computer-generated chart showing how much money you will spend on variable discretionary items* in one month. Your chart should include: (1) a list of your variable discretionary items for one month; (2) the amount of money you will spend on each variable discretionary item in one month; (3) the amount of money you will set aside biweekly for each variable discretionary item; (4) the total amount of money you will spend on variable discretionary items in one month; and (5) the total amount of money you will set aside biweekly for variable discretionary items. Next, create a computer-generated pie graph showing the amount of money you will spend on each variable discretionary item in one month. Include a title and key with your pie graph. **SYNTHESIS**

8. Discretionary Items Opportunity Costs (4 points): Identify and explain at least five opportunity costs* for the decisions you made while budgeting for fixed and variable discretionary items. **COMPREHENSION**

9. Total Monthly Budget Pie Graph (6 points): Create a comprehensive computer-generated pie graph showing the amount you will spend on each necessity, savings account, investment and discretionary item. Include a title and key with your pie graph. **SYNTHESIS**

Portfolio Section 3: Making Purchases To Set Up a Home

1. Necessary Purchases Chart and Pie Graph (5 points): Create a computer-generated chart showing how much money you will spend on necessary purchases* for your home. Your chart should include: (1) a list of the necessary purchases, grouped together by room; (2) the cost of each necessary purchase; (3) applicable sales tax for each purchase; (4) the total amount for each purchase; and (5) the total amount of money you will spend on necessary purchases for your home. Next, create a computer-generated pie graph showing the amount of money you will spend on each necessary purchase. Include a title and key with your pie graph. **SYNTHESIS**

2. Discretionary Purchases Chart and Pie Graph (5 points): Create a computer-generated chart showing how much money you will spend on discretionary purchases* for your home. Your chart should include: (1) a list of the discretionary purchases, grouped together by room; (2) the cost of each discretionary purchase; (3) applicable sales tax for each purchase; (4) the total amount for each purchase; and (5) the total amount of money you will spend on discretionary purchases. Next, create a computer-generated pie graph showing the amount of money you will spend on each discretionary purchase. Include a title and key with your pie graph. **SYNTHESIS**

3. Purchases Opportunity Costs (4 points): Identify and explain at least five opportunity costs for the decisions you made while budgeting for necessary and discretionary purchases for your home. **EVALUATION**

4. Total Purchases Pie Graph (6 points): Create a comprehensive computer-generated pie graph showing (1) the amount you will spend on each necessary and discretionary purchase you will make for your home, and (2) the amount of "cushion" you will have left over. Include a title and key. **SYNTHESIS**

5. Analysis of Credit (4 points): Research and explain the positive and negative aspects of using credit. **EVALUATION**

Remaining Portfolio Materials

1. Table of Contents (1 point): Write a table of contents that lists all the sections of your portfolio along with their corresponding page numbers. **COMPREHENSION**

2. Cover Page (1 point): Create an eye-catching cover page for your portfolio that includes an original title for your project as well as your name and the Classroom Presentation date. **SYNTHESIS**

3. Portfolio (1 point): Organize all of your materials in a three-ring binder. The table of contents should come first, followed by your work from Portfolio Sections 1, 2 and 3 above in the order presented. Your cover page should be placed on the front of the portfolio. **SYNTHESIS**

COMPONENT 2

Creating Your Financial Adventure Exhibit

Total Possible Exhibit Points: 11 out of 100 total possible for project

1. Floor Plan or Three-Dimensional Model (4 points): Design or recreate a floor plan or three-dimensional model of your future home. Be creative. Use a computer if you like. **SYNTHESIS**

2. Display Board (4 points): Use a large two- or three-panel display board to show pictures that represent your budgeted expenses and purchases. Use half of your board to organize the pictures of your budgeted expenses and the other half to organize the pictures of your purchases. Your display board must include your project's title and your name. You may add any additional materials that you wish. **SYNTHESIS**

3. Exhibit (3 points): Arrange your exhibit items, your portfolio and any additional materials you wish to include in an appealing and informative way. **SYNTHESIS**

COMPONENT 3:

Giving Your Classroom Presentation

Total Possible Classroom Presentation Points: 15 out of 100 total possible for project

1. What to Include in Your Presentation:

- Job Acceptance (2 points): Share various aspects of the position you accepted. **COMPREHENSION**

- Total Monthly Budget Pie Graph and Portfolio (2 points): Show your portfolio and share your final budget pie graph including some of the necessities and some of your discretionary items. **COMPREHENSION**

- Budget Opportunity Cost (2 points): Share one opportunity cost for your budgeted necessities, savings and investments or discretionary items. **EVALUATION**

- Total Purchases Pie Graph (2 points): Share your final purchases pie graph including some of your necessary purchases and some of your discretionary purchases. **COMPREHENSION**

- Purchases Opportunity Cost (2 points): Share one opportunity cost for your purchased necessities and discretionary purchases. **EVALUATION**

- Display Board (3 points): Point to and explain select features of your display board. **COMPREHENSION**

- Floor Plan or Three-Dimensional Model (2 points): Show the floor plan or three-dimensional model of your future residence and explain some of its key features. **COMPREHENSION**

TEACHER COPY CHART

Step Number	Form Title	Number of Copies
1.1	Teacher Planning Guide	1 only
2.1-2.3	Parent Financial Adventure Introduction Letter Student Financial Adventure Introduction Letter Student Instruction Guide	1 completed, then 1 per student 1 completed only 1 only
3.1-3.4	Teacher Forms Checklist Student Commitment Contract	1 completed only 1 completed, then 1 per student
3.5	Student Financial Adventure Introduction Letter* Student Instruction Guide* Financial Adventure Resource Card Appendix Pages* (optional) Financial Adventure Glossary* Roommate Questionnaire* Roommate Discussion Guide*	1 completed, then one per student 1 per student 1 per student 1 per student 1 per student 1 per student
4.1-4.2	Student Checkpoint Organizer Teacher Checkpoint Record	1 per student 1 completed only
5.1-5.2	Student Expo Invitation	1 completed, then one per student
5.9-5.11	Student Certificate Student Name Sign (optional) Left Arrow Sign Right Arrow Sign	1 per student, then each completed 1 per student, then each completed Amount needed Amount needed
5.12-5.13	Teacher Assessment Student Self-Assessment	1 per student 1 per student

* Staple these items into a packet for each student

TEACHER PLANNING GUIDE

*Events scheduled with the class are in black.

Week	Event (Step Numbers)	Day and Date	Time
1	Planning and Preparing for the Quarter (1.1-1.2)		
	Prepare for Financial Adventure Introduction (2.1-2.3)		
	Financial Adventure Introduction (2.4-2.7)		
	Preparation for Financial Adventure Implementation (3.1-3.6)		
	Financial Adventure Implementation (3.7-3.17)		
3	Preparation for the Checkpoint Meetings (4.1-4.2)		
	Distribute Checkpoint Organizers (4.3-4.6)		
	Checkpoint Meetings (4.7-4.12)		
5	Preparation for the Checkpoint Meetings (4.1-4.2)		
	Distribute Checkpoint Organizers (4.3-4.6)		
	Checkpoint Meetings (4.7-4.12)		
7	Preparation for the Checkpoint Meetings (4.1-4.2)		
	Distribute Checkpoint Organizers (4.3-4.6)		
	Checkpoint Meetings (4.7-4.12)		
8	Preparation for the Financial Adventure Expo (5.1-5.2)		
	Invite Families to the Financial Adventure Expo (5.3-5.4)		
	Preparation for the Financial Adventure Expo Ctd. (5.5-5.11)		
9	Preparation for Classroom Presentations and the Financial Adventure Expo (5.12-5.15)		
	Classroom Presentations (6A.1-6A.13 or 6B.1-6B.12)		
	Classroom Expo and Student Self-Assessment (7A.1-7A.9 or 7B.1-7B.10)		
10	Final Preparation for Financial Adventure Expo (8.1-8.10)		
	Financial Adventure Expo (9.1-9.4)		
	Conclusion and Teacher Assessment (10.1-10.8)		
	Student Review (10.9-10.10)		

parent financial adventure introduction letter

Dear Parent(s),

Welcome to Financial Adventure, an Envision project that will challenge and inspire your child. Financial Adventure offers your child the opportunity to research and plan a financial future based on the salary he or she might earn from a chosen career.

After formally accepting a fictional job offer in his or her chosen field, your child will chart how, and how much to spend and save of his or her monthly income, research the positive and negative aspects of using credit, select a home and plan how to furnish that home within a specified budget. Some of the materials generated from these tasks will go into a project portfolio; others will become part of a colorful and informative visual exhibit.

A Student Instruction Guide will be provided to guide your child, step by step, through this process. The Instruction Guide is a comprehensive list of project requirements and is designed to engage higher-level thinking. The guide also references helpful Resource Cards, which provide additional explanations, ideas, tips and directions. There will be a set of these cards in our classroom to which your child may refer.

Financial Adventure is designed to be worked on independently during class time, free time and at home. By scheduling several Checkpoint Meeting dates throughout the quarter, I will be able to monitor each student's progress. On these dates, I will meet with each student to discuss accomplishments and plan goals for the next checkpoint. I will also address any difficulties students might be having.

Financial Adventure will conclude with a Project Expo. The expo will be your child's opportunity to share his or her finished project with family, friends and other guests. You will receive a detailed invitation to the Project Expo later in the quarter.

Dates to Remember:

Checkpoint 1: _____

Checkpoint 2: _____

Checkpoint 3: _____

Classroom Presentation: _____

Financial Adventure Expo: _____ , _____

Sincerely,

_____

_____

student financial adventure introduction letter

Dear Student,

Welcome to Financial Adventure! This isa project you will embark on as part of your Envision Program experience. Financial Adventure challenges you to explore many financial choices you will have to make later in life. It will be a voyage of personal discovery and an opportunity for you to learn about some of the financial realities of being an adult.

After formally accepting a fictional job offer in your chosen field, you will break down your yearly salary to see how much money you can expect to earn each month and each week. You will then consider some other choices, such as whether to have a roommate and whether to rent or purchase a home. Next, you will look at your monthly income and decide what material goods and services you will be able to afford, and what, if any, you will have to do without. You will create a number of charts and graphs that will track where you expect your money to go each month. Next, you will create a detailed floor plan of the home you want to live in and, with a specified budget, decide how to furnish and decorate your home.

As with the other projects, some of the materials you create will go into a project portfolio, and others will become part of a colorful and informative project exhibit. You will formally share your finished project with the class by giving a brief presentation. The project will conclude, as the others have, with a fun project expo, at which you will share your project with invited family, friends and guests.

You will work on Financial Adventure throughout the school day, during your free time and at home. Generally, you will be expected to work on your own. You will consult with me periodically at Checkpoint Meetings to discuss your progress and receive guidance. Between the checkpoints, feel free to discuss your project with other Envision students.

The attached Student Instruction Guide contains all the information you will need to complete the required Financial Adventure Project successfully. The Instruction Guide will continue to challenge you to be resourceful, organized and to think at a higher level.

Dates to Remember:

Checkpoint 1: _____

Checkpoint 2: _____

Checkpoint 3: _____

Classroom Presentation: _____

Financial Adventure Expo: _____ , _____

After reading this introduction, you are ready to begin thinking about your personal financial future. Good luck and have fun!

Sincerely,

_____

_____

STUDENT INSTRUCTION GUIDE

**Building Your Project Portfolio • Creating Your Project Exhibit
Presenting Your Project • Attending the Expo**

BE CREATIVE!

IMPORTANT!

Available resource cards are denoted by a Financial Adventure icon . When you see one of these icons, you will know that there is a corresponding numbered resource card available that gives additional helpful information and visual examples for your reference. Also, be sure to visit www.mindvinepress.com, other trustworthy Internet sites, library reference materials and adult family members for additional resources and examples.

Terms marked with an asterisk (*) are defined in the "Financial Adventure Glossary" included with this instruction guide.

COMPONENT 1
Building Your Financial Adventure Portfolio
Total Possible Portfolio Points: 74 out of 100 total possible for project

With your chosen career path in mind, you are now ready to explore the type of financial future that might await you. Remember, financial decisions are about much more than just dollars and cents, so get ready to consider a number of interesting and challenging life choices. Complete the numbered requirements below, in the same order as they appear. The requirements build upon one another and will guide you smoothly through this financial adventure.

Note: "Component 1: Building Your Financial Adventure Portfolio" is separated into three sections: "Portfolio Section 1: Accepting a Job and Charting Your Salary", "Portfolio Section 2: Budgeting Your Monthly Expenses" and "Portfolio Section 3: Making Purchases To Set Up a Home". You might find it helpful to review all three sections before beginning.

Portfolio Section 1: Accepting a Job and Charting Your Salary

1. Job-Offer Acceptance Letter (5 points): Imagine that you have been offered the job you applied for in the Career Aspiration Project. Write a professional job-offer acceptance letter stating your acceptance of the position, your understanding of the job's terms and your enthusiasm for the company. Visit www.mindvinepress.com for helpful links and more information.

2. Salary Chart (2 points): Create a computer-generated salary chart that displays your gross annual income* and net annual income*. On the chart, also show your net annual income in its monthly, biweekly, weekly, daily and hourly amounts. Your gross annual income should be based on the starting salary for the position you accepted.

Portfolio Section 2: Budgeting Your Monthly Expenses

1. Housing and Roommate Decision (1 point): The requirements below ask you to create a budget for your living expenses. Before beginning, consider having one of your Envision classmates as a roommate to help share costs. If you choose to have a roommate, choose a place of residence together and plan to share only rent and utility expenses. Each roommate will work on his or her project independently, creating his or her own portfolio and exhibit, and presenting independently to the class. In order to be roommates, you must complete a Roommate Questionnaire and a Roommate Discussion Guide. If you decide to live alone, choose a specific home to rent or purchase. Write a paragraph explaining the rationale for your roommate and housing decisions and include it in your portfolio.

> Important: The requirements below ask you to consider living expenses in two ways. First, they ask you to estimate how much money you will spend on various goods and services each month. Then, they ask you to calculate how much money you will have to put aside every two weeks in order to meet those monthly expenses. Remember, the only monthly expenses that can be divided between roommates are rent and utilities. It is a good idea to consult adult family members about the estimated cost of these expenses. The Internet is also an excellent resource for this information.

2. ⓢ **Fixed Necessities Chart and Pie Graph** (5 points): Create a computer-generated chart showing how much money you will spend on fixed necessities* in one month. Your chart should include: (1) a list of your fixed necessities for one month; (2) the amount of money you will spend on each fixed necessity in one month; (3) the amount of money you will set aside biweekly for each fixed necessity; (4) the total amount of money you will spend on fixed necessities in one month; and (5) the total amount of money you will set aside biweekly for fixed necessities. Next, create a computer-generated pie graph showing the amount of money you will spend on each fixed necessity in one month. Include a title and key with your pie graph.

3. ⓢ **Variable Necessities Chart and Pie Graph** (5 points): Create a computer-generated chart showing how much money you will spend on variable necessities* in one month. Your chart should include: (1) a list of your variable necessities for one month; (2) the amount of money you will spend on each variable necessity in one month; (3) the amount of money you will set aside biweekly for each variable necessity; (4) the total amount of money you will spend on variable necessities in one month; and (5) the total amount of money you will set aside biweekly for variable necessities. Next, create a computer-generated pie graph showing the amount of money you will spend on each variable necessity in one month. Include a title and key with your pie graph.

4. ⓢ **Savings and Investing Chart and Pie Graph** (5 points): Create a computer-generated chart showing how much money you will contribute to savings* and financial investments* each month. Your chart should include: (1) a list of the savings accounts and investments you will contribute to each month; (2) the amount of money you will put into each account and investment each month; (3) the amount of money you will set aside biweekly for each account and investment; (4) the combined total amount of money you will contribute to savings accounts and investments each month; and (5) the total amount of money you will set aside biweekly for savings and investments. Next, create a computer-generated pie graph showing the amount of money you will contribute to each savings account and investment each month. Include a title and key with your pie graph.

5. Budget Opportunity Costs (4 points): Describe at least five opportunity costs* for the decisions that you made in budgeting for your necessities, savings and investments.

6. ⓢ **Fixed Discretionary Items Chart and Pie Graph** (5 points): Create a computer-generated chart showing how much money you will spend on fixed discretionary items* in one month. Your chart should include: (1) a list of your fixed discretionary items for one month; (2) the amount of money you will spend on each fixed discretionary item in one month; (3) the amount of money you will set aside biweekly for each fixed discretionary item; (4) the total amount of money you will spend on fixed discretionary items in one month; and (5) the total amount of money you will set aside biweekly for fixed discretionary items. Next, create a computer-generated pie graph showing the amount of money you will spend on each fixed discretionary item in one month. Include a title and key with your pie graph.

7. (S) **Variable Discretionary Items Chart and Pie Graph** (5 points): Create a computer-generated chart showing how much money you will spend on variable discretionary items * in one month. Your chart should include: (1) a list of your variable discretionary items for one month; (2) the amount of money you will spend on each variable discretionary item in one month; (3) the amount of money you will set aside biweekly for each variable discretionary item; (4) the total amount of money you will spend on variable discretionary items in one month; and (5) the total amount of money you will set aside biweekly for variable discretionary items. Next, create a computer-generated pie graph showing the amount of money you will spend on each variable discretionary item in one month. Include a title and key with your pie graph.

8. Discretionary Items Opportunity Costs (4 points): Identify and explain at least five opportunity costs* for the decisions you made while budgeting for fixed and variable discretionary items.

9. (S) **Total Monthly Budget Pie Graph** (6 points): Create a comprehensive computer-generated pie graph showing the amount you will spend on each necessity, savings account, investment and discretionary item. Include a title and key with your pie graph.

Portfolio Section 3: Making Purchases To Set Up a Home

Important: The requirements for this section are based on the assumption that you receive a signing bonus of $5,000 from your new employer. You may also assume that you have another $5,000 in the bank that you have saved over the years. You will use part of this total amount of $10,000 to make purchases for your home as you begin your new job. However, you should keep a sizable "cushion" in your bank account for unexpected expenses that may arise. Also, as you "shop" for your purchases, be sure to save any pictures of items you "buy." You will use the pictures for your display board.

Roommate Option: If you have a roommate, you may share the cost of any purchases that will be utilized by both of you in your home including appliances, living area furniture, dishes and other items. Remember that the requirements below must be completed by each of you separately and put into your own portfolios.

1. (S) **Necessary Purchases Chart and Pie Graph** (5 points): Create a computer-generated chart showing how much money you will spend on necessary purchases* for your home. Your chart should include: (1) a list of the necessary purchases, grouped together by room; (2) the cost of each necessary purchase; (3) applicable sales tax for each purchase; (4) the total amount for each purchase; and (5) the total amount of money you will spend on necessary purchases for your home. Next, create a computer-generated pie graph showing the amount of money you will spend on each necessary purchase. Include a title and key with your pie graph.

2. (S) **Discretionary Purchases Chart and Pie Graph** (5 points): Create a computer-generated chart showing how much money you will spend on discretionary purchases* for your home. Your chart should include: (1) a list of the discretionary purchases, grouped together by room; (2) the cost of each discretionary purchase; (3) applicable sales tax for each purchase; (4) the total amount for each purchase; and (5) the total amount of money you will spend on discretionary purchases. Next, create a computer-generated pie graph showing the amount of money you will spend on each discretionary purchase. Include a title and key with your pie graph.

3. Purchases Opportunity Costs (4 points): Identify and explain at least five opportunity costs* for the decisions you made while budgeting for necessary and discretionary purchases for your home.

4. (S) **Total Purchases Pie Graph** (6 points): Create a comprehensive computer-generated pie graph showing (1) the amount you will spend on each necessary and discretionary purchase you will make for your home, and (2) the amount of "cushion" you will have left over. Include a title and key.

5. Analysis of Credit (4 points): Research and explain the positive and negative aspects of using credit.

Remaining Portfolio Materials

1.  **Table of Contents** (1 point): Write a table of contents that lists all the sections of your portfolio along with their corresponding page numbers.

2. **Cover Page** (1 point): Create an eye-catching cover page for your portfolio that includes an original title for your project as well as your name and the Classroom Presentation date.

3. **Portfolio** (1 point): Organize all of your materials in a three-ring binder. The table of contents should come first, followed by your work from Portfolio Sections 1, 2 and 3 above in the order presented. Your cover page should be placed on the front of the portfolio.

You have now completed Component 1 of the Financial Adventure Project. By completing your portfolio, you have created an important resource that will help you work on Components 2 and 3. Though several worthy challenges lie ahead, you are now prepared to meet each of them, knowing that you have laid the necessary groundwork that will increase your chances for success. Good luck as you move on to creating your project exhibit items.

COMPONENT 2

Creating Your Financial Adventure Exhibit

Total Possible Exhibit Points: 11 out of 100 total possible for project

Having completed your budget and purchased items for your home, it is now time to design and create an informative and appealing exhibit of your plans. The items you complete will be viewed by your classmates on the day of your Classroom Presentation and also by everyone who attends the Financial Adventure Expo at the end of the term. As always, put your best work into designing, creating and integrating your exhibit items.

> **Note:**
> Keep in mind that each item is only one part of the overall exhibit. In other words, no single item has to say everything about your project. Decide upon a purpose for each item. Consider how best to arrange your exhibit for the greatest effect.

1. **Floor Plan or Three-Dimensional Model** (4 points): Design or recreate a floor plan or three-dimensional model of your future home. Be creative. Use a computer if you like.

2. **Display Board** (4 points): Use a large two- or three-panel display board to show pictures that represent your budgeted expenses and purchases. Use half of your board to organize the pictures of your budgeted expenses and the other half to organize the pictures of your purchases. Your display board must include your project's title and your name. You may add any additional materials that you wish.

3. **Exhibit** (3 points): Arrange your exhibit items, your portfolio and any additional materials you wish to include in an appealing and informative way.

You have now completed Component 2 of the Financial Adventure Project, an important exhibit that creatively displays your budget and purchasing plans. Now that you have finished your portfolio and exhibit, you are ready to confidently prepare for your Classroom Presentation (Component 3). Enjoy sharing your project with your peers and teacher!

COMPONENT 3:

Giving Your Classroom Presentation

Total Possible Classroom Presentation Points: 15 out of 100 total possible for project

It is now time to share your plans with others. Your Classroom Presentation is an opportunity to formally present some of your goals and to share some of your hard work. Your portfolio and exhibit contain all the information you will need to refer to for the presentation, so relax and have fun with it.

1. Ⓢ **What to Include in Your Presentation:**

- **Job Acceptance (2 points):** Share various aspects of the position you accepted.
- **Total Monthly Budget Pie Graph and Portfolio (2 points):** Show your portfolio and share your final budget pie graph including some of the necessities and some of your discretionary items.
- **Budget Opportunity Cost (2 points):** Share one opportunity cost for your budgeted necessities, savings and investments or discretionary items.
- **Total Purchases Pie Graph (2 points):** Share your final purchases pie graph including some of your necessary purchases and some of your discretionary purchases.
- **Purchases Opportunity Cost (2 points):** Share one opportunity cost for your purchased necessities and discretionary purchases.
- **Display Board (3 points):** Point to and explain select features of your display board.
- **Floor Plan or Three-Dimensional Model (2 points):** Show the floor plan or three-dimensional model of your future residence and explain some of its key features.

> **Note:** Your classroom presentation should last three to four minutes and should be rehearsed, but not memorized. If you forget to include any required information, your teacher will ask you in a question form so that you have a chance to include it.

Bring to the Classroom Presentation:
All of your exhibit items including anything extra that you think will enhance your exhibit.

You are now finished with Components 1, 2 and 3 – all of the assessed portions of your project. The final component, Attending the Financial Adventure Expo, provides a festive closure to the Financial Adventure Project.

COMPONENT 4:

Attending the Financial Adventure Expo (The expo does not involve any points.)

Now that you have completed your project and presented it to your peers, it is time to share your work with family and friends at the Financial Adventure Expo. The expo is an event that recognizes and celebrates the hard work you have done on your Financial Adventure Project. At the expo, you will set up and stand by your exhibit as invited guests walk around informally and view the projects. Guests may ask you friendly questions about your project as they visit your exhibit, so have fun sharing your Financial Adventure experiences with them.

Bring to the Expo: all of your exhibit items and anything extra that you think will enhance your exhibit.

CONGRATULATIONS ON YOUR COMPLETED FINANCIAL ADVENTURE PROJECT!

TEACHER FORMS CHECKLIST

use this checklist to record forms submitted by the students

student name	student commitment contract	student checkpoint organizer 1	student checkpoint organizer 2	student checkpoint organizer 3	expo invitation response number attending	special equip.needed
1.						
2.						
3.						
4.						
5.						
6.						
7.						
8.						
9.						
10.						
11.						
12.						
13.						
14.						
15.						
16.						
17.						
18.						
19.						
20.						
21.						
22.						
23.						
24.						
25.						

STUDENT COMMITMENT CONTRACT

expectations

project work time

I agree to:

- be responsible for following my Student Instruction Guide to do my work.
- keep track of all my project materials.
- work hard on Envision without disturbing others.
- save my unanswered questions until my teacher is free to talk.

checkpoint meetings

I will come prepared with:

- my Student Instruction Guide.
- my completed Student Checkpoint Organizer.
- all of my project materials.

important dates and times

Checkpoint 1: _____

Checkpoint 2: _____

Checkpoint 3: _____

Classroom Presentation: _____

Financial Adventure Expo: _____

_____

signatures

I agree to:

- meet expectations on the dates listed above.
- complete each of the Financial Adventure requirements to the best of my ability.
- bring my project work to school each day so that I can work on it during extra time.
- take my project work from school each night so that I can work on it at home.

I understand that the Envision Financial Adventure Aspiration Project is a special opportunity, and that if I do not meet the above expectations, I may be asked to return to normal classroom activities.

Student Signature: _____ Date: _____

Parent Signature: _____ Date: _____

Please return this contract by: _____

The following terms are listed and defined in the same order in which they appear in the Student Instruction Guide.

Portfolio Section 1: Accepting a Job and Charting Your Salary

Gross Annual Income: The total amount of money a person earns in a year before paying any income tax.

Net Annual Income: The amount of a person's income that he or she keeps after paying any federal, state and local income taxes.

Portfolio Section 2: Budgeting your Monthly Expenses

Fixed Necessities: Goods and services that a person decides are necessary, and whose costs are the same from month to month. Some fixed necessities are expensive goods that are paid for over time, such as a car, a home, a leased apartment, a student loan and various kinds of insurance. Other fixed necessities are inexpensive services that are used continually, and also paid for over time. These can include a phone plan, a monthly bus pass and various utilities, such as gas and electric.

Variable Necessities: Goods and services that a person decides are necessary, but whose costs may change from month to month. Variable necessities may include food, clothing, health care items, household supplies (cleaning products, toiletries), gasoline and occasional public transportation.

Savings: Money that has been collected and put away, usually in a savings account at a bank.

Financial Investments: Using money in hopes of gaining a profit. Investments can be high-risk or low-risk. High-risk investments usually produce a higher profit if they are successful, but are considered more insecure. Low-risk investments usually produce a lower profit if they are successful, but are considered fairly safe. Kinds of investments include: stocks, CD's (certificates of deposit), money-market accounts, 401K plans, individual retirement accounts, real estate and entrepreneurial ventures.

Budget Opportunity Costs: A necessity, savings or investment that a person gives up in order to have a more desirable necessity, savings or investment. For example, you may choose to give up buying expensive name-brand clothing so that you can put more money in your savings account. Giving up name-brand clothing is the opportunity cost of putting more money in your savings account.

Fixed Discretionary Items: Goods and services that a person decides are desirable, but not necessary, and whose costs are the same, or fixed, from month to month. Fixed discretionary items may include cable or satellite television service, Internet service, magazine subscriptions and membership to a gym.

Variable Discretionary Items: Goods and services that a person decides are desirable, but not necessary, and whose costs may change from month to month. Variable discretionary items may include eating out, going to the movies, participating in recreational activities and traveling.

Discretionary Items Opportunity Costs: A discretionary item that a person gives up in order to have a more desirable discretionary item. For example, you may choose to give up satellite television service so you can afford to go to the movies more often. Living without satellite television service is the opportunity cost of going to the movies more often.

Portfolio Section 3: Making Purchases To Set Up a Home

Necessary Purchases: Goods a person decides are necessary to purchase. Necessary purchases may include basic kinds of furniture, dishes, bedding, some major appliances (clothes washer and dryer, stove, or refrigerator), basic home-maintenance items (lawn mower, rake, broom or garbage cans) and basic home accessories (shower curtains, wastebaskets and other items).

Discretionary Purchases: Goods that a person decides are not necessary, but still desirable enough to purchase. Discretionary purchases may include pets and pet supplies, small appliances (microwave or coffee maker), a computer, specialized home-maintenance items (snow blower, edger or table saw) and decorative home accessories (artwork, plants or throw pillows).

Purchases Opportunity Costs: A good that a person decides not to purchase in order to purchase a more desirable good. For example, a person may choose not to purchase a home entertainment system in order to be able to purchase a snow blower. Not purchasing the entertainment system is the opportunity cost of purchasing the snow blower.

ROOMMATE QUESTIONNAIRE

Instructions: Complete this questionnaire by yourself. Read each question below, and circle the statement or response that best matches how you would answer. After you and your roommate have each completed a questionnaire, meet with each other and fill out the Roommate Discussion Guide together.

1. How would you best describe your sleep habits?

❏ I like to stay up late and sleep in.　　　❏ I like to go to bed early and get up early.

2. What time of day is it best for you to do your homework?

❏ before school　　　❏ after school　　　❏ after dinner

3. When you are studying, which best describes the atmosphere you prefer?

❏ I like to have it quiet.　　　❏ I like to have background noise.

4. Which statement best describes your bedroom?

❏ It's usually pretty messy.　　　❏ It's usually neat and clean.

5. What do you usually do when you take a phone message for someone?

❏ I write the message down right away.

❏ I remember the message and tell the person later.

❏ I try to remember the message, but sometimes I forget.

6. How do you manage your money?

❏ I usually manage my money sensibly and have enough for the things I need without having to borrow from others.

❏ I often overspend and have to ask others for small loans.

7. When you get upset with someone, what do you usually do?

❏ I usually try to talk about it with the person.

❏ I usually try to forget about it and not say anything.

❏ I usually try to talk to someone else about it.

❏ I either stop talking to the person for a while, or I yell at him or her.

ROOMMATE DISCUSSION GUIDE

Instructions: Roommates are to work on this Discussion Guide together. The seven questions below correlate to the seven questions on your Roommate Questionnaires. Refer to your questionnaires as you read and respond to the following questions.

1. For question 1, did you both choose the same statement about sleep habits?

❏ yes (If yes, go to question 2)   ❏ no

If no, how will you show consideration for each other when one of you wants to sleep and the other is up doing something that might make noise like watching television or talking on the phone?

2. For question 2, did you both choose the same time of day?

❏ yes (If yes, go to question 3)   ❏ no

If no, how will you show each other consideration when one of you is trying to study while the other is doing something that may be distracting?

3. For question 3, did you both choose the same statement about noise and studying?

❏ yes (If yes, go to question 4)   ❏ no

If no, what will you do when you both need to study and one of you wants background noise while the other wants quiet?

4. For question 4, did you both choose the same statement about the condition of your bedrooms?

❏ yes (If yes, go to question 5)   ❏ no

If no, how will you manage the upkeep of the rooms in your apartment or house that you have to share?

5. For question 5, did you both choose the same statement about phone messages?

❑ yes (If yes, go to question 6)   ❑ no

If no, what system will you work out to be sure messages are communicated in a timely manner?

6. For question 6, did you both answer that you usually have enough money for the things you need?

❑ yes (If yes, go to question 7)   ❑ no

If no, how will you make sure that you will both have enough money to pay shared bills when they are due?

7. For question 7, did you both answer that you usually talk to the person about why you are upset?

❑ yes (If yes, you are finished with the discussion guide.)   ❑ no

If no, discuss the possible problems with the other options. List three different phrases that you both agree would be appropriate to say when you approach each other with a concern.

- _____

- _____

- _____

STUDENT CHECKPOINT ORGANIZER

Student Name: _____ Checkpoint Date: _____

Job I Accepted: _____

directions

1. Using your Student Instruction Guide, check off any requirements that you have completed up to this point.
2. Bring the following items to the Checkpoint Meeting:
• your Student Instruction Guide.
• your completed Student Checkpoint Organizer.
• all of your project materials.

questions

1. Which requirements have you completed up to this point?

_____

_____

2. Is there anything you need help with?

_____

_____

3. Is there anything else about your project that you would like to discuss?

_____

_____

4. List at least three goals you expect to accomplish by the next checkpoint.

_____

_____

TEACHER CHECKPOINT RECORD

student name	job accepted	checkpoint 1 notes	checkpoint 2 notes	checkpoint 3 notes
1.				
2.				
3.				
4.				
5.				
6.				
7.				
8.				
9.				
10.				

YOU'RE INVITED!

FINANCIAL ADVENTURE

EXPO INVITATION RESPONSE

Please fill out and return by: _____

Student Name: _____

Student Attending? ☐ Yes ☐ No

Number of Student Guests Attending: _____

Will your child need any special school equipment for the expo (i.e., computer or TV)? Please List: _____

_____

Thank you.

We look forward to seeing you at this special event!

PLEASE JOIN US FOR OUR ENVISION FINANCIAL ADVENTURE EXPO!

Why? _____

Who? _____

Where? _____

When? _____

Remember to bring your camera!

CERTIFICATE OF ACHIEVEMENT

FINANCIAL ADVENTURE

AWARDED TO

DATE

SIGNATURE

envision®

FINANCIAL ADVENTURE PROJECT

STUDENT

envision®

financial adventure expo

envision®

financial adventure expo

envision®

TEACHER ASSESSMENT

Component 1: Building Your Financial Adventure Portfolio
Total Possible Portfolio Points: 74 out of 100 total possible for project

Requirements	Possible Points	Teacher Points	Average Points
Portfolio Section 1: Accepting a Job and Charting Your Salary			
1. Job-Offer Acceptance Letter: Imagine that you have been offered the job you applied for in the Career Aspiration Project. Write a professional job-offer acceptance letter stating your acceptance of the position, your understanding of the job's terms and your enthusiasm for the company. Visit www.mindvinepress.com for helpful links and more information.	5		
2. Salary Chart: Create a computer-generated salary chart that displays your gross annual income* and net annual income*. On the chart, also show your net annual income in its monthly, biweekly, weekly, daily and hourly amounts. Your gross annual income should be based on the starting salary for the position you accepted.	2		
Portfolio Section 2: Budgeting Your Monthly Expenses			
1. Housing and Roommate Decision: The requirements below ask you to create a budget for your living expenses. Before beginning, consider having one of your Envision classmates as a roommate to help share costs. If you choose to have a roommate, choose a place of residence together and plan to share only rent and utility expenses. Each roommate will work on his or her project independently, creating his or her own portfolio and exhibit, and presenting independently to the class. In order to be roommates, you must complete a Roommate Questionnaire and a Roommate Discussion Guide. If you decide to live alone, choose a specific home to rent or purchase. Write a paragraph explaining the rationale for your roommate and housing decisions and include it in your portfolio.	1		
2. Fixed Necessities Chart and Pie Graph: Create a computer-generated chart showing how much money you will spend on fixed necessities* in one month. Your chart should include: (1) a list of your fixed necessities for one month; (2) the amount of money you will spend on each fixed necessity in one month; (3) the amount of money you will set aside biweekly for each fixed necessity; (4) the total amount of money you will spend on fixed necessities in one month; and (5) the total amount of money you will set aside biweekly for fixed necessities. Next, create a computer-generated pie graph showing the amount of money you will spend on each fixed necessity in one month. Include a title and key with your pie graph.	5		
3. Variable Necessities Chart and Pie Graph: Create a computer-generated chart showing how much money you will spend on variable necessities* in one month. Your chart should include: (1) a list of your variable necessities for one month; (2) the amount of money you will spend on each variable necessity in one month; (3) the amount of money you will set aside biweekly for each variable necessity; (4) the total amount of money you will spend on variable necessities in one month; and (5) the total amount of money you will set aside biweekly for variable necessities. Next, create a computer-generated pie graph showing the amount of money you will spend on each variable necessity in one month. Include a title and key with your pie graph.	5		

4. Savings and Investing Chart and Pie Graph: Create a computer-generated chart showing how much money you will contribute to savings* and financial investments* each month. Your chart should include: (1) a list of the savings accounts and investments you will contribute to each month; (2) the amount of money you will put into each account and investment each month; (3) the amount of money you will set aside biweekly for each account and investment; (4) the combined total amount of money you will contribute to savings accounts and investments each month; and (5) the total amount of money you will set aside biweekly for savings and investments. Next, create a computer-generated pie graph showing the amount of money you will contribute to each savings account and investment each month. Include a title and key with your pie graph.	5		
5. Budget Opportunity Costs: Describe at least five opportunity costs* for the decisions that you made in budgeting for your necessities, savings and investments.	4		
6. Fixed Discretionary Items Chart and Pie Graph: Create a computer-generated chart showing how much money you will spend on fixed discretionary items* in one month. Your chart should include: (1) a list of your fixed discretionary items for one month; (2) the amount of money you will spend on each fixed discretionary item in one month; (3) the amount of money you will set aside biweekly for each fixed discretionary item; (4) the total amount of money you will spend on fixed discretionary items in one month; and (5) the total amount of money you will set aside biweekly for fixed discretionary items. Next, create a computer-generated pie graph showing the amount of money you will spend on each fixed discretionary item in one month. Include a title and key with your pie graph.	5		
7. Variable Discretionary Items Chart and Pie Graph: Create a computer-generated chart showing how much money you will spend on variable discretionary items * in one month. Your chart should include: (1) a list of your variable discretionary items for one month; (2) the amount of money you will spend on each variable discretionary item in one month; (3) the amount of money you will set aside biweekly for each variable discretionary item; (4) the total amount of money you will spend on variable discretionary items in one month; and (5) the total amount of money you will set aside biweekly for variable discretionary items. Next, create a computer-generated pie graph showing the amount of money you will spend on each variable discretionary item in one month. Include a title and key with your pie graph.	5		
8. Discretionary Items Opportunity Costs: Identify and explain at least five opportunity costs* for the decisions you made while budgeting for fixed and variable discretionary items.	4		
9. Total Monthly Budget Pie Graph: Create a comprehensive computer-generated pie graph showing the amount you will spend on each necessity, savings account, investment and discretionary item. Include a title and key with your pie graph.	6		

Portfolio Section 3: Making Purchases To Set Up a Home

1. Necessary Purchases Chart and Pie Graph: Create a computer-generated chart showing how much money you will spend on necessary purchases* for your home. Your chart should include: (1) a list of the necessary purchases, grouped together by room; (2) the cost of each necessary purchase; (3) applicable sales tax for each purchase; (4) the total amount for each purchase; and (5) the total amount of money you will spend on necessary purchases for your home. Next, create a computer-generated pie graph showing the amount of money you will spend on each necessary purchase. Include a title and key with your pie graph.	5		
2. Discretionary Purchases Chart and Pie Graph: Create a computer-generated chart showing how much money you will spend on discretionary purchases* for your home. Your chart should include: (1) a list of the discretionary purchases, grouped together by room; (2) the cost of each discretionary purchase; (3) applicable sales tax for each purchase; (4) the total amount for each purchase; and (5) the total amount of money you will spend on discretionary purchases. Next, create a computer-generated pie graph showing the amount of money you will spend on each discretionary purchase. Include a title and key with your pie graph.	5		
3. Purchases Opportunity Costs: Identify and explain at least five opportunity costs for the decisions you made while budgeting for necessary and discretionary purchases for your home.	4		
4. Total Purchases Pie Graph: Create a comprehensive computer-generated pie graph showing (1) the amount you will spend on each necessary and discretionary purchase you will make for your home, and (2) the amount of "cushion" you will have left over. Include a title and key.	6		
5. Analysis of Credit: Research and explain the positive and negative aspects of using credit.	4		
Remaining Portfolio Materials			
1. Table of Contents: Write a table of contents that lists all the sections of your portfolio along with their corresponding page numbers.	1		
2. Cover Page: Create an eye-catching cover page for your portfolio that includes an original title for your project as well as your name and the Classroom Presentation date.	1		
3. Portfolio: Organize all of your materials in a three-ring binder (portfolio). The table of contents should come first, followed by your work from Portfolio Sections 1, 2 and 3 above in the order presented. Your cover page should be placed on the front of the portfolio.	1		
TOTAL PORTFOLIO POINTS	**74**		

TEACHER ASSESSMENT

Component 2: Creating Your Financial Adventure Exhibit
Total Possible Exhibit Points: 11 out of 100 total possible for project

1. Floor Plan or Three-Dimensional Model: Design or recreate a floor plan or three-dimensional model of your future home. Be creative. Use a computer if you like.	4		
2. Display Board: Use a large two- or three-panel display board to show pictures that represent your budgeted expenses and purchases. Use half of your board to organize the pictures of your budgeted expenses and the other half to organize the pictures of your purchases. Your display board must include your project's title and your name. You may add any additional materials that you wish.	4		
3. Exhibit: Arrange your exhibit items, your portfolio and any additional materials you wish to include in an appealing and informative way.	3		
TOTAL EXHIBIT POINTS	**11**		

Component 3: Giving Your Classroom Presentation
Total Possible Classroom Presentation Points: 15 out of 100 total possible for project

1. What to Include in Your Presentation:			
• Job Acceptance: Share various aspects of the position you accepted	2		
• Total Monthly Budget Pie Graph and Portfolio: Show your portfolio and share your final budget pie graph including some of the necessities and some of your discretionary items.	2		
• Budget Opportunity Cost: Share one opportunity cost for your budgeted necessities, savings and investments or discretionary items.	2		
• Total Purchases Pie Graph: Share your final purchases pie graph including some of your necessary purchases and some of your discretionary purchases.	2		
• Purchases Opportunity Cost: Share one opportunity cost for your purchased necessities and discretionary purchases.	2		
• Display Board: Point to and explain select features of your display board.	3		
• Floor Plan or Three-Dimensional Model: Show the floor plan or three-dimensional model of your future residence and explain some of its key features.	2		
TOTAL CLASSROOM PRESENTATION POINTS	**15**		
TOTAL PROJECT POINTS	**100**		

STUDENT SELF-ASSESSMENT

Component 1: Building Your Financial Adventure Portfolio
Total Possible Portfolio Points: 74 out of 100 total possible for project

Requirements	Possible Points	Student Points
Portfolio Section 1: Accepting a Job and Charting Your Salary		
1. Job-Offer Acceptance Letter: Imagine that you have been offered the job you applied for in the Career Aspiration Project. Write a professional job-offer acceptance letter stating your acceptance of the position, your understanding of the job's terms and your enthusiasm for the company. Visit www.mindvinepress.com for helpful links and more information.	5	
2. Salary Chart: Create a computer-generated salary chart that displays your gross annual income* and net annual income*. On the chart, also show your net annual income in its monthly, biweekly, weekly, daily and hourly amounts. Your gross annual income should be based on the starting salary for the position you accepted.	2	
Portfolio Section 2: Budgeting Your Monthly Expenses		
1. Housing and Roommate Decision: The requirements below ask you to create a budget for your living expenses. Before beginning, consider having one of your Envision classmates as a roommate to help share costs. If you choose to have a roommate, choose a place of residence together and plan to share only rent and utility expenses. Each roommate will work on his or her project independently, creating his or her own portfolio and exhibit, and presenting independently to the class. In order to be roommates, you must complete a Roommate Questionnaire and a Roommate Discussion Guide. If you decide to live alone, choose a specific home to rent or purchase. Write a paragraph explaining the rationale for your roommate and housing decisions and include it in your portfolio.	1	
2. Fixed Necessities Chart and Pie Graph: Create a computer-generated chart showing how much money you will spend on fixed necessities* in one month. Your chart should include: (1) a list of your fixed necessities for one month; (2) the amount of money you will spend on each fixed necessity in one month; (3) the amount of money you will set aside biweekly for each fixed necessity; (4) the total amount of money you will spend on fixed necessities in one month; and (5) the total amount of money you will set aside biweekly for fixed necessities. Next, create a computer-generated pie graph showing the amount of money you will spend on each fixed necessity in one month. Include a title and key with your pie graph.	5	
3. Variable Necessities Chart and Pie Graph: Create a computer-generated chart showing how much money you will spend on variable necessities* in one month. Your chart should include: (1) a list of your variable necessities for one month; (2) the amount of money you will spend on each variable necessity in one month; (3) the amount of money you will set aside biweekly for each variable necessity; (4) the total amount of money you will spend on variable necessities in one month; and (5) the total amount of money you will set aside biweekly for variable necessities. Next, create a computer-generated pie graph showing the amount of money you will spend on each variable necessity in one month. Include a title and key with your pie graph.	5	

4. Savings and Investing Chart and Pie Graph: Create a computer-generated chart showing how much money you will contribute to savings* and financial investments* each month. Your chart should include: (1) a list of the savings accounts and investments you will contribute to each month; (2) the amount of money you will put into each account and investment each month; (3) the amount of money you will set aside biweekly for each account and investment; (4) the combined total amount of money you will contribute to savings accounts and investments each month; and (5) the total amount of money you will set aside biweekly for savings and investments. Next, create a computer-generated pie graph showing the amount of money you will contribute to each savings account and investment each month. Include a title and key with your pie graph.	5	
5. Budget Opportunity Costs: Describe at least five opportunity costs* for the decisions that you made in budgeting for your necessities, savings and investments.	4	
6. Fixed Discretionary Items Chart and Pie Graph: Create a computer-generated chart showing how much money you will spend on fixed discretionary items* in one month. Your chart should include: (1) a list of your fixed discretionary items for one month; (2) the amount of money you will spend on each fixed discretionary item in one month; (3) the amount of money you will set aside biweekly for each fixed discretionary item; (4) the total amount of money you will spend on fixed discretionary items in one month; and (5) the total amount of money you will set aside biweekly for fixed discretionary items. Next, create a computer-generated pie graph showing the amount of money you will spend on each fixed discretionary item in one month. Include a title and key with your pie graph.	5	
7. Variable Discretionary Items Chart and Pie Graph: Create a computer-generated chart showing how much money you will spend on variable discretionary items * in one month. Your chart should include: (1) a list of your variable discretionary items for one month; (2) the amount of money you will spend on each variable discretionary item in one month; (3) the amount of money you will set aside biweekly for each variable discretionary item; (4) the total amount of money you will spend on variable discretionary items in one month; and (5) the total amount of money you will set aside biweekly for variable discretionary items. Next, create a computer-generated pie graph showing the amount of money you will spend on each variable discretionary item in one month. Include a title and key with your pie graph.	5	
8. Discretionary Items Opportunity Costs: Identify and explain at least five opportunity costs* for the decisions you made while budgeting for fixed and variable discretionary items.	4	
9. Total Monthly Budget Pie Graph: Create a comprehensive computer-generated pie graph showing the amount you will spend on each necessity, savings account, investment and discretionary item. Include a title and key with your pie graph.	6	

STUDENT SELF-ASSESSMENT

1. Necessary Purchases Chart and Pie Graph: Create a computer-generated chart showing how much money you will spend on necessary purchases* for your home. Your chart should include: (1) a list of the necessary purchases, grouped together by room; (2) the cost of each necessary purchase; (3) applicable sales tax for each purchase; (4) the total amount for each purchase; and (5) the total amount of money you will spend on necessary purchases for your home. Next, create a computer-generated pie graph showing the amount of money you will spend on each necessary purchase. Include a title and key with your pie graph.	5	
2. Discretionary Purchases Chart and Pie Graph: Create a computer-generated chart showing how much money you will spend on discretionary purchases* for your home. Your chart should include: (1) a list of the discretionary purchases, grouped together by room; (2) the cost of each discretionary purchase; (3) applicable sales tax for each purchase; (4) the total amount for each purchase; and (5) the total amount of money you will spend on discretionary purchases. Next, create a computer-generated pie graph showing the amount of money you will spend on each discretionary purchase. Include a title and key with your pie graph.	5	
3. Purchases Opportunity Costs: Identify and explain at least five opportunity costs for the decisions you made while budgeting for necessary and discretionary purchases for your home.	4	
4. Total Purchases Pie Graph: Create a comprehensive computer-generated pie graph showing (1) the amount you will spend on each necessary and discretionary purchase you will make for your home, and (2) the amount of "cushion" you will have left over. Include a title and key.	6	
5. Analysis of Credit: Research and explain the positive and negative aspects of using credit.	4	
Remaining Portfolio Materials		
1. Table of Contents: Write a table of contents that lists all the sections of your portfolio along with their corresponding page numbers.	1	
2. Cover Page: Create an eye-catching cover page for your portfolio that includes an original title for your project as well as your name and the Classroom Presentation date.	1	
3. Portfolio: Organize all of your materials in a three-ring binder (portfolio). The table of contents should come first, followed by your work from Portfolio Sections 1, 2 and 3 above in the order presented. Your cover page should be placed on the front of the portfolio.	1	
TOTAL PORTFOLIO POINTS	**74**	

Component 2: Creating Your Financial Adventure Exhibit
Total Possible Exhibit Points: 11 out of 100 total possible for project

1. Floor Plan or Three-Dimensional Model: Design or recreate a floor plan or three-dimensional model of your future home. Be creative. Use a computer if you like.	4	
2. Display Board: Use a large two- or three-panel display board to show pictures that represent your budgeted expenses and purchases. Use half of your board to organize the pictures of your budgeted expenses and the other half to organize the pictures of your purchases. Your display board must include your project's title and your name. You may add any additional materials that you wish.	4	
3. Exhibit: Arrange your exhibit items, your portfolio and any additional materials you wish to include in an appealing and informative way.	3	
TOTAL EXHIBIT POINTS	**11**	

Component 3: Giving Your Classroom Presentation
Total Possible Classroom Presentation Points: 15 out of 100 total possible for project

1. What to Include in Your Presentation:		
• Job Acceptance: Share various aspects of the position you accepted	2	
• Total Monthly Budget Pie Graph and Portfolio: Show your portfolio and share your final budget pie graph including some of the necessities and some of your discretionary items.	2	
• Budget Opportunity Cost: Share one opportunity cost for your budgeted necessities, savings and investments or discretionary items.	2	
• Total Purchases Pie Graph: Share your final purchases pie graph including some of your necessary purchases and some of your discretionary purchases.	2	
• Purchases Opportunity Cost: Share one opportunity cost for your purchased necessities and discretionary purchases.	2	
• Display Board: Point to and explain select features of your display board.	3	
• Floor Plan or Three-Dimensional Model: Show the floor plan or three-dimensional model of your future residence and explain some of its key features.	2	
TOTAL CLASSROOM PRESENTATION POINTS	**15**	
TOTAL PROJECT POINTS	**100**	

SPANISH TRANSLATIONS OF PARENT FORMS AND STUDENT INSTRUCTION GUIDE

carta de introducción para padres del proyecto aventura financiera

Estimados Padres,

Bienvenidos al proyecto "Aventura Financiera", un proyecto de "Envision" que inspirará y mantendrá la atención educativa de su hijo/a. "Aventura Financiera" le ofrece a su hijo/a la oportunidad de investigar y planificar su futuro basado en el sueldo que él o ella ganará en la profesión que elija.

Después de aceptar formalmente la oferta de un trabajo ficticio en su área elegida, su hijo/a hará una tabla que demostrará cómo y cuánto gastará y ahorrará. Toda esta información será basada en sus ingresos mensuales. Además, investigará los aspectos positivos y negativos de usar crédito, elegirá un hogar, y planificará como amueblar ese hogar dentro de un presupuesto específico. Algunos de los materiales generados durante estas tareas serán designados al portafolio del proyecto; y otros se convertirán en parte de una exhibición colorida e informativa.

Una Guía Estudiantil será proveída para orientar al estudiante paso por paso y guiarlo por este proceso. La Guía Estudiantil es una lista completa que indica los requisitos de este proyecto y está diseñada para guiar al alumno a que comience a pensar usando un nivel superior. La guía también menciona las Tarjetas de Recursos que proveen explicaciones adicionales, ideas, consejos, y otra información. Estas tarjetas también estarán disponibles en el salón de su hijo/a para el uso de él/ella.

El proyecto "Aventura Financiera" está diseñado para que el alumno pueda trabajar independientemente en su salón, durante su tiempo libre y en casa. "Juntas de Revisión" están programadas durante el proyecto para que yo esté al pendiente del progreso del estudiante. En las fechas indicadas, el estudiante y yo nos reuniremos para discutir sus logros y para planear nuevas metas para la siguiente junta. También, veremos si el estudiante ha tenido dificultades o si tiene algunas preguntas.

"Aventura Financiera" se terminará en una "Exposición de Proyectos". Esta Exposición dará una oportunidad al estudiante a que comparta su trabajo y sus experiencias con su familia, amigos, e invitados. Usted recibirá una invitación para la "Exposición de Proyectos" más adelante en el trimestre.

Fechas para recordar:

Revisión 1: _____

Revisión 2: _____

Revisión 3: _____

Presentación en el Salón de Clase: _____

Exposición de "Aventura Financiera": _____ , _____

Sinceramente,

_____

_____

CONTRATO DE COMPROMISO ESTUDIANTIL

expectativas

tiempo de proyecto

Acepto:

- seguir los pasos indicados en mi guía estudiantil mientras que hago mi trabajo.
- mantener en orden mis materiales de proyecto.
- trabajar duro en Envision sin molestar a otros.
- mantener mis preguntas para mi mismo, hasta que mi maestro/a esté libre para hablar.

juntas de reviso

Vendré preparado con:

- mi Guía Estudiantil.
- mi Organizador Estudiantil.
- todos los materiales necesarios para el proyecto.

fechas importantes

Revisión 1: _____

Revisión 2: _____

Revisión 3: _____

Presentación en el Salón de Clase: _____

Exposición de Aventura Financiera: _____

_____

firmas

Acepto:

- cumplir con las expectativas en las fechas citadas anteriormente.
- utilizaré mis mejores habilidades y conocimientos para completar los requisitos de Aventura Financiera.
- traer mi proyecto a la escuela todos los días, así podré trabajar en él durante mi tiempo libre.
- llevar mi proyecto a la casa todos los días, así podré trabajar en casa.

Entiendo que el proyecto Aventura Financiera de Envision es una oportunidad especial, y si no cumplo con las expectativas mencionadas existe la posibilidad de que tenga que regresar a las actividades normales de mi salón.

Firma del Estudiante: _____ Fecha: _____

Firma del Padre: _____ Fecha: _____

Por favor devuelva este contrato antes de: _____

Construyendo el Portafolio de Tu Proyecto • Creando La Exhibición de Tu Proyecto
Presentación de Tu Proyecto • Asistiendo a la Exposición

SE CREATIVO!

IMPORTANTE!

Las tarjetas de recursos disponibles están señaladas por un icono de Aventura Financiera. Cuando veas uno de estos símbolos, sabrás que hay una tarjeta correspondiente numerada disponible que te da información adicional útil y ejemplos visuales para tu referencia. También, asegúrate de visitar www. mindvinepress.com, otros sitios de Internet confiables, materiales de referencia de la biblioteca, y la ayuda de adultos de tu familia para tener recursos y ejemplos adicionales.

Los Términos marcados con un asterisco (*) son definidos en el "Glosario de Aventura Financiera" incluida con este instructivo.

COMPONENTE 1

Construyendo tu Portafolio de Aventura Financiera

Total de Puntos Posibles por el Portafolio: 74 de un total de 100 por el proyecto

Con el trayecto profesional que elegiste en mente, estás ahora listo para explorar el tipo de futuro financiero que puedes esperar. Recuerda, las decisiones financieras son acerca de mucho más que tan solo dólares y centavos, así que debes de estar listo para considerar un gran número de interesantes y desafiantes alternativas de vida. Completa los requisitos enumerados a continuación, en el mismo orden en que estos se presentan. Estos requisitos se basan en cada uno de ellos y te guiarán sin problemas a través de esta aventura financiera.

Nota: "Componente 1: Construir tu Portafolio de Aventura Financiera" se divide en tres secciones: "Sección 1 del Portafolio: Aceptando un Trabajo y Definiendo tu Salario", "Sección 2 del Portafolio: Presupuestando tus Gastos Mensuales", y "Sección 3 del Portafolio": Haciendo las Compras para Establecer un Hogar". Puedes encontrar útil revisar estas tres secciones antes de empezar.

Sección 1 del Portafolio: Aceptando un Trabajo y Definiendo tu Salario

1. Carta de Aceptación de una Oferta de Trabajo (5 puntos): Imagina que se te ha ofrecido el trabajo que solicitaste en tu Proyecto de Aspiración a una Carrera. Escribe una carta de aceptación de la oferta de trabajo estableciendo que estás aceptando la posición, tu entendimiento de los términos del trabajo y tu entusiasmo por la compañía. Visita www.mindvinepress.com para encontrar enlaces útiles en el internet y más información.

2. Tabla Salarial (2 puntos): Crea una tabla salarial utilizando la computadora que muestre tu ingreso anual bruto* y tu ingreso anual neto*. En la tabla, muestra también tu ingreso anual neto, mensual, quincenal, semanal, diario, y por hora. Tu ingreso anual bruto deberá ser basado en el salario inicial para la posición que aceptaste.

Sección 2 del Portafolio: Presupuestando tus Gastos Mensuales

1. Decisiones Sobre Vivienda y Compañero de Habitación (1 punto): Los requisitos siguientes te piden un presupuesto de tus gastos de vivienda. Antes de comenzar, considera a alguno de tus compañeros de Envision como un compañero de habitación que te ayudará compartiendo costos. Si escoges tener un compañero de habitación, escojan un lugar de residencia y planeen compartir solamente los gastos de la renta y servicios. Cada compañero de habitación trabajará en su proyecto independientemente, creando su portafolio y exhibición y lo presentará independientemente a la clase. Para poder ser compañeros de habitación, deberán completar un Cuestionario de Compañero de Habitación y una Guía de Discusión de Compañero de Habitación. Si decides vivir solo, elige una casa específica para rentarla o comprarla. Escribe un párrafo explicando la razón de un compañero de habitación y gastos de vivienda e inclúyelo en tu portafolio.

> Importante: Los siguientes requerimientos te piden considerar los gastos de vivienda en dos maneras. Primero, te piden estimar cuánto dinero gastarás en varios bienes y servicios cada mes. Después, te piden calcular cuánto dinero separarás cada dos semanas para poder pagar esos gastos mensuales. Recuerda que los únicos gastos mensuales que pueden compartirse entre compañeros de habitación son la renta y servicios. Es una buena idea consultar con los miembros adultos de tu familia acerca del costo estimado de estos gastos. El Internet es también un excelente recurso para esta información.

2. 💲 Tabla y Gráfica Circular de Necesidades Fijas (5 puntos): Crea una tabla generada en la computadora que muestre cuánto dinero vas a gastar en tus necesidades fijas* en un mes. Tu tabla deberá incluir: (1) una lista de tus necesidades fijas en un mes (2) la cantidad de dinero que gastarás en cada una de las necesidades básicas en un mes; (3) la cantidad de dinero que separarás cada dos semanas para cada una de tus necesidades básicas; (4) la cantidad total de dinero que gastarás en tus necesidades básicas en un mes; y (5) la cantidad total de dinero que separarás cada dos semanas para tus necesidades básicas. Después, haz una gráfica circular usando la computadora que muestre la cantidad de dinero que gastarás en cada una de tus necesidades básicas en un mes. Incluye el título y los símbolos clave con tu gráfica circular.

3. 💲 Tabla y Gráfica Circular de Necesidades Variables (5 puntos): Crea una tabla usando la computadora que muestre cuánto dinero gastarás en tus necesidades variables* en un mes. Tu tabla deberá incluir: (1) una lista de tus necesidades variables en un mes; (2) la cantidad de dinero que gastarás en cada una de tus necesidades variables en un mes; (3) la cantidad de dinero que separarás cada dos semanas para cada una de tus necesidades variables; (4) la cantidad total de dinero que gastarás en tus necesidades variables de un mes; y (5) la cantidad total de dinero que separarás cada dos semanas para tus necesidades variables. Enseguida, haz una gráfica circular usando la computadora que muestre la cantidad de dinero que gastarás en cada una de tus necesidades variables en un mes. Incluye un título y la clave de símbolos con tu gráfica circular.

4. 💲 Tabla y Gráfica Circular de Ahorros e Inversiones (5 puntos): Crea una tabla usando la computadora que muestre cuánto dinero usarás para ahorros* e inversiones financieras* cada mes. Tu tabla deberá incluir: (1) una lista de las cuentas de ahorros e inversiones a las que contribuirás cada mes; (2) la cantidad de dinero que pondrás en cada cuenta e inversiones cada mes; (3) la cantidad de dinero que separarás cada dos semanas para cada cuenta e inversiones; (4) el total de dinero combinado que pondrás en las cuentas de ahorro e inversiones cada mes; y (5) la cantidad total de dinero que separarás cada dos semanas para ahorros e inversiones. Después, crea una gráfica circular utilizando la computadora que muestre la cantidad de dinero que pondrás en cada cuenta individual de ahorros e inversiones cada mes. Incluye el título y la clave de símbolos en tu gráfica circular.

5. Presupuesto de Costos de Oportunidad (4 puntos): Describe al menos cinco costos de oportunidad* para las decisiones que hiciste al presupuestar tus necesidades, ahorros e inversiones.

6. 💲 Tabla y Gráfica Circular de Artículos Discrecionales Fijos (5 puntos): Haz una tabla usando la computadora que muestre cuánto dinero gastarás en artículos discrecionales fijos* en un mes. Tu tabla deberá incluir: (1) una lista de los artículos discrecionales fijos para un mes; (2) la cantidad de dinero que gastarás en cada uno de los artículos discrecionales fijos en un mes; (3) la cantidad de dinero que separarás cada dos semanas para cada uno de los artículos discrecionales fijos; (4) la cantidad total de dinero que gastarás en artículos discrecionales fijos en un mes; y (5) la cantidad total de dinero que separarás cada dos semanas para artículos discrecionales fijos. Después, crea una gráfica circular utilizando la computadora que muestre la cantidad de dinero que gastarás en artículos discrecionales fijos en un mes. Incluye el título y la clave de símbolos en tu gráfica circular.

7. **Tabla y Gráfica Circular de Artículos Discrecionales Variables** (5 puntos): Haz una tabla usando la computadora que muestre cuánto dinero gastarás en artículos discrecionales variables* en un mes. Tu tabla deberá incluir: (1) una lista de los artículos discrecionales variables para un mes; (2) la cantidad de dinero que gastarás en cada uno de los artículos discrecionales variables en un mes; (3) la cantidad de dinero que separarás cada dos semanas para cada uno de los artículos discrecionales variables; (4) la cantidad total de dinero que gastarás en artículos discrecionales variables en un mes; y (5) la cantidad total de dinero que separarás cada dos semanas para artículos discrecionales variables. Después, haz una gráfica circular utilizando la computadora que muestre la cantidad de dinero que gastarás en artículos discrecionales variables en un mes. Incluye el título y la clave de símbolos en tu gráfica circular.

8. Costos de Oportunidad de Artículos Discrecionales (4 puntos): Identifica y explica al menos cinco costos de oportunidad* para las decisiones que hiciste mientras presupuestabas los artículos discrecionales fijos y variables.

9. **Gráfica Circular del Presupuesto Mensual Total** (6 puntos): Crea una gráfica circular utilizando la computadora que muestre la cantidad que gastarás en cada una de las necesidades, cuentas de ahorros, inversiones y artículos discrecionales. Incluye un título y la clave de símbolos en tu gráfica circular.

Portafolio Sección 3: Haciendo Compras para Establecer un Hogar

> Importante: Los requerimientos para esta sección están basados en la presunción de que recibiste un bono por firmar de $5,000 de tu nuevo empleador. También debes asumir que tú tienes también otros $5,000 en el banco que has ahorrado a través de los años. Tú usarás parte de estos $10,000 para hacer compras para tu casa cuando comiences tu nuevo trabajo. Sin embargo, deberás dejar en tu banco un considerable "colchón" para aquellos gastos inesperados que pudieran presentarse. También, mientras haces tus compras, asegúrate de guardar todas las fotografías de los artículos que "compras." Usarás las fotografías para tu tablero de exhibición.

Opciones de Compañero de Habitación: Si tienes un compañero de habitación, deberán compartir el costo de todas las compras de artículos que serán utilizados por los dos en su casa incluyendo accesorios, muebles de la sala, vajilla, etc. Recuera que cada uno de los requerimientos que siguen deberá ser completado por cada uno de ustedes por separado e incluidos en sus portafolios.

1. **Tabla y Gráfica Circular de las Compras Necesarias** (5 puntos): Haz una tabla utilizando tu computadora que muestre cuánto dinero gastarás en las compras necesarias* para tu hogar. Tu tabla deberá incluir: (1) una lista de todas las compras necesarias, agrupadas por cada uno de los cuartos; (2) el costo de cada una de las compras necesarias; (3) los impuestos de ventas aplicables a cada compra; (4) la cantidad total por cada compra; y (5) la cantidad de dinero que gastarás en las compras necesarias para tu hogar. Después, crea una gráfica circular usando la computadora que muestre la cantidad de dinero que gastarás en cada una de las compras necesarias. Incluye un título y la clave de símbolos en tu gráfica circular.

2. **Tabla y Gráfica Circular de los Gastos Discrecionales** (5 puntos): Crea una tabla utilizando la computadora que muestre cuánto dinero gastarás en compras discrecionales* para tu hogar. Tu tabla deberá incluir: (1) una lista de las compras discrecionales, agrupadas por cada uno de los cuartos; (2) el costo de cada una de las compras discrecionales; (3) el impuesto de ventas aplicable a cada compra; (4) la cantidad total por cada una de las compras; y (5) la cantidad total de dinero que gastarás en compras discrecionales. Después, crea una gráfica circular usando la computadora que muestre la cantidad de dinero que gastarás en cada una de las compras discrecionales. Incluye un título y la clave de símbolos en tu gráfica circular.

3. Costos de Oportunidades en las Compras (4 puntos): Identifica y explica al menos cinco costos de oportunidad* para las decisiones que hiciste mientras presupuestabas las compras necesarias y discrecionales para tu hogar.

4. **Gráfica Circular de las Compras Totales** (6 puntos): Crea una gráfica circular utilizando la computadora que muestre (1) la cantidad que gastarás en cada una de las compras necesarias y discrecionales que harás para tu hogar, y (2) la cantidad de "colchón" que te quedará. Incluye un título y la clave de símbolos.

5. Análisis del Crédito (4 puntos): Investiga y explica los aspectos positivos y negativos de usar crédito.

Materiales Restantes del Portafolio

1. ⑤ **Tabla de Contenido o Índice** (1 punto): Escribe una tabla de contenido que muestre todas las secciones de tu portafolio juntamente con los números de páginas correspondientes.

2. ⑤ **Cubierta o Portada** (1 punto): Crea una página de cubierta llamativa para tu portafolio que incluya un título original para tu proyecto así como también tu nombre y la fecha de presentación en el salón de clase.

3. ⑤ **Portafolio** (1 punto): Organiza todos tus materiales en una carpeta de tres argollas. La tabla de contenido o índice deberá ir primero, seguida de tu trabajo para el Portafolio Secciones 1, 2 y 3 en el orden en que se presentan. La página de cubierta deberá ir en el frente de tu portafolio.

Has completado el Componente 1 de tu Proyecto de Aventura Financiera. Al completar tu portafolio, has creado un importante recurso que te ayudará a trabajar en tus componentes 2 y 3. Aun cuando tienes algunos retos importantes por venir, tú estás ahora preparado para llevarlos a cabo, sabiendo que has puesto los fundamentos necesarios para aumentar tus posibilidades de éxito. Buena suerte en tanto avanzas a la creación de los artículos a exhibir en tu proyecto.

COMPONENTE 2
Creando la Exhibición de Tu Aventura Financiera

Puntos Posibles por tu Exhibición: 11 de un total de 100 puntos por el proyecto

Habiendo completado tu presupuesto y comprado los artículos para tu hogar, es tiempo de diseñar y crear una exhibición informativa y llamativa de tus planes. Lo que has completado será visto por tus compañeros de clase en el día de la Presentación en el Salón de Clase y también por cada una de las personas que asistan a La Exposición de Aventura Financiera al final del término. Como siempre, pon tu mejor esfuerzo en el diseño, creación e integración de los artículos que vas a exhibir.

> **Nota:**
> Recuerda que cada uno de los elementos es solo una parte de tu exhibición total. En otras palabras, un solo elemento no tiene que decir todo acerca de tu proyecto. Decide cual es el propósito de cada elemento. Considera la mejor manera de organizar tu exhibición para lograr un mayor efecto.

1. ⑤ **Plano o Modelo Tridimensional** (4 puntos): Diseña o recrea un plano o un modelo tridimensional de tu futura casa. Se creativo. Si tú quieres usa una computadora para hacerlo.

2. ⑤ **Tablero de Exhibición** (4 puntos): Usa un tablero de exhibición de dos o tres páneles (secciones) para mostrar las fotografías que representan tus gastos y compras presupuestados. Usa la mitad del tablero para organizar las fotografías de tus gastos presupuestados y la otra mitad para organizar las fotografías de tus compras. Tu tablero de exhibición debe incluir el título de tu proyecto y tu nombre. Puedes incluir los materiales adicionales que tú desees.

3. ⑤ **Exhibición** (3 puntos): Organiza y ordena las cosas que vas a exhibir, tu portafolio y todos los materiales adicionales que hayas querido incluir en una manera informativa y atractiva.

Has completado el componente 2 de tu Proyecto de Aventura Financiera, una importante exhibición que de una manera creativa muestra tu presupuesto y tus planes de compra. Ahora que has terminado tu portafolio y tu exhibición, estás listo para prepararte con confianza para tu Presentación en el Salón de Clase (Componente 3). Disfruta compartiendo tu proyecto con tus compañeros y maestro!

COMPONENTE 3:

Dando tu Presentación en el Salón de Clase:
Puntos Posibles por la Presentación en el Salón de Clase: 15 de un total de 100 por el proyecto

Ahora es tiempo de compartir tus planes con otros. La presentación en el salón de clase es una oportunidad para que formalmente presentes algunas de tus metas y compartir algo del arduo trabajo que has hecho. Tu portafolio y tu exhibición contienen toda la información que necesitas para tu presentación, así que relájate y diviértete con esto.

1. ⑤ Que Incluir en Tu Presentación:

• Aceptación del Trabajo (2 puntos): **Camparte varios aspectos de la posición que aceptaste.**

• Gráfica Circular del Presupuesto Total Mensual y el Portafolio (2 puntos): **Muestra tu portafolio y comparte acerca de tu gráfica circular del presupuesto final incluyendo algunas de las necesidades y algunos de los artículos discrecionales.**

• Presupuesto de Costo de Oportunidad (2 puntos): **Comparte un costo de oportunidad para tus necesidades presupuestadas, ahorros, inversiones o artículos discrecionales.**

• Gráfica Circular de las Compras Totales (2 puntos): **Comparte tu gráfica circular de tus compras finales y algunas de las compras discrecionales.**

• Costo de Oportunidad en las Compras (2 puntos): **Comparte un costo de oportunidad de tus compras de necesidades y de tus compras discrecionales.**

• Tablero de Exhibición (3 puntos): **Señala y explica algunas características que hayas seleccionado de tu tablero de exhibición.**

• Plano o Modelo Tridimensional (2 puntos): **Muestra el plano o el modelo tridimensional de tu futura residencia y explica algunas de sus características claves.**

> **Nota:** La presentación en tu salón deberá durar de tres a cuatro minutos y debe ser ensayada pero no memorizada. Si olvidas incluir alguna información requerida, tu maestro te hará una pregunta acerca de esta para que tengas oportunidad de incluirla.

Que Traer a Tu Presentación en el Salón de Clase:
Todos tus artículos de exhibición incluyendo cualquier cosa extra que te permita mejorar y ampliar tu exhibición.

Ya has terminado con los Componentes 1, 2 y 3 – y todas las partes que se requirieron para tu proyecto. El Componente final será asistir a la Exposición de Aventura Financiera, donde habrá una celebración para clausurar este proyecto.

COMPONENTE 4:

Asistiendo a la Exposición de Aventura Financiera (La exposición no te da puntos.)

Ahora que has terminado tu proyecto y lo has presentado a tus compañeros, es tiempo de compartir tu trabajo con tu familia y amigos en la Exposición de Aventura Financiera. La exposición es un evento que reconoce y celebra el duro trabajo que has hecho para hacer tu Proyecto de Aventura Financiera. En la exposición, tú colocarás tu exhibición y permanecerás al lado de tu proyecto mientras los invitados caminan observando los proyectos. Los invitados pueden hacer algunas preguntas acerca de tu proyecto, así que disfruta y diviértete compartiendo las experiencias de tu Aventura Financiera con ellos.

Que Traer a la Exposición: Todos tus artículos de exhibición incluyendo cualquier cosa extra que te permita mejorar y ampliar tu exhibición.

Los siguientes términos están enumerados y definidos en el mismo orden en el que aparecen en la Guía de Instrucciones para el Estudiante.

Portafolio Sección 1: Aceptando un Trabajo y Haciendo una Gráfica de tu Salario

Ingreso Anual Bruto: La cantidad de dinero que una persona gana en un año antes de pagar impuestos sobre sus ingresos.

Ingreso Anual Neto: La cantidad de ingresos que le queda a una persona después de pagar los impuestos federales, estatales, y locales sobre sus ingresos.

Portafolio Sección 2: Presupuestando tus Gastos Mensuales

Necesidades Fijas: Los bienes y servicios que una persona decide que son necesarios, y que los costos son los mismos de mes a mes. Algunos gastos fijos son bienes caros que se pagan por un periodo de tiempo, como lo es un carro, una casa, el alquiler de un apartamento, un préstamo estudiantil y varias clases de seguros. Otras necesidades fijas son servicios de bajo costo que se usan continuamente, y también se pagan a cierto tiempo. Estas pueden incluir el plan telefónico, un pase mensual del autobús, y algunos servicios, como el gas y la electricidad.

Necesidades Variables: Los bienes y servicios que una persona decide que son necesarios, pero que cuyos costos pueden variar de mes a mes. Las necesidades variables pueden incluir, alimentos, ropa, artículos para la salud, artículos para el hogar, (productos de limpieza, artículos del tocador), gasolina y transporte público ocasional.

Ahorros: El dinero que ha sido ahorrado y puesto en una cuenta de ahorros, usualmente en un banco.

Inversiones Financieras: El dinero que se invierte esperando obtener una utilidad. Las inversiones pueden ser de alto o bajo riesgo. Las inversiones de alto riesgo por lo general producen mayor ganancia si tienen éxito, pero se consideran inseguras. Las inversiones de bajo riesgo por lo general producen menor ganancia si tienen éxito, pero se consideran bastante seguras. Algunas clases de inversiones incluyen: acciones, CD (certificados de depósito), cuentas del mercado monetario, planes 401K, cuentas individuales de jubilación, bienes raíces e inversiones en empresas.

Presupuestos de Costos de Oportunidad: Una necesidad, ahorros o inversiones a los que una persona renuncia con el fin de tener una necesidad , ahorros o inversiones más convenientes. Por ejemplo, puede ser que tu optes por renunciar a comprar ropa cara de marca para poder poner más dinero en tu cuenta de ahorros. Renunciar a la ropa de marca es el costo de oportunidad de poner más dinero en tu cuenta de ahorros.

Artículos Fijos Discrecionales: Bienes y servicios que una persona decide que son deseables, pero no necesarios, y cuyos costos son los mismos de mes a mes. Los artículos fijos discrecionales pueden incluir el servicio de televisión por cable o satélite, servicio de Internet, suscripciones de revistas y membresía a un gimnasio.

Artículos Variables Discrecionales: Bienes y servicios que una persona decide que son deseables, pero no necesarios, y cuyos costos pueden variar de mes a mes. Los artículos variables discrecionales pueden incluir el comer fuera, ir al cine, participar en actividades recreativas y viajar.

Costo de Oportunidad de Artículos Discrecionales: Un artículo discrecional al cual una persona renuncia para poder tener otro artículo discrecional que desea más. Por ejemplo, puede ser que optes por renunciar a la televisión por satélite para poder ir al cine con más frecuencia.

Portafolio Sección 3: Haciendo las Compras para Establecer un Hogar

Compras Necesarias: Las cosas que una persona decide comprar porque son necesarias. Las compras necesarias pueden incluir muebles básicos, vajilla, ropa de cama, algunos electrodomésticos importantes (lavadora y secadora de ropa, estufa, o refrigerador), artículos básicos para el mantenimiento del hogar (cortadora del césped, rastrillo, escoba o botes de basura) y los accesorios básicos del hogar (cortinas de baño, papeleras, etc.).

Compras Discrecionales: Las cosas que una persona decide que no son necesarias, pero lo suficientemente deseables para comprarlas. Las compras discrecionales pueden incluir mascotas, artículos para mascota, electrodomésticos pequeños, (microondas y cafetera), una computadora, artículos especializados para el mantenimiento del hogar, (limpiadora de nieve, cortadora de bordes o sierra) y accesorios decorativos para el hogar (obras de arte, plantas o cojines).

Costo de Oportunidad en las Compras: Un bien que una persona decide no comprar para poder comprar otro bien que es más deseable. Por ejemplo, una persona puede optar por no comprar un sistema de entretenimiento para el hogar para poder comprar la limpiadora de nieve. No comprar el sistema de entretenimiento para el hogar es el costo de oportunidad para poder comprar la limpiadora de nieve.

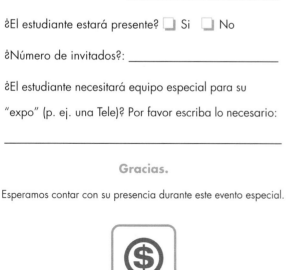

¡ESTA INVITADO!

RESPUESTA A LA "EXPO"

Por favor complete y regrese antes de: _____

Nombre del estudiante: _____

¿El estudiante estará presente? ☐ Si ☐ No

¿Número de invitados?: _____

¿El estudiante necesitará equipo especial para su "expo" (p. ej. una Tele)? Por favor escriba lo necesario:
_____

Gracias.

Esperamos contar con su presencia durante este evento especial.

¡POR FAVOR VENGAN A VISITARNOS A LA EXPO AVENTURA FINANCIERA!

¿Por qué? _____

¿Quién?_____

¿Dónde? _____

¿Cuándo? _____

Recuerde de traer su cámara!

FINANCIAL ADVENTURE
RESOURCE CARDS
FOR STUDENTS

JOB-OFFER ACCEPTANCE LETTER

A formal job offer is usually made in writing. This is so the employer can state the terms of the offer clearly. It is then appropriate that you reply to that offer in writing. A job-offer acceptance letter uses the standard business-letter style and format. In your acceptance letter, you should thank the company or individual for the offer, clearly state that you accept the offer and restate the terms of the contract as you understand them (salary, benefits and other items), as well as any special details about your hire, such as your start date.

> 111 Oak Street
> Newtown, MI 49999
>
> September 23, 20XX
>
> Mr. Robert L. Black
>
> Personnel Director
> Big Bank
> 25 Main Street
> Capital City, MI 45588
>
> Dear Mr. Black:
>
> I am writing to thank you for offering me the job of senior loan officer, and to say that I am happy to accept. I understand that my beginning salary will be . . .

EXAMPLE

SALARY CHART

A salary chart shows detailed information about a person's yearly income from a given job. Your salary chart should show your gross annual income* from the job you have accepted, your net annual income*, your monthly net income, bi-weekly net income, daily net income, and hourly net income (hourly wage). These amounts will help you later as you plan various aspects of your budget. Your hourly net income is based on the average number of hours you expect to work each day. A typical workday is eight hours, but it could be longer or shorter depending on the type of work and the job.

SALARY CHART

Gross Annual Income	$35,783.00
Net Annual Income	$29,963.09
Monthly	$2,496.92
Bi-Weekly	$1,248.46
Weekly	$624,23
Daily	$89.18
Hourly (based on 8-hour work day)	$11.15

EXAMPLE

FIXED NECESSITIES CHART AND PIE GRAPH

A fixed necessities chart lists all of the fixed necessities you plan to spend money on each month, along with the financial information needed to plan your monthly and bi-weekly budgets. Your chart should include the following: the amount you plan to spend monthly on each fixed necessity; the amount you will need to set aside bi-weekly to meet each monthly expense; totals for all monthly expenses and bi-weekly budgeted amounts.

A fixed necessities pie graph visually represents the proportions of the money you plan to spend on each fixed necessity each month.

FIXED NECESSITIES CHART		
Fixed Necessity	Amount Needed Each Month	Amount to Set Aside Bi-Weekly
Rent	$400.00	$200.00
Renter's Insurance	$12.58	$6.29
Car Payment	$172.00	$86.00
Totals	$584.58	$292.29

FIXED NECESSITIES PIE GRAPH

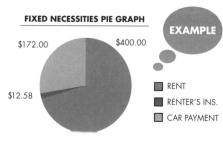

$172.00 $400.00

$12.58

■ RENT
■ RENTER'S INS.
□ CAR PAYMENT

EXAMPLE

VARIABLE NECESSITIES CHART AND PIE GRAPH

A variable necessities chart lists all of the variable necessities you plan to spend money on each month, along with the financial information needed to plan your monthly and bi-weekly budgets. Your chart should include the following: the amount you plan to spend monthly on each variable necessity; the amount you will need to set aside bi-weekly to meet each monthly expense; totals for all monthly expenses and bi-weekly budgeted amounts.

A variable necessities pie graph visually represents the proportions of the money you plan to spend on each variable necessity each month.

VARIABLE NECESSITIES CHART		
Variable Necessity	Amount Needed Each Month	Amount to Set Aside Bi-Weekly
Grocery	$200.00	$100.00
Clothing	$40.00	$20.00
Medical Bills	$15.00	$7.50
Totals	$255.00	$127.50

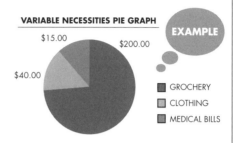

VARIABLE NECESSITIES PIE GRAPH

EXAMPLE

- GROCHERY
- CLOTHING
- MEDICAL BILLS

SAVINGS AND INVESTING CHART AND PIE GRAPH

A savings and investment chart lists all of the savings accounts and investments you plan to contribute to each month, along with the financial information needed to plan your monthly and bi-weekly budgets. Your chart should include the following: the amount you plan to contribute monthly to each savings account and investment; the amount you will need to set aside bi-weekly to meet each monthly contribution; totals for all monthly contributions and bi-weekly budgeted amounts.

A savings and investment pie graph visually represents the proportions of money you plan to contribute to each savings account and investment each month.

SAVINGS AND INVESTMENTS CHART		
Savings Account or Investment	Monthly Contribution	Amount to Set Aside Bi-Weekly
Personal Savings Account	100.00	$50.00
Individual Stocks	$50.00	$25.00
Mutual Fund	$50.00	$25.00
Totals	$200.00	$100.00

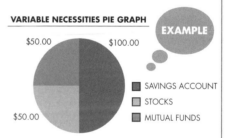

VARIABLE NECESSITIES PIE GRAPH

EXAMPLE

- SAVINGS ACCOUNT
- STOCKS
- MUTUAL FUNDS

FIXED DISCRETIONARY ITEMS CHART AND PIE GRAPH

A fixed discretionary items chart lists all of the fixed discretionary items you plan to spend money on each month, along with the financial information needed to plan your monthly and bi-weekly budgets. Your chart should include the following: the amount you plan to spend monthly on each fixed discretionary item; the amount you will need to set aside bi-weekly to meet each monthly expense; totals for all monthly expenses and bi-weekly budgeted amounts.

A fixed discretionary items pie graph visually represents the proportions of the money you plan to spend on each fixed discretionary items each month.

FIXED DISCRETIONARY ITEMS CHART		
Fixed Discretionary Items	Amount Needed Each Month	Amount to Set Aside Bi-Weekly
Cable	$36.50	$18.25
Internet	$19.98	$9.99
Haircut	$26.00	$13.00
Totals	$82.48	$41.24

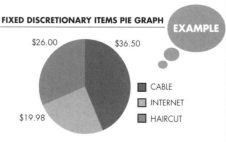

FIXED DISCRETIONARY ITEMS PIE GRAPH

EXAMPLE

- CABLE
- INTERNET
- HAIRCUT

VARIABLE DISCRETIONARY ITEMS CHART AND PIE GRAPH

A variable discretionary items chart lists all of the variable discretionary items you plan to spend money on each month, along with the financial information needed to plan your monthly and bi-weekly budgets. Your chart should include the following: the amount you plan to spend monthly on each variable discretionary item; the amount you will need to set aside bi-weekly to meet each monthly expense; totals for all monthly expenses and bi-weekly budgeted amounts.

A variable discretionary items pie graph visually represents the proportions of the money you plan to spend on each variable discretionary item each month.

VARIABLE DISCRETIONARY ITEMS CHART		
Variable Discretionary Items	Amount Needed Each Month	Amount to Set Aside Bi-Weekly
Books	$16.00	$8.00
Eating Out	$20.00	$10.00
Movies	$10.00	$5.00
Totals	$46.00	$23.00

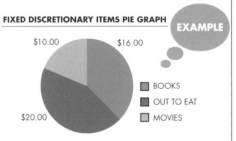

FIXED DISCRETIONARY ITEMS PIE GRAPH

EXAMPLE

$10.00 $16.00

$20.00

- BOOKS
- OUT TO EAT
- MOVIES

TOTAL MONTHLY BUDGET PIE GRAPH

A total monthly budget pie graph visually represents the proportions of the money you plan to spend on each necessity, savings, investment, and discretionary item each month. (Your total monthly budgeted amounts for all these items cannot exceed your monthly net income.)

TOTAL MONTHLY BUDGET PIE GRAPH

$36.50
$50.00
$50.00
$100.00
$15.00
$40.00
$200.00
$400.00
$12.58
$172.00

- RENT
- RENTER'S INSURANCE
- CAR PAYMENT
- GROCERY
- CLOTHING
- MEDICAL BILLS
- SAVINGS' ACCOUNT
- STOCKS
- MUTUAL FUND
- CABLE

EXAMPLE

TOTAL MONTHLY EXPENSES:
$1,076.08

NECESSARY PURCHASES CHART AND PIE GRAPH

A necessary purchases chart lists the basic household items you will need to set up your home, along with the retail price of each item, any applicable sales tax and a total cost. Remember to organize your chart by room. (If you chose to have a roommate, you may share the cost of any purchases that will be utilized by both of you in your home: appliances, living area furniture, dishes and other items). You have $10,000 in the bank, but only a portion of that is to be budgeted for necessary purchases. Some will be budgeted for discretionary purchases, and the rest will stay in the bank as savings.

A necessary purchases pie graph visually represents the proportions of the money you plan to spend on each necessary purchase.

NECESSARY PURCHASES CHART			
Kitchen Items	Retail Price	6% Sales Tax	Total Cost
Table and Chairs	$250.00	$15.00	$265.00
Dishes	$37.99	$2.28	$40.27
Total Kitchen	$287.99	$17.28	$305.27
Bathroom Items			
Towels	$41.88	$2.51	$44.39
Shower Curtain	$15.99	$0.96	$16.95
Total Bathroom	$57.87	$3.47	$61.34
Grand Totals:	**$345.86**	**$20.75**	**$366.61**

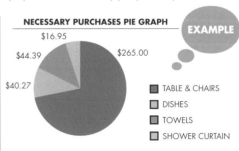

NECESSARY PURCHASES PIE GRAPH

EXAMPLE

$16.95
$44.39
$265.00
$40.27

- TABLE & CHAIRS
- DISHES
- TOWELS
- SHOWER CURTAIN

A discretionary purchases chart lists household items you do not feel you need but that you wish to have, along with the retail price of each item, any applicable sales tax, and a total cost. Remember to organize your chart by room. (If you chose to have a roommate, you may share the cost of any purchases that will be utilized by both of you in your home (television, pet, plants, etc.). Each student has $10,000 in the bank, but only a portion of that is to be budgeted for discretionary purchases. Some will have already been budgeted for necessary-choice purchases, and the rest will stay in the bank as savings.)

A discretionary purchases pie graph visually represents the proportions of the money you plan to spend on each discretionary purchase.

DISCRETIONARY PURCHASES CHART			
Kitchen Items	**Retail Price**	**6% Sales Tax**	**Total Cost**
Toaster Oven	$50.00	$3.00	$53.00
Electric Mixer	$9.99	$.60	$10.59
Total Kitchen	$59.99	$3.60	$63.59
Bathroom Items			
Wall Hanging	$19.98	$1.20	$21.18
Soap Dispenser	$8.99	$0.54	$9.53
Total Bathroom	$28.97	$1.74	$30.71
Grand Totals:	**$88.96**	**$5.34**	**$94.30**

NECESSARY PURCHASES PIE GRAPH

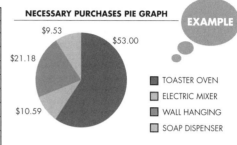

- ■ TOASTER OVEN
- ☐ ELECTRIC MIXER
- ■ WALL HANGING
- ☐ SOAP DISPENSER

A total purchases pie graph visually represents the proportions of the money you plan to spend on each necessary and discretionary purchase. (Your total budgeted amounts for all these items cannot exceed your $10,000 spending amount and should, in fact, reflect a "cushion" amount that will remain in your savings account.)

TOTAL PURCHASES PIE GRAPH

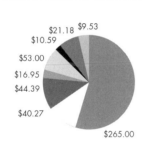

- ■ TABLE & CHAIRS
- ☐ DISHES
- ■ TOWELS
- ■ SHOWER CURTAIN
- ☐ TOASTER OVEN
- ■ ELECTRIC MIXER
- ■ WALL HANGING
- ☐ SOAP DISPENSER

TOTAL PURCHASES:
$460.91

Your table of contents should be the first page in your portfolio, although you write it after you finish all of the pages on the inside. Writing it after finishing the contents allows you to be accurate with your page numbers and titles in case you make any last-minute changes. Your table of contents should list each section and the page it begins on. It should be neat and well organized, but feel free to be creative with your own layout.

Table of Contents

Page	Section Title
1	Acceptance Letter
2	Salary Chart
3	Fixed Necessities Chart and Graph
4	Variable Necessities Chart and Graph
5	Savings and Investing Chart and Graph
6	Opportunity Costs
7	Fixed Discretionary Items Chart and Graph
8	Variable Discretionary Items Chart and Graph

COVER PAGE AND PORTFOLIO

The cover page of your portfolio should entice people to read about your project. It should include an original title, your name and the Classroom Presentation date. Your portfolio is used to organize most of your paper items. A one- to two-inch binder with a clear cover works well. Arrange your papers in the order listed in your Student Instruction Guide. You may choose to add tab dividers, page protectors and creative touches.

FRONT COVER   SPINE   BACK COVER

FLOOR PLAN OR THREE-DIMENSIONAL MODEL

A home floor plan is basically an interior map of your living space. It shows the entire layout and indicates the dimensions, in feet, of each room of the home you want to live in. A more detailed plan might include the location of furniture within the home, as well as exterior features such as porches, landscaping and yard space. A three-dimensional model can be used with or instead of a two-dimensional floor plan.

MY APARTMENT

DISPLAY BOARD AND EXHIBIT

The purpose of your display board and exhibit is to draw people's attention to your project. It should be neat, colorful and creative. You should include the items listed in your Student Instruction Guide and any additional materials you wish to bring. The example below is to be used only as a guide; feel free to rearrange. Tip: Two- or three-panel display boards can be purchased at most craft or office stores. If you prefer to make one, you can ask an adult to help construct one from a large cardboard box.

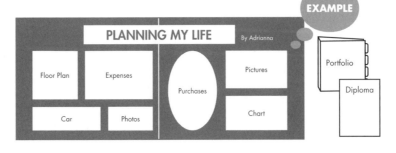

Your presentation is a formal delivery of what you learned and produced for your project. It should be practiced until you are comfortable with the things you will say (not a memorized speech). It should fit into the 3-4 minute time frame and include the bulleted information listed on your Student Instruction Guide. Also, remember to dress in clothing that reflects your career. The additional suggestions below may help you prepare.

REMEMBER TO:

- Take a deep breath, relax and enjoy sharing.
- Greet your audience and introduce yourself.
- Speak clearly, loudly enough so everyone can hear you, and at a natural pace.
- Stand still and calm; don't fidget.
- Point to and show various visuals as you speak about them.
- Have fun while presenting. Show your excitement about your experiences.
- Make eye contact with your audience, looking around the room naturally.
- Thank your audience when you are finished.

APPENDIX 4:
KNOWLEDGE QUEST FORMS
AND RESOURCE CARDS

Levels From Lowest to Highest:
KNOWLEDGE • COMPREHENSION • APPLICATION • ANALYSIS • EVALUATION • SYNTHESIS

Below you will find each Knowledge Quest requirement, along with its corresponding level of Bloom's Taxonomy.

> **IMPORTANT!**
> The levels listed above are cumulative. For example, the highest level of thinking, Synthesis, incorporates all other levels of thinking: Knowledge, Comprehension, Application, Analysis and Evaluation.

COMPONENT 1
Building Your Knowledge Quest Portfolio
Total Possible Portfolio Points: 75 out of 100 total possible for project

Portfolio Section 1: Choosing and Researching Your Topic

1. Research Topic and Question (2 points): Think of a topic that you are interested in and do not know much about. Compose an interesting question about your topic that will guide your research. Below the question, write a paragraph or two explaining why you chose your topic. **SYNTHESIS**

2. Semantic Map (4 points): Create a semantic map using a computer. Begin by typing your topic question in the center of your document, then draw a circle around the question. In the space surrounding your question, add related questions that come to mind. Circle the new questions and draw lines that connect the newer questions to the older ones they relate to. Your semantic map should contain a minimum of ten new topic sub-questions that you would like to consider as you explore your main topic question. Use this semantic map to guide your project research. **SYNTHESIS**

3. Research and Notes (6 points): Using at least ten different sources such as Internet websites, books, periodicals, journals and knowledgeable people you know, thoroughly research each of your semantic-map questions. Feel free to add to your map of questions as you go along, and to revise any existing questions. As you conduct your research, take careful notes using your own words on sheets of paper to place in your portfolio. Be sure to record the bibliographic information for each source as you take notes from it. You will need this information to identify your sources for the two portfolio requirements below. You may want to review the resource cards for the type of bibliographic information you should record. **SYNTHESIS**

4. Hot-List Chart (2 points): Create a chart that lists four to six of the most useful websites you found while researching your semantic-map questions. Your hot-list chart should include the name of each website, its web address and a brief summary of its content. **COMPREHENSION**

5. Works Cited (3 points): Create a works cited listing of all the books, articles, websites or other sources you received information from for your research and note taking. Follow the MLA style of documentation. **COMPREHENSION**

6. Survey (3 points): Create and conduct a survey based on your research to learn people's opinions or understanding about one or more interesting features of your topic. Survey a minimum of ten people. Be sure to record the gender and age of each person you talk to. You will need this demographic information to create the double bar graph described below. **SYNTHESIS**

7. Computer-Generated Double Bar Graph (3 points): Choose one question from your survey that produced interesting or surprising results. Classify the survey results for this question into two groups, such as gender groups or age groups, based on the demographic information that you recorded. Using a computer, create a double bar graph that compares the responses of each group for the question you chose. **SYNTHESIS**

Portfolio Section 2: Reporting Your Findings

1. Newspaper: For this portfolio section, you will design, write articles for and edit a newspaper dedicated to your topic. To begin, analyze various newspapers for layouts, features and writing styles. After becoming familiar with the format and content of a newspaper, you will be ready to begin working on yours. Your newspaper should be created on a computer and should include each of the elements listed below. In addition to your informational writing, feel free to use your creative writing skills. Follow the steps of the writing process when creating your newspaper and remember to include a newspaper title, day, date and index. **SYNTHESIS**

- Newspaper Articles (2 points each, total of 16 points): Write a minimum of eight articles for your newspaper. Each article should focus on one of the semantic-map questions you researched. Though your articles will contain information you gathered during your research, each must be written in your own words. Each article should begin with an intriguing lead sentence and conclude with a strong ending sentence. **SYNTHESIS**

- Newspaper Informational Text Structures (2 points each, total of 16 points): Six of your eight articles should be written using a different informational text structure. The informational text structures are as follows: (1) Cause and Effect, (2) Compare and Contrast, (3) Description, (4) Problem and Solution, (5) Question and Answer and (6) Sequence. The remaining two or more articles can use any text structure you choose. **COMPREHENSION**

- Newspaper Text Features (1 point each, total of 7 points): Use each of the following text features at least one time throughout your newspaper. Try to spread them out rather than cluster them all in one or two articles. As you use the various text features in your newspaper, jot down the page number, article title and line number where the feature was added. When the final copy of your newspaper is completed, double check that you have recorded the locations correctly and list them on a separate page in your portfolio so that your teacher can locate them quickly. Title the page "Locations of Text Features." **COMPREHENSION**

- Newspaper Photos and Pictures (1 point each, total of 4 points): Insert a minimum of two photos and two pictures, clipart pictures or drawings, into your newspaper. **COMPREHENSION**

- Newspaper Choice Extras (2 points each, total of 6 points): Newspapers are made up of more than just articles, photos and pictures. They also contain "extra" items such as editorials, letters to the editor, advertisements, cartoons, classified ads, word search puzzles, crossword puzzles, graphs, charts and notices of all kinds. Go over the newspapers you analyzed earlier, and choose three of these "extras" to add to your newspaper. Create these three "extras" making them relevant to your central topic, and include them in your newspaper. **SYNTHESIS**

Remaining Portfolio Materials

1. Table of Contents (1 point): Write a table of contents that lists all the sections of your portfolio along with their corresponding page numbers. **COMPREHENSION**

2. Cover Page (1 point): Create an eye-catching cover page for your portfolio that includes an original title for your project as well as your name and the Classroom Presentation date. **SYNTHESIS**

3. Portfolio (1 point): Organize all of your materials in a three-ring binder. The table of contents should come first, followed by your work from Portfolio Sections 1 and 2 above in the order presented. Your cover page should be placed on the front of the portfolio. **SYNTHESIS**

COMPONENT 2

Creating Your Knowledge Quest Exhibit

Total Possible Exhibit Points: 16 out of 100 total possible for project

1. Game (5 points): Create and design a game based on your topic. The game should include information that will help others learn about your topic. Write a set of instructions that includes the following sections: (1) Number of Players, 2) Materials Needed to Play, (3) Object of the Game, (4) Rules, (5) Set-Up, (6) How to Play and (7) Scoring. Remember, this is a game; it should be fun as well as educational. **SYNTHESIS**

2. Prediction Illustration (4 points): Careful research about a topic's past and present can often give us clues about how that topic will develop in the future. Based on your research, create an illustration or series of illustrations that show how you think one aspect of your topic might change over time. Include descriptions and labels with your illustration. **SYNTHESIS**

3. Display Board (4 points): Use a large two- or three-panel display board to create an "advertisement" for your topic. Your display board must include your project's title, your name, an extra copy of your newspaper and your prediction illustration. You may then choose to add any additional materials that you wish. **SYNTHESIS**

4. Exhibit (3 points): Arrange your exhibit items, your portfolio and any additional materials you wish to include in an appealing and informative way. **SYNTHESIS**

COMPONENT 3:

Giving Your Classroom Presentation

Total Possible Classroom Presentation Points: 9 out of 100 total possible for project

1. What to Include in Your Presentation:

- Research Topic and Question (1 point): Share your topic and your original topic question, and explain why you chose them. **EVALUATION**

- Newspaper (2 points): Point out some special features of your newspaper, and read one of the articles aloud. **COMPREHENSION**

- Demonstration (5 points): Design and prepare a demonstration that teaches something about your topic. Your demonstration should last between one and three minutes. For your use, ahead of time, make a list of the materials you will use, along with the steps you will perform and the main point or points you wish to make. **SYNTHESIS**

2. Attire (1 point): Dress in clothing that relates to your topic. **SYNTHESIS**

TEACHER COPY CHART

Step Number	Form Title	Number of Copies
1.1	Teacher Planning Guide	1 only
2.1-2.3	Parent Knowledge Quest Introduction Letter Student Knowledge Quest Introduction Letter Student Instruction Guide	1 completed, then 1 per student 1 completed only 1 only
3.1-3.4	Teacher Forms Checklist Student Commitment Contract	1 completed only 1 completed, then 1 per student
3.5	Student Knowledge Quest Introduction Letter* Student Instruction Guide* Knowledge Quest Resource Card Appendix Pages* (optional)	1 completed, then one per student 1 per student 1 per student
4.1-4.2	Student Checkpoint Organizer Teacher Checkpoint Record	1 per student 1 completed only
5.1-5.2	Student Expo Invitation	1 completed, then one per student
5.9-5.11	Student Certificate Student Name Sign (optional) Left Arrow Sign Right Arrow Sign	1 per student, then each completed 1 per student, then each completed Amount needed Amount needed
5.12-5.13	Teacher Assessment Student Self-Assessment	1 per student 1 per student

* Staple these items into a packet for each student

*Events scheduled with the class are in black.

Week	Event (Step Numbers)	Day and Date	Time
1	Planning and Preparing for the Quarter (1.1-1.2)		
	Prepare for Knowledge Quest Introduction (2.1-2.3)		
	Knowledge Quest Introduction Day (2.4-2.7)		
	Preparation for Knowledge Quest Implementation (3.1-3.6)		
	Knowledge Quest Implementation Day (3.7-3.17)		
3	Preparation for the Checkpoint Meetings (4.1-4.2)		
	Distribute Checkpoint Organizers (4.3-4.6)		
	Checkpoint Meeting Day (4.7-4.12)		
5	Preparation for the Checkpoint Meetings (4.1-4.2)		
	Distribute Checkpoint Organizers (4.3-4.6)		
	Checkpoint Meeting Day (4.7-4.12)		
7	Preparation for the Checkpoint Meetings (4.1-4.2)		
	Distribute Checkpoint Organizers (4.3-4.6)		
	Checkpoint Meeting Day (4.7-4.12)		
8	Preparation for the Knowledge Quest Expo (5.1-5.2)		
	Invite Families to the Knowledge Quest Expo (5.3-5.4)		
	Preparation for the Knowledge Quest Expo Ctd. (5.5-5.11)		
9	Preparation for Classroom Presentations and the Knowledge Quest Expo (5.12-5.15)		
	Classroom Presentations Day (6A.1-6A.13 or 6B.1-6B.12)		
	Classroom Expo and Student Self-Assessment Day (7A.1-7A.9 or 7B.1-7B.10)		
10	Final Preparation for the Knowledge Quest Expo (8.1-8.10)		
	Knowledge Quest Expo Day (9.1-9.4)		
	Conclusion and Teacher Assessment (10.1-10.8)		
	Student Review (10.9-10.10)		

parent knowledge quest introduction letter

Dear Parent(s),

Welcome to Knowledge Quest, an Envision project that will challenge and inspire your child. Knowledge Quest is designed to enlighten your child about a topic of his or her choice. Your child will have the opportunity to choose a topic of interest and thoroughly research it, answering his or her own personal questions about it.

For this project, students will create a semantic map to explore their chosen topic. Their research will be showcased in a newspaper format created using the computer that requires the incorporation of various informational text structures and text features. They will also create and conduct a survey, create a double bar graph, compile a hot-list chart of websites and write a works cited list. For their exhibits, each student will design a game, make an illustration of personal predictions for the future of their topic and arrange a display board related to their topic of study. They will also prepare a demonstration that teaches something about their topic and present it during their Classroom Presentation and at the Knowledge Quest Expo.

A Student Instruction Guide will be provided to guide your child, step by step, through this process. The instruction guide is a comprehensive list of project requirements and is designed to engage higher-level thinking. The guide also references helpful resource cards, which provide additional explanation, ideas, tips and directions. There will be a set of these cards in our classroom to which your child may refer.

Knowledge Quest is designed to be worked on independently during class time, free time and at home. By scheduling several Checkpoint Meeting dates throughout the quarter, I will be able to monitor each student's progress. On these dates, I will meet with each student to discuss accomplishments and plan goals for the next checkpoint. I will also address any difficulties students might be having.

Knowledge Quest will conclude with a Project Expo. The expo will be your child's opportunity to share his or her finished project with family, friends and other guests. You will receive a detailed invitation to the Project Expo later in the quarter.

Dates to Remember:

Checkpoint 1: _____

Checkpoint 2: _____

Checkpoint 3: _____

Classroom Presentation: _____

Knowledge Quest Expo: _____ , _____

Sincerely,

_____

_____

student knowledge quest introduction letter

Dear Student,

Welcome to Knowledge Quest! This is a project you will embark on as part of the Envision Program experience. Knowledge Quest is about choosing a topic that you are interested in and investigating numerous aspects of it. It will be a voyage of discovery and an opportunity to learn information that you have always wondered about.

The project begins with creating a semantic map using the computer. You will use this map of questions to guide your research and discovery. You will showcase your findings by creating a newspaper that includes various articles and extra items. You will also create a survey, a computer-generated graph, a game and a demonstration.

This project contains four components. The first is to organize your research and project materials in a project portfolio. The second will be to create an exhibit of your topic and findings. The third will be to share your completed portfolio and exhibit with your classmates. To do this, you will give a brief formal presentation. During your presentation, you will explain key aspects of your topic findings and perform your demonstration. Fourth is the Project Expo, an event that celebrates your hard work and achievements. This final component allows you the opportunity to invite family and friends to share in your success. You will also perform your demonstration at the expo.

You will work on Knowledge Quest throughout the school day and, of course, during your free time and at home. Generally, you will be expected to work on your own. You will consult with me periodically at Checkpoint Meetings to discuss your progress and receive guidance. Between the checkpoints, feel free to discuss your project with other Envision students.

The attached Student Instruction Guide contains all the information you will need to complete the required Knowledge Quest Project successfully. The instruction guide will challenge you to be resourceful, organized and to think at a higher level.

Dates to Remember:

Checkpoint 1: _____

Checkpoint 2: _____

Checkpoint 3: _____

Classroom Presentation: _____

Knowledge Quest Expo: _____ , _____

After reading this introduction, you are now ready to begin thinking about a topic you would like to explore. Good luck and have fun!

Sincerely,

_____

_____

Building Your Project Portfolio • Creating Your Project Exhibit
Presenting Your Project • Attending the Expo

BE
CREATIVE!

IMPORTANT!

Resource cards are denoted by a Knowledge Quest icon . When you see one of these icons, you will know that there is a corresponding numbered resource card available that gives additional helpful information and examples. Also, be sure to visit www.mindvinepress.com, other trustworthy Internet sites, various newspapers and library reference materials for helpful resources and examples.

COMPONENT 1

Building Your Knowledge Quest Portfolio

Total Possible Portfolio Points: 75 out of 100 total possible for project

You are about to begin a quest for knowledge on a topic of your choice. This will be an opportunity to engage your curiosity, research new information and report your findings. Complete the numbered requirements below in order, as they build upon one another to guide you smoothly through the project.

Note: "Component 1: Building Your Project Portfolio" is separated into two sections: "Portfolio Section 1: Choosing and Researching Your Topic" and "Portfolio Section 2: Reporting Your Findings". Knowing ahead of time that Component 1 is made up of two related sections will help you organize your thoughts as you proceed.

Portfolio Section 1: Choosing and Researching Your Topic

1. Research Topic and Question (2 points): Think of a topic that you are interested in and do not know much about. Compose an interesting question about your topic that will guide your research. Below the question, write a paragraph or two explaining why you chose your topic.

2. Semantic Map (4 points): Create a semantic map using a computer. Begin by typing your topic question in the center of your document, then draw a circle around the question. In the space surrounding your question, add related questions that come to mind. Circle the new questions and draw lines that connect the newer questions to the older ones they relate to. Your semantic map should contain a minimum of ten new topic sub-questions that you would like to consider as you explore your main topic question. Use this semantic map to guide your project research.

3. Research and Notes (6 points): Using at least ten different sources, such as Internet websites, books, periodicals, journals and knowledgeable people you know, thoroughly research each of your semantic-map questions. Feel free to add to your map of questions as you go along, and to revise any existing questions. As you conduct your research, take careful notes using your own words on sheets of paper to place in your portfolio. Be sure to record the bibliographic information for each source as you take notes from it. You will need this information to identify your sources for the two portfolio requirements below. You may want to review the resource cards for the type of bibliographic information you should record.

4. Hot-List Chart (2 points): Create a chart that lists four to six of the most useful websites you found while researching your semantic-map questions. Your hot-list chart should include the name of each website, its web address and a brief summary of its content.

5. Works Cited (3 points): Create a works cited listing of all the books, articles, websites or other sources you received information from for your research and note taking. Follow the MLA style of documentation.

6. Survey (3 points): Create and conduct a survey based on your research to learn people's opinions or understanding about one or more interesting features of your topic. Survey a minimum of ten people. Be sure to record the gender and age of each person you talk to. You will need this demographic information to create the double bar graph described below.

7. Computer-Generated Double Bar Graph (3 points): Choose one question from your survey that produced interesting or surprising results. Classify the survey results for this question into two groups, such as gender groups or age groups, based on the demographic information that you recorded. Using a computer, create a double bar graph that compares the responses of each group for the question you chose.

Portfolio Section 2: Reporting Your Findings

1. Newspaper: For this portfolio section, you will design, write articles for and edit a newspaper dedicated to your topic. To begin, analyze various newspapers for layouts, features and writing styles. After becoming familiar with the format and content of a newspaper, you will be ready to begin working on yours. Your newspaper should be created on a computer and should include each of the elements listed below. In addition to your informational writing, feel free to use your creative writing skills. Follow the steps of the writing process when creating your newspaper and remember to include a newspaper title, day, date and index.

- Newspaper Articles (2 points each, total of 16 points): Write a minimum of eight articles for your newspaper. Each article should focus on one of the semantic-map questions you researched. Though your articles will contain information you gathered during your research, each must be written in your own words. Each article should begin with an intriguing lead sentence and conclude with a strong ending sentence. Read below first.

- Newspaper Informational Text Structures (2 points each, total of 16 points): Six of your eight articles should be written using a different informational text structure. The informational text structures are as follows: (1) Cause and Effect, (2) Compare and Contrast, (3) Description, (4) Problem and Solution, (5) Question and Answer and (6) Sequence. The remaining two or more articles can use any text structure you choose.

- Newspaper Text Features (1 point each, total of 7 points): Use each of the following text features at least one time throughout your newspaper. Try to spread them out rather than cluster them all in one or two articles. As you use the various text features in your newspaper, jot down the page number, article title and line number where the feature was added. When the final copy of your newspaper is completed, double check that you have recorded the locations correctly, and list them on a separate page in your portfolio so that your teacher can locate them quickly. Title the page "Locations of Text Features."

  ❑ centered headline or title   ❑ bullet points

  ❑ bold, italicized or underlined words   ❑ indented paragraph

  ❑ various font sizes   ❑ various font styles

  ❑ various font colors or highlights

- Newspaper Photos and Pictures (1 point each, total of 4 points): Insert a minimum of two photos and two pictures, clipart pictures or drawings, into your newspaper.

- Newspaper Choice Extras (2 points each, total of 6 points): Newspapers are made up of more than just articles, photos and pictures. They also contain "extra" items such as editorials, letters to the editor, advertisements, cartoons, classified ads, word search puzzles, crossword puzzles, graphs, charts and notices of all kinds. Go over the newspapers you analyzed earlier, and choose three of these "extras" to add to your newspaper. Create these three "extras" making them relevant to your central topic, and include them in your newspaper.

Remaining Portfolio Materials

1. **Table of Contents** (1 point): Write a table of contents that lists all the sections of your portfolio along with their corresponding page numbers.

2. **Cover Page** (1 point): Create an eye-catching cover page for your portfolio that includes an original title for your project as well as your name and the Classroom Presentation date.

3. **Portfolio** (1 point): Organize all of your materials in a three-ring binder. The table of contents should come first, followed by your work from Portfolio Sections 1 and 2 above in the order presented. Your cover page should be placed on the front of the portfolio.

You have completed Component 1 of the Knowledge Quest Project. By completing your portfolio, you have created an important resource that will help you work on Components 2 and 3. Though several worthy challenges lie ahead, you are now prepared to meet each of them, knowing that you have laid the necessary groundwork that will increase your chances for success. Good luck as you move on to creating your project exhibit items.

STUDENT INSTRUCTION GUIDE

COMPONENT 2

CREATING YOUR KNOWLEDGE QUEST EXHIBIT

Total Possible Exhibit Points: 16 out of 100 total possible for project

Having thoroughly researched your topic and organized the information you learned, it is now time to design and create an informative and appealing exhibit of your findings. The items you complete will be viewed by your classmates on the day of your Classroom Presentation and also by everyone who attends the Knowledge Quest Expo at the end of the term. As always, put your best work into designing, creating and integrating your exhibit items.

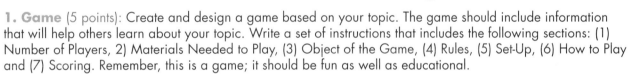

Note: Keep in mind that each item is only one part of the overall exhibit. In other words, no single item has to say everything about your project. Decide upon a purpose for each item. Consider how best to arrange your exhibit for the greatest effect.

1. Game (5 points): Create and design a game based on your topic. The game should include information that will help others learn about your topic. Write a set of instructions that includes the following sections: (1) Number of Players, 2) Materials Needed to Play, (3) Object of the Game, (4) Rules, (5) Set-Up, (6) How to Play and (7) Scoring. Remember, this is a game; it should be fun as well as educational.

2. Prediction Illustration (4 points): Careful research about a topic's past and present can often give us clues about how that topic will develop in the future. Based on your research, create an illustration or series of illustrations that show how you think one aspect of your topic might change over time. Include descriptions and labels with your illustration.

3. 📖 Display Board (4 points): Use a large two- or three-panel display board to create an "advertisement" for your topic. Your display board must include your project's title, your name, an extra copy of your newspaper and your prediction illustration. You may then choose to add any additional materials that you wish.

4. 📖 Exhibit (3 points): Arrange your exhibit items, your portfolio and any additional materials you wish to include in an appealing and informative way.

You have now completed Component 2 of the Knowledge Quest Project, an important exhibit that creatively displays your topic and findings. Now that you have finished your portfolio and exhibit, you are ready to confidently prepare for your Classroom Presentation (Component 3). Enjoy sharing your exciting project with your peers and teacher!

COMPONENT 3:

Giving Your Classroom Presentation
Total Possible Classroom Presentation Points: 9 out of 100 total possible for project

It is now time to share your topic knowledge with others. Your Classroom Presentation is an opportunity to formally present some of your findings and to share some of your hard work. Relax and have fun with it.

1. **What to Include in Your Presentation:**

• Research Topic and Question (1 point): Share your topic and your original topic question, and explain why you chose them.

• Newspaper (2 points): Point out some special features of your newspaper, and read one of the articles aloud.

• Demonstration (5 points): Design and prepare a demonstration that teaches something about your topic. Your demonstration should last between one and three minutes. For your use, ahead of time, make a list of the materials you will use, along with the steps you will perform and the main point or points you wish to make.

Note: Your classroom presentation should last three to four minutes and should be rehearsed, but not memorized. If you forget to include any required information, your teacher will ask you in a question form so that you have a chance to include it.

2. Attire (1 point): Dress in clothing that relates to your topic.

Bring to the Classroom Presentation:
All of your exhibit items and anything extra that you would like to enhance your exhibit. Also, remember to dress in clothing that reflects your topic.

You are now finished with Components 1, 2 and 3 - all of the assessed portions of your project. The final Component, Attending the Knowledge Quest Expo, provides a festive closure to the Knowledge Quest Project.

COMPONENT 4:

Attending the Knowledge Quest Expo (The expo does not involve any points.)

Now that you have completed your project and presented it to your peers, it's time to share your work with family and friends at the Knowledge Quest Expo. The expo is an event that recognizes and celebrates the hard work you have done on your Knowledge Quest Project. At the expo, you will set up and stand by your exhibit as invited guests walk around informally and view the projects. Guests may ask you friendly questions about your project as they visit your exhibit, so have fun sharing your Knowledge Quest findings with them. You will also be asked, each student in turn, to perform your demonstration for the attendees.

Bring to the Expo: all of your exhibit items, including your demonstration materials, and anything extra that you would like to enhance your exhibit. Also, remember to dress in clothing that reflects your topic.

CONGRATULATIONS ON YOUR COMPLETED KNOWLEDGE QUEST PROJECT!

TEACHER FORMS CHECKLIST

use this checklist to record forms submitted by the students

student name	student commitment contract	student checkpoint organizer 1	student checkpoint organizer 2	student checkpoint organizer 3	expo invitation response	
					number attending	special equip.needed
1.						
2.						
3.						
4.						
5.						
6.						
7.						
8.						
9.						
10.						
11.						
12.						
13.						
14.						
15.						
16.						
17.						
18.						
19.						
20.						
21.						
22.						
23.						
24.						
25.						

STUDENT COMMITMENT CONTRACT

expectations

project work time

I agree to:

- be responsible for following my Student Instruction Guide to do my work.
- keep track of all my project materials.
- work hard on Envision without disturbing others.
- save my unanswered questions until my teacher is free to talk.

checkpoint meetings

I will come prepared with:

- my Student Instruction Guide.
- my completed Student Checkpoint Organizer.
- all of my project materials.

important dates and times

Checkpoint 1: _____

Checkpoint 2: _____

Checkpoint 3: _____

Classroom Presentation: _____

Knowledge Quest Expo: _____

_____

signatures

I agree to:

- meet expectations on the dates listed above.
- complete each of the Knowledge Quest requirements to the best of my ability.
- bring my project work to school each day so that I can work on it during extra time.
- take my project work from school each night so that I can work on it at home.

I understand that the Envision Knowledge Quest Project is a special opportunity, and that if I do not meet the above expectations, I may be asked to return to normal classroom activities.

Student Signature: _____ Date: _____

Parent Signature: _____ Date: _____

Please return this contract by: _____

STUDENT CHECKPOINT ORGANIZER

Student Name: _____ Checkpoint Date: _____

My Topic Question: _____

directions

1. Using your Student Instruction Guide, check off any requirements that you have completed up to this point.

2. Bring the following items to the Checkpoint Meeting:

• your Student Instruction Guide.

• your completed Student Checkpoint Organizer.

• all of your project materials.

questions

1. Which requirements have you completed up to this point?

_____

_____

2. Is there anything you need help with?

_____

_____

3. Is there anything else about your project that you would like to discuss?

_____

_____

4. List at least three goals you expect to accomplish by the next checkpoint.

_____

_____

TEACHER CHECKPOINT RECORD

student name	research topic	checkpoint 1 notes	checkpoint 2 notes	checkpoint 3 notes
1.				
2.				
3.				
4.				
5.				
6.				
7.				
8.				
9.				
10.				

KNOWLEDGE QUEST

YOU'RE INVITED!

EXPO INVITATION RESPONSE

Please fill out and return by: _____

Student Name: _____

Student Attending? ☐ Yes ☐ No

Number of Student Guests Attending: _____

Will your child need any special school equipment for

the expo (i.e., computer or TV)? Please List: _____

_____

Thank you.

We look forward to seeing you at this special event!

KNOWLEDGE QUEST

PLEASE JOIN US FOR OUR ENVISION KNOWLEDGE QUEST EXPO!

Why? _____

Who? _____

Where? _____

When? _____

Remember to bring your camera!

KNOWLEDGE QUEST

CERTIFICATE OF ACHIEVEMENT

AWARDED TO

DATE

SIGNATURE

envision®

KNOWLEDGE QUEST PROJECT

STUDENT

envision®

knowledge quest quest expo

envision®

knowledge quest expo

envision®

TEACHER ASSESSMENT

Component 1: Building Your Knowledge Quest Portfolio
Total Possible Portfolio Points: 75 out of 100 total possible for project

Requirements	Possible Points	Teacher Points	Average Points
Portfolio Section 1: Choosing and Researching Your Topic			
1. Research Topic and Question: Think of a topic that you are interested in and do not know much about. Compose an interesting question about your topic that will guide your research. Below the question, write a paragraph or two explaining why you chose your topic.	2		
2. Semantic Map: Create a semantic map using a computer. Begin by typing your topic question in the center of your document, then draw a circle around the question. In the space surrounding your question, add related questions that come to mind. Circle the new questions and draw lines that connect the newer questions to the older ones they relate to. Your semantic map should contain a minimum of ten new topic sub-questions that you would like to consider as you explore your main topic question. Use this semantic map to guide your project research.	4		
3. Research and Notes: Using at least ten different sources, such as Internet websites, books, periodicals, journals and knowledgeable people you know, thoroughly research each of your semantic-map questions. Feel free to add to your map of questions as you go along, and to revise any existing questions. As you conduct your research, take careful notes using your own words on sheets of paper to place in your portfolio. Be sure to record the bibliographic information for each source as you take notes from it. You will need this information to identify your sources for the two portfolio requirements below. You may want to review the resource cards for the type of bibliographic information you should record.	6		
4. Hot-List Chart: Create a chart that lists four to six of the most useful websites you found while researching your semantic-map questions. Your hot-list chart should include the name of each website, its web address and a brief summary of its content.	2		
5. Works Cited: Create a works cited listing of all the books, articles, websites or other sources you received information from for your research and note taking. Follow the MLA style of documentation.	3		
6. Survey: Create and conduct a survey based on your research to learn people's opinions or understanding about one or more interesting features of your topic. Survey a minimum of ten people. Be sure to record the gender and age of each person you talk to. You will need this demographic information to create the double bar graph described below.	3		
7. Computer-Generated Double Bar Graph: Choose one question from your survey that produced interesting or surprising results. Classify the survey results for this question into two groups, such as gender groups or age groups, based on the demographic information that you recorded. Using a computer, create a double bar graph that compares the responses of each group for the question you chose.	3		

Portfolio Section 2: Reporting Your Findings

1. Newspaper:			
• Newspaper Articles: Write a minimum of eight articles for your newspaper. Each article should focus on one of the semantic-map questions you researched. Though your articles will contain information you gathered during your research, each must be written in your own words. Each article should begin with an intriguing lead sentence and conclude with a strong ending sentence.	16		
• Newspaper Informational Text Structures: Six of your eight articles should be written using a different informational text structure. The informational text structures are as follows: (1) Cause and Effect, (2) Compare and Contrast, (3) Description, (4) Problem and Solution, (5) Question and Answer and (6) Sequence. The remaining two or more articles can use any text structure you choose.	16		
• Newspaper Text Features: Use each of the following text features at least one time throughout your newspaper. Try to spread them out rather than cluster them all in one or two articles. As you use the various text features in your newspaper, jot down the page number, article title and line number where the feature was added. When the final copy of your newspaper is completed, double check that you have recorded the locations correctly, and list them on a separate page in your portfolio so that your teacher can locate them quickly. Title the page "Locations of Text Features." ❑ centered headline or title; ❑ bullet points, ❑ bold, italicized or underlined words; ❑ indented paragraph; ❑ various font sizes; ❑ various font styles; ❑ various font colors or highlights	7		
• Newspaper Photos and Pictures: Insert a minimum of two photos and two pictures, clipart pictures or drawings, into your newspaper.	4		
• Newspaper Choice Extras: Newspapers are made up of more than just articles, photos and pictures. They also contain "extra" items such as editorials, letters to the editor, advertisements, cartoons, classified ads, word search puzzles, crossword puzzles, graphs, charts and notices of all kinds. Go over the newspapers you analyzed earlier, and choose three of these "extras" to add to your newspaper. Create these three "extras" making them relevant to your central topic, and include them in your newspaper.	6		
Remaining Portfolio Materials			
1. Table of Contents: Write a table of contents that lists all the sections of your portfolio along with their corresponding page numbers.	1		
2. Cover Page: Create an eye-catching cover page for your portfolio that includes an original title for your project as well as your name and the Classroom Presentation date.	1		
3. Portfolio: Organize all of your materials in a three-ring binder (portfolio). The table of contents should come first, followed by your work from Portfolio Sections 1, 2 and 3 above in the order presented. Your cover page should be placed on the front of the portfolio.	1		
TOTAL PORTFOLIO POINTS	**75**		

Component 2: Creating Your Knowledge Quest Exhibit
Total Possible Exhibit Points: 16 out of 100 total possible for project

1. Game: Create and design a game based on your topic. The game should include information that will help others learn about your topic. Write a set of instructions that includes the following sections: (1) Number of Players, 2) Materials Needed to Play, (3) Object of the Game, (4) Rules, (5) Set-Up, (6) How to Play and (7) Scoring. Remember, this is a game; it should be fun as well as educational.	5		
2. Prediction Illustration: Careful research about a topic's past and present can often give us clues about how that topic will develop in the future. Based on your research, create an illustration or series of illustrations that show how you think one aspect of your topic might change over time. Include descriptions and labels with your illustration.	4		
3. Display Board: Use a large two- or three-panel display board to create an "advertisement" for your topic. Your display board must include your project's title, your name, an extra copy of your newspaper and your prediction illustration. You may then choose to add any additional materials that you wish.	4		
4. Exhibit: Arrange your exhibit items, your portfolio and any additional materials you wish to include in an appealing and informative way.	3		
TOTAL EXHIBIT POINTS	**16**		

Component 3: Giving Your Classroom Presentation
Total Possible Classroom Presentation Points: 9 out of 100 total possible for project

1. What to Include in Your Presentation: • Research Topic and Question: Share your topic and your original topic question, and explain why you chose them.	1		
• Newspaper: Point out some special features of your newspaper, and read one of the articles aloud.	2		
• Demonstration: Design and prepare a demonstration that teaches something about your topic. Your demonstration should last between one and three minutes. For your use, ahead of time, make a list of the materials you will use, along with the steps you will perform and the main point or points you wish to make.	5		
2. Attire: Dress in clothing that relates to your topic.	1		
TOTAL CLASSROOM PRESENTATION POINTS	**9**		
TOTAL PROJECT POINTS	**100**		

STUDENT SELF-ASSESSMENT

Component 1: Building Your Knowledge Quest Portfolio
Total Possible Portfolio Points: 75 out of 100 total possible for project

Requirements	Possible Points	Student Points
Portfolio Section 1: Choosing and Researching Your Topic		
1. Research Topic and Question: Think of a topic that you are interested in and do not know much about. Compose an interesting question about your topic that will guide your research. Below the question, write a paragraph or two explaining why you chose your topic.	2	
2. Semantic Map: Create a semantic map using a computer. Begin by typing your topic question in the center of your document, then draw a circle around the question. In the space surrounding your question, add related questions that come to mind. Circle the new questions and draw lines that connect the newer questions to the older ones they relate to. Your semantic map should contain a minimum of ten new topic sub-questions that you would like to consider as you explore your main topic question. Use this semantic map to guide your project research.	4	
3. Research and Notes: Using at least ten different sources, such as Internet websites, books, periodicals, journals and knowledgeable people you know, thoroughly research each of your semantic-map questions. Feel free to add to your map of questions as you go along, and to revise any existing questions. As you conduct your research, take careful notes using your own words on sheets of paper to place in your portfolio. Be sure to record the bibliographic information for each source as you take notes from it. You will need this information to identify your sources for the two portfolio requirements below. You may want to review the resource cards for the type of bibliographic information you should record.	6	
4. Hot-List Chart: Create a chart that lists four to six of the most useful websites you found while researching your semantic-map questions. Your hot-list chart should include the name of each website, its web address and a brief summary of its content.	2	
5. Works Cited: Create a works cited listing of all the books, articles, websites or other sources you received information from for your research and note taking. Follow the MLA style of documentation.	3	
6. Survey: Create and conduct a survey based on your research to learn people's opinions or understanding about one or more interesting features of your topic. Survey a minimum of ten people. Be sure to record the gender and age of each person you talk to. You will need this demographic information to create the double bar graph described below.	3	
7. Computer-Generated Double Bar Graph: Choose one question from your survey that produced interesting or surprising results. Classify the survey results for this question into two groups, such as gender groups or age groups, based on the demographic information that you recorded. Using a computer, create a double bar graph that compares the responses of each group for the question you chose.	3	

Portfolio Section 2: Reporting Your Findings

1. Newspaper:		
• Newspaper Articles: Write a minimum of eight articles for your newspaper. Each article should focus on one of the semantic-map questions you researched. Though your articles will contain information you gathered during your research, each must be written in your own words. Each article should begin with an intriguing lead sentence and conclude with a strong ending sentence.	16	
• Newspaper Informational Text Structures: Six of your eight articles should be written using a different informational text structure. The informational text structures are as follows: (1) Cause and Effect, (2) Compare and Contrast, (3) Description, (4) Problem and Solution, (5) Question and Answer and (6) Sequence. The remaining two or more articles can use any text structure you choose.	16	
• Newspaper Text Features: Use each of the following text features at least one time throughout your newspaper. Try to spread them out rather than cluster them all in one or two articles. As you use the various text features in your newspaper, jot down the page number, article title and line number where the feature was added. When the final copy of your newspaper is completed, double check that you have recorded the locations correctly, and list them on a separate page in your portfolio so that your teacher can locate them quickly. Title the page "Locations of Text Features." ❑ centered headline or title; ❑ bullet points, ❑ bold, italicized or underlined words; ❑ indented paragraph; ❑ various font sizes; ❑ various font styles; ❑ various font colors or highlights	7	
• Newspaper Photos and Pictures: Insert a minimum of two photos and two pictures, clipart pictures or drawings, into your newspaper.	4	
• Newspaper Choice Extras: Newspapers are made up of more than just articles, photos and pictures. They also contain "extra" items such as editorials, letters to the editor, advertisements, cartoons, classified ads, word search puzzles, crossword puzzles, graphs, charts and notices of all kinds. Go over the newspapers you analyzed earlier, and choose three of these "extras" to add to your newspaper. Create these three "extras" making them relevant to your central topic, and include them in your newspaper.	6	
Remaining Portfolio Materials		
1. Table of Contents: Write a table of contents that lists all the sections of your portfolio along with their corresponding page numbers.	1	
2. Cover Page: Create an eye-catching cover page for your portfolio that includes an original title for your project as well as your name and the Classroom Presentation date.	1	
3. Portfolio: Organize all of your materials in a three-ring binder (portfolio). The table of contents should come first, followed by your work from Portfolio Sections 1, 2 and 3 above in the order presented. Your cover page should be placed on the front of the portfolio.	1	
TOTAL PORTFOLIO POINTS	**75**	

Component 2: Creating Your Knowledge Quest Exhibit
Total Possible Exhibit Points: 16 out of 100 total possible for project

1. Game: Create and design a game based on your topic. The game should include information that will help others learn about your topic. Write a set of instructions that includes the following sections: (1) Number of Players, 2) Materials Needed to Play, (3) Object of the Game, (4) Rules, (5) Set-Up, (6) How to Play and (7) Scoring. Remember, this is a game; it should be fun as well as educational.	5	
2. Prediction Illustration: Careful research about a topic's past and present can often give us clues about how that topic will develop in the future. Based on your research, create an illustration or series of illustrations that show how you think one aspect of your topic might change over time. Include descriptions and labels with your illustration.	4	
3. Display Board: Use a large two- or three-panel display board to create an "advertisement" for your topic. Your display board must include your project's title, your name, an extra copy of your newspaper and your prediction illustration. You may then choose to add any additional materials that you wish.	4	
4. Exhibit: Arrange your exhibit items, your portfolio and any additional materials you wish to include in an appealing and informative way.	3	
TOTAL EXHIBIT POINTS	**16**	

Component 3: Giving Your Classroom Presentation
Total Possible Classroom Presentation Points: 9 out of 100 total possible for project

1. What to Include in Your Presentation:		
• Research Topic and Question: Share your topic and your original topic question, and explain why you chose them.	1	
• Newspaper: Point out some special features of your newspaper, and read one of the articles aloud.	2	
• Demonstration: Design and prepare a demonstration that teaches something about your topic. Your demonstration should last between one and three minutes. For your use, ahead of time, make a list of the materials you will use, along with the steps you will perform and the main point or points you wish to make.	5	
2. Attire: Dress in clothing that relates to your topic.	1	
TOTAL CLASSROOM PRESENTATION POINTS	**9**	
TOTAL PROJECT POINTS	**100**	

SPANISH TRANSLATIONS OF PARENT FORMS AND STUDENT INSTRUCTION GUIDE

carta de introducción para padres del proyecto búsqueda de conocimiento

Estimados Padres,

Bienvenidos a "Búsqueda de Conocimiento", un proyecto de "Envision" que inspirará y mantendrá la atención educativa de su hijo/a. "Búsqueda de Conocimiento" está diseñado para informar a su hijo/a acerca de un tema de su elección. Su hijo/a tendrá la oportunidad de elegir un tema de interés, investigarlo a fondo, y responder sus propias preguntas sobre el tema.

Para este proyecto, los estudiantes crearán un mapa semántico para explorar el tema que eligieron. Sus investigaciones se presentarán en un formato de periódico hecho en computadora, que requiere la incorporación de estructuras informativas de texto y características de texto. Los estudiantes crearán y realizarán una encuesta, elaborarán una gráfica de barras dobles, recopilarán una lista de los sitios web más populares y escribirán una bibliografía. Para sus exhibiciones cada estudiante diseñará un juego, harán una ilustración de sus predicciones personales para el futuro de su tema y organizarán un tablero para mostrar su tema de estudio. Ellos también prepararán una demostración que enseñe algo acerca de su tema y lo presentarán en la Presentación en el Salón de Clase y en la Exposición "Búsqueda de Conocimiento".

Una Guía Estudiantil será proveída para orientar al estudiante paso por paso y guiarlo por este proceso. La Guía Estudiantil es una lista completa que indica los requisitos de este proyecto y está diseñada para guiar al alumno a que comience a pensar usando un nivel superior. La guía también menciona las Tarjetas de Recursos que proveen explicaciones adicionales, ideas, consejos, y otra información. Estas tarjetas también estarán disponibles en el salón de su hijo/a para el uso de él/ella.

El proyecto "Búsqueda de Conocimiento" está diseñado para que el alumno pueda trabajar independientemente en su salón, durante su tiempo libre y en casa. "Juntas de Revisión" están programadas durante el proyecto para que yo esté al pendiente del progreso del estudiante. En las fechas indicadas, el estudiante y yo nos reuniremos para discutir sus logros y para planear nuevas metas para la siguiente junta. También, veremos si el estudiante ha tenido dificultades o si tiene algunas preguntas.

"Búsqueda de Conocimiento" se terminará en una "Exposición de Proyectos". Esta Exposición dará una oportunidad al estudiante a que comparta su trabajo y sus experiencias con su familia, amigos, e invitados. Usted recibirá una invitación para la "Exposición de Proyectos" más adelante en el trimestre.

Fechas para recordar:

Revisión 1: _____

Revisión 2: _____

Revisión 3: _____

Presentación en el Salón de Clase: _____

Exposición "Búsqueda de Conocimiento": _____ , _____

Sinceramente,

_____

_____

CONTRATO DE COMPROMISO ESTUDIANTIL

expectativas

tiempo de proyecto

Acepto:

- seguir los pasos indicados en mi guía estudiantil mientras que hago mi trabajo.
- mantener en orden mis materiales de proyecto.
- trabajar duro en Envision sin molestar a otros.
- mantener mis preguntas para mi mismo, hasta que mi maestro/a esté libre para hablar.

juntas de revisión

Vendré preparado con:

- mi Guía Estudiantil.
- mi Organizador Estudiantil.
- todos los materiales necesarios para el proyecto.

fechas importantes

Revisión 1: _____

Revisión 2: _____

Revisión 3: _____

Presentación en el Salón de Clase: _____

Exposición "Búsqueda de Conocimiento": _____

_____

firmas

Acepto:

- cumplir con las expectativas en las fechas citadas anteriormente.
- utilizaré mis mejores habilidades y conocimientos para completar los requisitos de "Búsqueda de Conocimiento".
- traer mi proyecto a la escuela todos los días, así podré trabajar en él durante mi tiempo libre.
- llevar mi proyecto a la casa todos los días, así podré trabajar en casa.

Entiendo que el proyecto Búsqueda de " Conocimiento" de Envision es una oportunidad especial, y si no cumplo con las expectativas mencionadas existe la posibilidad de que tenga que regresar a las actividades normales de mi salón de clase.

Firma del Estudiante: _____ Fecha: _____

Firma del Padre: _____ Fecha: _____

Por favor devuelva este contrato antes de: _____

Construyendo el Portafolio de Tu Proyecto • Creando la Exhibición de tu Proyecto • Presentando tu Proyecto • Asistiendo a la Exposición

SE CREATIVO!

IMPORTANTE!

Las tarjetas de recursos se indican mediante un ícono de Búsqueda de Conocimiento. Cuando veas uno de estos símbolos, sabrás que hay una tarjeta correspondiente numerada disponible que te da información adicional útil y ejemplos visuales para tu referencia. También, asegúrate de visitar www.mindvinepress.com, otros sitios de Internet confiables, varios periódicos y materiales de referencia de la biblioteca para encontrar recursos útiles y ejemplos.

COMPONENTE 1
Construyendo tu Portafolio de Búsqueda de Conocimiento
Total de Puntos Posibles por el Portafolio: 75 de un total de 100 por el proyecto

Estás a punto de empezar una búsqueda de conocimiento sobre un tema que tú escogiste. Esta será una oportunidad para despertar tu curiosidad, investigar nueva información y reportar lo que hayas encontrado. Completa los requisitos enumerados a continuación en el mismo orden en que estos se presentan. Estos requisitos dependen uno de otro y te guiarán sin problemas a través de este proyecto.

Nota: "Componente 1: Construyendo tu "Portafolio de Proyecto" está separado en dos secciones: "Portafolio Sección 1: Escogiendo e Investigando tu Tema" y 2: "Reportando lo que Encontraste". Saber de antemano que el Componente 1 tiene dos secciones relacionadas te ayudará a organizar tus ideas mientras lo haces.

Portafolio Sección 1: Escogiendo e Investigando tu Tema

1. **Tema de Investigación y Pregunta** (2 puntos): Piensa en un tema que te interese y del cual no sepas mucho acerca de este. Elabora una pregunta interesante acerca de tu tema que guiará tu investigación. Enseguida de tu pregunta, escribe un párrafo o dos explicando por qué elegiste este tema.

2. Mapa Semántico (4 puntos): Crea un mapa semántico usando una computadora. Empieza por escribir tu pregunta del tema en el centro de tu documento. Luego dibuja un círculo alrededor de la pregunta. En el espacio que rodea a tu pregunta, añade preguntas relacionadas que te vengan a la mente. Circula las preguntas nuevas y dibuja o traza líneas que conecten las preguntas más nuevas con las primeras que estén relacionadas. Tu mapa semántico deberá incluir un mínimo de diez nuevas sub-preguntas que se relacionen con tu tema y que te gustaría considerar mientras exploras la pregunta principal de tu tema. Usa este mapa semántico para guiar la investigación de tu proyecto.

3. Investigación y Notas (6 puntos): Usando al menos diez diferentes fuentes, tales como sitios de Internet, libros, periódicos, revistas, y personas con conocimiento que conozcas, haz una investigación que complete y amplíe cada una de las preguntas de tu mapa semántico. Siéntete libre de añadir preguntas a tu mapa semántico durante tu investigación y de revisar cualquiera de las que ya tenías. Mientras llevas a cabo tu investigación, toma notas usando tus propias palabras en hojas de papel que puedas poner en tu portafolio. Asegúrate de anotar la información bibliográfica de cada una de las fuentes mientras tomas notas de ellas. Necesitarás esta información para identificar tus fuentes para los dos requisitos de tu portafolio a continuación. Sería bueno que revisaras las tarjetas de recursos para saber el tipo de información bibliográfica que deberás registrar.

4. Lista de Sitios de Internet Útiles (2 puntos): Haz una tabla que incluya de cuatro a seis de los sitios de internet más útiles que hayas encontrado mientras investigabas las preguntas de tu mapa semántico. Tu tabla deberá incluir el nombre de cada sitio, la dirección electrónica y una breve descripción de su contenido.

5. Bibliografía (3 puntos): Crea una fuente bibliográfica listando todos los libros, artículos, sitios de internet u otras fuentes de las cuales recibiste información y tomaste notas durante tu investigación. Sigue el estilo de documentación de MLA (Asociación de Lenguaje Moderno).

6. Encuesta (3 puntos): Crea y realiza una entrevista basada en tu investigación para conocer la opinión de la gente o su entendimiento acerca de una o más de las características interesantes de tu tema. Entrevista a un mínimo de 10 personas. Asegúrate de registrar el género y edad de cada una de las personas con las que hables. Vas a necesitar esta información para crear la gráfica de doble barra descrita enseguida.

7. Gráfica de Doble Barra hecha con Computadora (3 puntos): Escoge una pregunta de tu encuesta que haya producido resultados interesantes o sorprendentes. Clasifica los resultados de tu encuesta para esta pregunta en dos grupos, tales como grupos por género o grupos por edad, basado en la información demográfica que registraste. Usando una computadora, haz una gráfica de doble barra que compare las respuestas de cada grupo para la pregunta que elegiste.

Portafolio Sección 2: Reportando lo que Encontraste

1. Periódico: Para esta sección del portafolio, vas a diseñar, escribir artículos y editar un periódico dedicado a tu tema. Para empezar, analiza varios periódicos para informarte de los formatos, características y estilos de escritura. Después de familiarizarte con el formato y contenido de un periódico, tú estarás listo para empezar a trabajar en el tuyo. Tu periódico deberá ser hecho en computadora y deberá incluir los elementos que se listan enseguida. Adicionalmente a tu escritura informal, siéntete libre de usar tus habilidades creativas de escritura. Cuando crees tu periódico, sigue los pasos del proceso de escritura y recuerda incluir el título del periódico, día, fecha y un índice.

- Artículos para el Periódico (2 puntos cada uno, de un total 16 puntos): Escribe un mínimo de ocho artículos para el periódico. Cada artículo deberá enfocarse en una de las preguntas de tu mapa semántico que investigaste. Aun cuando los artículos contendrán información que reuniste durante tu investigación, cada uno deberá estar escrito en tus propias palabras. Cada artículo deberá comenzar con una oración intrigante (una oración que haga al lector interesarse), y terminar con una oración firme al final. Primero lee lo siguiente.

- Estructura Informativa del Texto para el Periódico (2 puntos cada uno, de un total de 16 puntos): Seis de tus ocho artículos deberán ser escritos utilizando diferentes estructuras informativas de texto. Las estructuras informativas de texto son como sigue: (1) Causa y Efecto, (2) Comparación y Contraste, (3) Descripción, (4) Problema y Solución, (5) Pregunta y Respuesta y (6) Secuencia. Los dos artículos restantes pueden usar la estructura de texto que tú elijas.

- Características del Texto para un Periódico (1 punto cada una, de un total de 7 puntos): Usa cada una de las siguientes características de texto por lo menos una vez en tu periódico. Trata de repartirlas en lugar de poner todas ellas en uno o dos artículos. Cuando vayas usando las diferentes características de texto en tu periódico, anota el número de página, título del artículo y número de línea en donde usaste esa característica. Una vez que la copia final de tu periódico este completa, verifica doblemente que hayas registrado los lugares correctamente y haz una lista de ellas en una hoja aparte en tu portafolio para que tu maestro pueda localizarlas rápidamente. Titula la página "Localización de las Características de Texto."

    ❏ título o encabezado centrado
    ❏ palabras subrayadas, recalcadas o cursivas
    ❏ varios tamaños de letra
    ❏ varias fuentes de colores o resaltado

    ❏ puntos importantes
    ❏ párrafo sangrado
    ❏ varias fuentes de estilo de letras

- Fotos y Dibujos para el Periódico (1 punto cada una, de un total de 4 puntos): Inserta un mínimo de dos fotos, dos imágenes, imágenes prediseñadas o dibujos, en tu periódico.

- Extras en el Periódico (2 puntos cada una, de un total de 6 puntos): Los periódicos no solo se componen de artículos, fotos e imágenes. También contienen "extras" tales como los editoriales, cartas al editor, anuncios, caricaturas, anuncios clasificados, crucigramas, gráficas, tablas y noticias de todo tipo. Repasa los periódicos que analizaste primero y elige tres "extras" para añadir a tu periódico. Crea estos tres tipos de "extras" de manera que se relacionen con tu tema central e inclúyelos en tu periódico.

Materiales Restantes del Portafolio

1. **Tabla de Contenido o Índice** (1 punto): Escribe una tabla de contenido o índice que indique todas las secciones de tu portafolio y los números de páginas correspondientes.

2. **Cubierta o Portada** (1 punto): Crea una cubierta o portada llamativa para tu portafolio que incluya un título original para tu proyecto así como también tu nombre y la fecha de presentación en el Salón de Clase.

3. **Portafolio** (1 punto): Organiza todos tus materiales en una carpeta de tres argollas. La tabla de contenido o índice deberá ir primero, seguida de tu trabajo para el Portafolio de las Secciones 1 y 2 en el orden en que se presentan. Tu cubierta debe ir al frente de tu portafolio.

Has completado el Componente número 1 de tu Proyecto de Búsqueda de Conocimiento. Al completar tu portafolio, has creado un importante recurso que te ayudará para trabajar en los Componentes 2 y 3. Aun cuando tienes algunos retos importantes por venir, tú estás ahora preparado para llevarlos a cabo, sabiendo que has puesto los fundamentos necesarios para aumentar tus posibilidades de éxito. Buena suerte en tanto avanzas a la creación de los artículos a exhibir en tu proyecto.

COMPONENTE 2

CREANDO TU EXHIBICION DE BUSQUEDA DE CONOCIMIENTO

Total de Puntos Posibles por la Exhibición: 16 de un total de 100 por el proyecto

Habiendo investigado minuciosamente tu tema y organizado la información que aprendiste, es ahora el tiempo de diseñar y crear una exhibición atractiva e informativa de lo que encontraste. El trabajo que has terminado será visto por tus compañeros el día de la Presentación en el Salón de Clase y también por aquellos que asistan a la Exposición de Búsqueda de Conocimiento al final del término. Como siempre, pon tu mejor esfuerzo para diseñar, crear e integrar las cosas que vas a exhibir.

Nota: Recuerda que cada elemento es solo una parte de tu exhibición total. En otras palabras, un solo elemento no tiene que decir todo acerca de tu proyecto. Decide el propósito de cada elemento. Considera la mejor manera de organizar tu exhibición para tener un mayor efecto.

1. Juego (5 puntos): Crea y diseña un juego basado en tu tema. El juego deberá incluir información que ayude a otros a aprender sobre tu tema. Escribe un grupo de instrucciones que incluya las siguientes secciones: (1) Número de Jugadores, 2) Materiales Necesarios para Jugar, (3) Objetivo del Juego, (4) Reglas, (5) Como Iniciarlo, (6) Como Jugarlo y (7) Puntaje. Recuerda, este es un juego; debe ser tanto divertido como educativo.

2. Ilustrar una Predicción (4 puntos): Una investigación cuidadosa acerca del pasado y presente de un tema puede a menudo darnos pistas acerca de cómo se desarrollará este tema en el futuro. Basado en tu investigación, crea una ilustración o una serie de ilustraciones que muestren como piensas que un aspecto de tu tema podría cambiar con el tiempo. Incluye descripciones y etiquetas con tu ilustración.

3. 📖 Tablero de Exhibición (4 puntos): Utiliza un tablero de exhibición de dos o tres paneles (secciones) para crear un "anuncio" de tu tema. Tu tablero de exhibición deberá incluir el título de tu proyecto, tu nombre, una copia extra de tu periódico y tu ilustración de predicción. Puedes elegir añadir el material adicional que tú desees.

4. 📖 Exhibición (3 puntos): Organiza y ordena las cosas que vas a exhibir, tu portafolio y todos los materiales adicionales que hayas decidido incluir de una manera informativa y atractiva.

Has completado el componente 2 de tu Proyecto Búsqueda de Conocimiento, una importante exhibición que de una manera creativa muestra tu tema y hallazgos. Ahora que has terminado tu portafolio y tu exhibición, estás listo para prepararte con confianza para tu Presentación en el Salón de Clase (Componente 3). Disfruta compartiendo tu proyecto con tus compañeros y maestro!

COMPONENTE 3:

Dando Tu Presentación en el Salón de Clase
Total de Puntos Posibles por tu Presentación en el Salón de Clase: 9 de un total de 100 por el proyecto

Ahora es tiempo de compartir tus planes con otros. La Presentación en el Salón de Clase es una oportunidad para que formalmente presentes algunas de tus metas y compartir algo del arduo trabajo que has hecho. Relájate y diviértete con esto.

1. Que Incluir en Tu Presentación:

- El Tema de Investigación y la Pregunta (1 punto): Comparte tu tema y tu pregunta original del tema, y explica por qué los elegiste.

- Periódico (2 puntos): Señala algunas de las características especiales de tu periódico, y lee en voz alta uno de los artículos que incluiste.

- Demostración (5 puntos): Diseña y prepara una demostración que muestre algo acerca de tu tema. Tu demostración deberá durar entre uno y tres minutos. Para tu uso, prepara desde antes una lista de los materiales que usarás, junto con los pasos que vas a seguir y el punto o puntos principales que quieres cubrir.

> **Nota:** La presentación en tu salón deberá durar de tres a cuatro minutos y puede ser ensayada pero no memorizada. Si olvidas incluir alguna información requerida, tu maestro te hará una pregunta relacionada para que puedas incluir esa parte en tu presentación.

2. Atuendo o Vestimenta (1 punto): Viste con ropa relacionada con tu tema.

Que Traer a tu Presentación en el Salón de Clase:
Todas las cosas de tu exhibición y cualquier cosa extra que tú creas que te pueda ayudar a ampliar y mejorar tu exhibición. Además, recuerda vestir ropa que se relacione con tu tema.

Has terminado los Componentes 1, 2 y 3 – todas las porciones que serán evaluadas de tu proyecto. El Componente final, Asistiendo a la Exposición de Búsqueda de Conocimiento, te da un cierre o final maravilloso para tu Proyecto de Búsqueda de Conocimiento.

COMPONENTE 4:

Asistiendo a la Exposición de Búsqueda de Conocimiento (La exposición no te da puntos.)

Ahora que has terminado tu proyecto y lo has presentado a tus compañeros, es tiempo de compartir tu trabajo con tu familia y amigos en la Exposición de Búsqueda de Conocimiento. La exposición es un evento que reconoce y celebra el duro trabajo que has hecho para hacer posible tu Proyecto de Búsqueda de Conocimiento. En la exposición, tú colocarás tu exhibición y permanecerás al lado de tu exhibición mientras los invitados caminan y observan los proyectos. Los invitados pueden hacer algunas preguntas acerca de tu proyecto, así que disfruta y diviértete compartiendo las experiencias de tu Búsqueda de Conocimiento con ellos. Se le pedirá a cada uno de los estudiantes por turno que haga una demostración para los asistentes.

Que Traer a la Exposición: Todas las cosas de tu exhibición y cualquier cosa extra que tú quieras que te pueda ayudar a ampliar y mejorar tu exhibición. Además, recuerda vestir ropa que se relacione con tu tema.

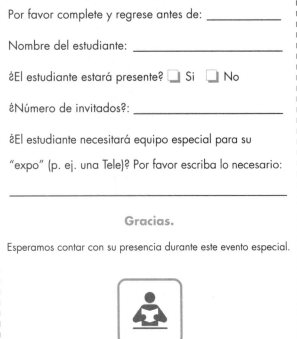

¡ESTA INVITADO!

envision

RESPUESTA A LA "EXPO"

Por favor complete y regrese antes de: _____

Nombre del estudiante: _____

¿El estudiante estará presente? ☐ Si ☐ No

¿Número de invitados?: _____

¿El estudiante necesitará equipo especial para su "expo" (p. ej. una Tele)? Por favor escriba lo necesario:

_____

Gracias.

Esperamos contar con su presencia durante este evento especial.

¡POR FAVOR VENGAN A VISITARNOS A LA EXPO BUSQUEDA DE CONOCIMIENTO!

¿Por qué? _____

¿Quién?_____

¿Dónde? _____

¿Cuándo? _____

Recuerde de traer su cámara!

KNOWLEDGE QUEST
RESOURCE CARDS
FOR STUDENTS

RESEARCH TOPIC AND QUESTION

In order to give your research focus and greater purpose, you need more than just a general topic to investigate. You need to create a specific question about your topic that will guide your research. The question should be narrow enough to be interesting while being broad enough to require investigation. Read through the chart of examples to help guide your topic question creation. Once you have written your topic question, be sure to explain why you chose it.

EXAMPLE

Questions That are Broad Enough for In-Depth Investigation	Questions That Are Too Narrow for In-Depth Investigation
What is the history of soccer?	Who created soccer?
Who were the ancient Egyptians?	When did the ancient Egyptians live?
How do telephones work?	What is a telephone?
Who was Thomas Jefferson?	When did Thomas Jefferson live?
What are the dynamics of a coral reef?	Where are coral reefs located?
Why can't you ever find the end of a rainbow?	What colors are in the rainbow?
How do various artists use tessellations?	What is a tessellation?
How does an automotive engine work?	When was the first car engine made?
What causes the moon to look different each night?	When was the moon discovered?

SEMANTIC MAP

Semantic maps are excellent planning tools. They allow you to generate ideas that are connected to one another, while being able to see all of your ideas and connections at one time. Your main topic question should be in the center of your semantic map. You should have many branches stemming off from the center, listing other sub-questions.

EXAMPLE

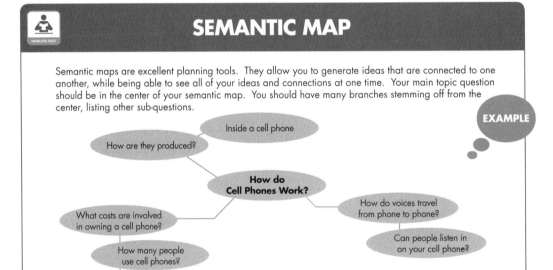

HOT-LIST CHART

A hot-list chart provides basic information about the websites you have found to be most useful in your research. When compiling a hot list, the idea is to be selective. Only the most reliable, most informative, most current and most accessible websites should be on your hot list. Therefore, as you visit various websites, ask yourself the following questions:

* Is the site maintained by a trustworthy source?   * Does the site contain useful information?
* Is the site up-to-date?   * Is the site easy to navigate?

Choose four to six of the best websites you find to include on your hot-list chart. List the name of each site, its web address and a brief description of its content.

EXAMPLE

Hot-List Chart

Name of Site	Address	Description
Mind Vine Press	www.mindvinepress.com	This website has excellent Envision support. It contains helpful links, photos and examples of students' work. It is maintained by Mind Vine Press, publisher of Envision.

WORKS CITED

A works cited list is an alphabetical list of all the sources you borrow information from for a research project. To compile your works cited list, you will need the bibliographic information that you recorded earlier. Individual entries vary slightly depending on the form of the source (whether the source is a book, a magazine article, a website, etc.). Below are three examples of works cited entries, written in the Modern Language Association (MLA) documentation style. Below each entry, in parentheses, is an explanation of how to read the entry. Model your entries after these examples, even if they do not match your sources exactly. For more examples and information on MLA guidelines, consult the Internet or your library's reference section.

For a Book with One Author: Bondy, Melanie. Envision: Grade 5. Lawton, Michigan: Mind Vine Press, 2006. (Author. Title. Location of Publisher: Publisher, Year of Publication.)

For an Article in a Monthly Magazine: Bondy, Scott. "Building a Dream." Mind Vine Press Quarterly, April 2005, 55-61. (Author. "Title of Article." Title of Magazine, Month and Year of Publication, Page Numbers.)

For Material from a World Wide Website: Bondy, Melanie. "Envision." Mind Vine Press 19 August 2004. Mind Vine Press. Mind Vine Press 5 October 2007 <http://www.mindvinepress.com>. (Author. "Title of Article." Title of Website and Date of Electronic Publication. Sponsoring Group or Organization. Date You Accessed the Material and <Web Address>.)

SURVEY

A survey involves asking individuals a set of questions on a specific topic. Good surveys are carefully prepared for and conducted among a wide range of people. The results of a good survey are considered an acceptable indication of knowledge and opinion among the public. Conducting your own survey will help you learn what people know and think about one or more features of your study. Your survey should include five to ten questions related to your research. You will also need to record some basic demographic information about each respondent, such as age and gender. You will need this information later. The more people you survey, the stronger your results, so be sure to survey a minimum of ten people.

EXAMPLE

Cell Phone Usage Survey:

Date:_____   Age:_____   Gender: ❑ Male ❑ Female

1. What is the main reason you have a cell phone?
   ❑ for emergencies ❑ for personal use ❑ for business ❑ other: _____

2. How or where do you use your cell phone most?
   ❑ while driving ❑ in a public place ❑ at home ❑ outdoors ❑ work ❑ other: _____

COMPUTER-GENERATED DOUBLE BAR GRAPH

A double bar graph allows you to show how the group of people you surveyed responded to a particular survey question. It also allows you to break that group of people into subgroups and show how each subgroup responded. The way you set up your double bars depends on how you classify your subgroups. There are options within most word processing programs to help you with creating this graph. Be sure to give your graph a title and provide a key.

EXAMPLE

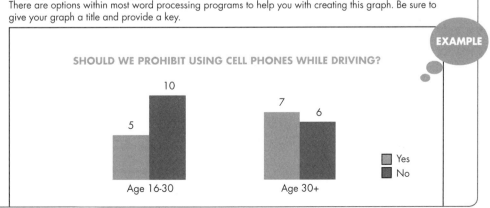

NEWSPAPER

Newspapers are informative sets of articles that are usually printed daily. Along with articles, they also contain other features such as advertisements, comics, photos, illustrations, graphs, maps, puzzles and more. Spend some time studying a few newspapers. Notice how they are laid out, the various sections, how certain features grab your attention and the way the articles are written.

═══ *American Times* ═══

Tuesday, December 9, 1941   15¢

Pearl Harbor Latest

On Sunday morning at 8:00 am, the U.S. Pacific Fleet, based at Pearl Harbor, was woken up to a surprise attack by six Japanese aircraft carriers, twenty-four supporting vessels, and a group of submarines. Just before 10:00 a.m., the attack ended with twenty-one ships of the U.S. Pacific Fleet sunk or damaged, 347 air crafts destroyed or damaged and a devastating loss of life. In all, 2,403 Americans were killed and many more injured in what has been the largest attack on

Recycle, Recycle, Recycle!

"Use it up, wear it out, make it do, or do without!"

We are all looking for ways to help with any war effort possible. One thing Americans are doing is recycling by conserving resources for the war effort. For example, rubber tires are being recycled into life saving rafts for downed pilots, washing machines are being used to make military trucks, and golf clubs are being melted down and converted into rifles. Everyone is being urged to cut back as a way to preserve supplies to support the troops.

For a drop-off location in your neighborhood, call your government service official.

EXAMPLE

NEWSPAPER INFORMATIONAL TEXT STRUCTURES

Articles (and other nonfiction texts) are generally written in one of six different text structures. Finding the right text structure for each of your articles will make your writing more interesting and effective. Use the chart below to help guide your writing. Be sure to use all six text structures at least once.

Text Structure	When to Use	Words/Phrases to Use
Cause and Effect	To describe what happened as a result of something else.	because, consequently, due to, for this reason, since, therefore
Compare and Contrast	To show similarities or differences between two or more things or events.	in the same manner, likewise, similarly/as opposed to, but, however
Description	To describe something's features usually using two or more of the five senses.	colors, feel, size characteristics, smell, sound, taste
Problem and Solution	To state the problem and then the solution or possible solutions.	the problem is, the issue is/one solution is, ways to correct this are
Question and Answer	To pose a question and give the answer or possible answers.	how, what, when, where, who, why/the answer is to, the conclusion is that
Sequence	To describe a series of many events that relate to one another.	after, at (time), before, finally, first, next, on (date), then

EXAMPLE

NEWSPAPER TEXT FEATURES

Text features are elements used within a written piece that help add meaning or emphasis. Using various text features helps different words, phrases, and titles stand out. Oftentimes, for example, the headline on the front page of a newspaper is written in a much larger text size than other article titles. This grabs the reader's attention and directs it to the article that should be read first.

TEXT FEATURES

Centered Headline or Title: p.1A, "It Started With One Idea," line 1.

Bold Words: p. 2B, "safety rules," Line 11.

Varied Font Size: p. 3A, "From Print to Press," Line 29.

EXAMPLE

230

TABLE OF CONTENTS

Your table of contents should be the first page in your portfolio, although you write it after you finish all of the other pages. Writing it after finishing the contents allows you to be accurate with your page numbers and titles in case you make any last-minute changes. Your table of contents should list each section and the page it begins on. It should be neat and well organized, but feel free to be creative with your own layout.

EXAMPLE

PORTFOLIO TABLE OF CONTENTS

Page Number	Section Title
Page	Section Title
1	Topic Question
2	Semantic Map
3	Research and Notes
10	Hot List
11	Bibliography
12	Survey

COVER PAGE AND PORTFOLIO

The cover page of your portfolio should entice people to read about your project. It should include an original title, your name and the Classroom Presentation date. Your portfolio is used to organize most of your paper items. A one- to two-inch binder with a clear cover works well. Arrange your papers in the order listed in your Student Instruction Guide. You may choose to add tab dividers, page protectors and creative touches.

FRONT COVER   SPINE   BACK COVER

EXAMPLE

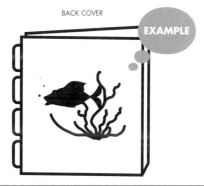

DISPLAY BOARD AND EXHIBIT

The purpose of your display board and exhibit is to draw people's attention to your project. It should be neat, colorful and creative. You should include the items listed in your Student Instruction Guide and any additional materials you wish to bring. The example below is to be used only as a guide; feel free to rearrange. Tip: Two- or three-panel display boards can be purchased at most craft or office stores. If you prefer to make one, you can ask an adult to help construct one from a large cardboard box.

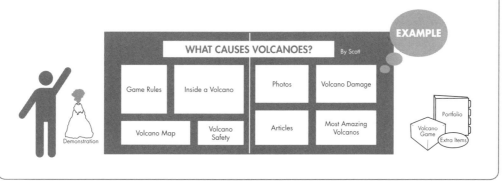

Your presentation will be a talk on what you learned, collected and produced for your project. You should practice until you are comfortable with what you will say, but do not memorize a speech. Your presentation should be three to four minutes long and address the bulleted information listed in Component 3 your Student Instruction Guide. Also, remember to dress in clothing that reflects your career. The additional suggestions below may help you prepare.

REMEMBER TO:

- Take a deep breath, relax and enjoy sharing.
- Greet your audience and introduce yourself.
- Speak clearly, loudly enough so everyone can hear you, and at a natural pace.
- Stand still and calm; don't fidget.
- Point to and show various visuals as you speak about them.
- Have fun while presenting. Show your excitement about your experiences.
- Make eye contact with your audience, looking around the room naturally.
- Thank your audience when you are finished.

ABOUT THE AUTHOR

ABOUT THE AUTHOR

Melanie Bondy taught elementary students for seven years before authoring the Envision program. She has always had a special interest in challenging students to reach their highest potential while making learning relevant and fun. When she saw a widespread need for higher quality materials for gifted students, she utilized her talents to create this unique educational program.

After publishing Envision programs for grades three, four and five, Melanie has also introduced Envision Singles to educators everywhere. The success of Envision has been overwhelming and its reviews have been purely positive. Melanie is planning to produce numerous Envision Singles appropriate for students in grades one through eight.

Melanie is a popular speaker in numerous states and has spoken at many educational conferences nationwide. She has also consulted for school districts across the nation. Melanie is happy to discuss the presentation of the Envision program to teachers in your district.

Mind Vine Press
70727 Copper Boulevard
Lawton, MI 49065
Phone: 269.978.7227
Fax: 269.978.6871
Email: info@mindvinepress.com

ORDER FORM

To place your Envision order, please fill out this form and submit it to **Mind Vine Press** by mail, fax, email or phone.

70727 Copper Blvd., Lawton, MI 49065
Phone: 269.978.7227 Fax: 269.978.6871
Email: info@mindvinepress.com

BILL TO:

District: _____

Name: _____

Street: _____

City: _____

State: _____ Zip: _____

Phone: _____ Fax: _____

Email: _____

SHIP TO:

School: _____

Name: _____

Street: _____

City: _____

State: _____ Zip: _____

Phone: _____ Fax: _____

Email: _____

Date: _____ Purchase Order #: _____

Tax Exempt #: _____

We accept purchase orders, checks and credit cards.

Credit Card #: _____

Exp. Date: _____

Name on Card: _____

Signature: _____

Description	Qty.	Price	Sub Total
Grade 3 Complete Program		$139.95	
Grade 4 Complete Program		$139.95	
Grade 5 Complete Program		$139.95	
Program Bundle: Grades 3, 4 and 5		$389.85	
Career Aspiration Single Project		$49.95	
Backyard Getaway Single Project		$49.95	
Pet Parade Single Project		$49.95	
Party Plan Single Project		$49.95	
Additional Set of Resource Cards Grades:		$39.95	
		S/H*	
		Subtotal	
		Tax (MI Only)	
		Total Due	

Comments: _____

_____

_____

_____

*S/H (Shipping/Handling): Priority Shipping (2-3 days).

$100 or less	$7	$1500 - 1999	$32
$100 - 299	$10	$2000 - 2499	$40
$300 - 699	$15	$2500 - 2999	$48
$700 - 999	$20	$3000 - 3999	$60
$1000 - 1499	$25	$4000 - 5000	$75

For next-day shipping or to purchase delivery insurance, please call 269.978.7227.

Please remit purchase order payment within 30 days of your order.

Thank you!

www.mindvinepress.com